UNIVERSITY OF NORTH CAROLINA AT CHAPEL HILL
DEPARTMENT OF ROMANCE LANGUAGES

NORTH CAROLINA STUDIES
IN THE ROMANCE LANGUAGES AND LITERATURES

*Founder:* URBAN TIGNER HOLMES
*Editor:* MARÍA A. SALGADO

*Distributed by:*

UNIVERSITY OF NORTH CAROLINA PRESS

CHAPEL HILL
North Carolina 27515-2288
U.S.A.

NORTH CAROLINA STUDIES IN THE
ROMANCE LANGUAGES AND LITERATURES
Number 245

THE *LIBRO DE ALEXANDRE*

# THE *LIBRO DE ALEXANDRE*

## MEDIEVAL EPIC AND SILVER LATIN

BY

CHARLES F. FRAKER

CHAPEL HILL

NORTH CAROLINA STUDIES IN THE ROMANCE
LANGUAGES AND LITERATURES
U.N.C. DEPARTMENT OF ROMANCE LANGUAGES

1993

**Library of Congress Cataloging-in-Publication Data**

Fraker, Charles F.
    The Libro de Alexandre: medieval epic and silver Latin / by Charles F. Fraker
    187 p. cm. –(North Carolina studies in the Romance languages and literatures; no. 245)
    Includes bibliographical references (p.).
    ISBN 0-8078-9249-1
    1. Libro de Alexandre. 2. Epic poetry, Latin – History and criticism. 3. Lucan, 39-65. Pharsalia. 4. Rhetoric, Medieval. 5. Narration (Rhetoric) I. Title. II. Series.
    PQ6411.L32F73    1993
    861'.1–dc20                                                                      92-56387
                                                                                      CIP

© 1993. Department of Romance Languages. The University of North Carolina at Chapel Hill.

ISBN 0-8078-9249-1

DEPÓSITO LEGAL: V. 1.996 - 1993        I.S.B.N. 84-599-3308-3

ARTES GRÁFICAS SOLER, S. A. - LA OLIVERETA, 28 - 46018 VALENCIA - 1993

## TABLE OF CONTENTS

|   | Page |
|---|---|
| Foreword | 9 |
| I. The *Libro de Alexandre* Itself | 15 |
| II. Ovid, Lucan and Others | 71 |
| III. Joseph of Exeter and Gautier of Châtillon | 125 |
| Bibliography | 184 |

# FOREWORD

The study which follows is about the influence of Silver Latin poetry on the *Libro de Alexandre*. It grows out of three great interests of mine. The first, obviously enough, is the *Libro* itself. Generations of students at the University of Michigan have had to endure my manifestos in favor of that work. I have taught it and, more than once, have read it for pleasure, as one would a novel; I hope I am not alone on the latter score. The second interest is Lucan. Years ago, a colleague at Wesleyan, the late Tom Tashiro, expressed to me his own enthusiasm for the *Pharsalia*, but alas, it was not until I started to read and study the *Primera crónica* that I came to know that great poem first hand. The present book is certainly not an apology for Lucan, but were my powers equal to the project, I would gladly compose one. This most Shakespearean of ancient poems does not deserve the second-class status accorded it by neoclassic critics and their heirs. We have all heard the tiresome recital: the *Pharsalia* is brilliant in parts, but uneven, the work of a poet of uncertain taste; too much given to bombast and rhetoric (we must remember that for some critics and readers rhetoric is a vice).

My third enthusiasm is one which in some ways might better be kept secret. It is for narrative theory. I am reluctant to make a display of this interest for two reasons. First, quite simply, my reading of the literature is spotty. Long years since I did come to know something about Russian formalism, and I must insist that at various times I have read Barthes, Genette and other theorists with attention and respect. But for all of that, I remain a Sunday-supplement student of narratology. In the remarks that follow I think I have saved myself from foolish utterance by keeping my analysis of narrative simple. My second reason for not wishing to highlight my interest in narrative theory is more complicated. My revered teacher

Raimundo Lida used to say that a critical theory should be like a piece of scaffolding, expendible once the building is finished: the actual critical performance should stand by itself, and the theories and principles that made it possible should be kept hidden. Nowadays this all-wise rule is observed hardly at all, but I would like to be a partial holdout. I so wish especially because I mean the following lines to be read as a learned essay, a study in philology. To put the matter less generally, I am designing my comments on the *Alexandre* and other texts in terms I imagine might be intelligible to their authors, as though the categories I drew upon to study their works might be something like the ones they used to compose them. If this is really what I am about, the fact that the whole project might have been inspired by Tomachevsky, for example, should be of little interest to anyone.

At the heart of this study is the belief that formal patterns in literature, devices of style, strategies of discourse, have a history, just as do themes, for example, or genres. To many this conviction may seem unremarkable. What is certain is that it is going to force large parts of this essay into a very special mold. Much of what follows is unquestionably going to be close reading, or practical criticism. But if indeed a large part of this study is given over to micro-analysis, that does not mean that my first aim is literary interpretation; my procedures are certainly not Spitzerian, passing from things local to things global, from the traits of style of the work to its total significance. This separates my work from that of other students of the *Libro*. Close readings of the *Alexandre* or of *cuaderna vía* poetry generally are not numerous, and as I say, many in this vein are quite unlike mine in that they do aim at what could broadly be called interpretation. Thus, Ian Michael's now classic work, *The Treatment of Classical Material in the 'Libro de Alexandre'*,[1] and the admirable study by P. A. Bly and A. J. Deyermond on "The Use of *Figura* in the *Libro de Alexandre*"[2] are both essays in practical criticism which marshal details of their text in order to establish certain broad propositions about the nature and intention of the work as a whole.

---

[1] Michael, Ian, *The Treatment of Classical Material in the 'Libro de Alexandre'* (Manchester, Manchester University Press, 1970).

[2] Bly, P. A., and Deyermond, A. D., "The Use of *Figura* in the *Libro de Alexandre*," *The Journal of Medieval and Renaissance Studies* 2 (1972), pp. 151-181.

By contrast, my intention is to draw upon my close reading of the *Alexandre* and other texts in order to make judgments about the external history of these works and of the historical relationships between them. For better or for worse, this enterprise is like Melchizedek, without known lineage. I do believe, however, that I might properly cite two authors whose work in some ways parallels mine, Francisco Marcos Marín and Isabel Uría Maqua. Both have worked in an area which could informally be called discourse analysis, the organization of texts and the distribution of material over their extent. My study on its synchronic side, if I could call it that, my close reading, in a word, sets out to do more or less the same kind of work. Marcos Marín's "La confusión de lenguas: el comentario filológico desde un fragmento del *Libro de Alexandre*"[3] glosses five stanzas of the *Libro*, in the versions of the two extensive manuscripts, from the points of view of orthography, phonology and versification, of lexicon, morphology, syntax and semantics. Obviously, much of this material is far afield from any interest of mine here. In the section on syntax however, he steers very close. He points to a feature of his text that poses an important paradox. The syntax in the *Alexandre*, in his text and generally, is simple, often close to parataxis, with little subordination, but the logical and semantic relationships between propositions are rich and complex. This coupling is without doubt one of the most important features of the style and composition of the *Alexandre* and of the earlier *cuaderna vía* poetry generally, and no account of the structure and fabric of any of these works can afford to lose sight of it. I certainly have taken note of it. It should be obvious that my own reflections about the *Libro* assume that, simple as its syntax is, its flow of themes and motifs is complex, and that the poet's management of that succession is subtle and artful.

Uría's utterances on the texture and design of *cuaderna vía* poetry are much more extensive and detailed, but some of her interests are akin to those of Marcos. She belongs to the great tradition of *clerecía* scholarship; her work grows out of decades of reflection by many about Berceo and his fellows. I must begin, alas, by noting my differences with her, ironically enough, with respect to her ideas

---

[3] Marcos Marín, Francisco, "La confusión de las lenguas. Comentario filológico desde un fragmento del *Libro de Alexandre*," *El Comentario de Textos, 4: La poesía medieval* (Madrid, Castalia, 1983), pp. 149-184, especially pp. 170-171.

about the *Alexandre*.[4] I do not share her views about the collective authorship of the poem, and I do not see why its supposed authors must be linked to the newly founded University of Palencia. But my admiration does not flag. Her reflections "Sobre la unidad del mester de clerecía"[5] are wise and learned, a full and detailed description of a common style. Her starting point is a perennial interest of Berceo scholars, the versification of the earlier *cuaderna vía* poems. The "sílabas contadas" of the second quatrain of the *Alexandre* has in her view a very exact meaning. It refers, in her terms, not to *isometría* but to *isosilabismo*. The former would mean that the length and syllable count of a *cuaderna vía* hemistich would always be the same, regardless of the number of syllables which actually made up the words of the half-verse. In other words, hemistichs that were simply isometric could admit *synalepha*; only the length of the half-verse as a whole would matter, and not the number of syllables in the first word plus that of the second, third and fourth. This, as Uría insists, is not the system of early *clerecía* verse. The hemistichs of the *Alexandre*, of Berceo's poem, of the *Apolonio* and the rest presuppose *dialepha*. In these poems vowels in contact between words belong to different syllables, and the only thing that counts in measuring half-verses is the number of syllables in the words that make up the segment. This principle of construction imposes on the texts that use it a certain stiffness in the flow of the discourse. Synalepha would permit more fluency and variety, but dialepha encourages processions of short phrases. But the *clerecía* poets partly compensate for this restriction by making the logical and semantic relationships between the short units interesting and varied. The feature of *cuaderna vía* she calls attention to particularly is the special role of the last line of the quatrain. The d-verse sums up the preceding three, offers the most striking image of the four, expresses a judgment in the narrator's voice, or otherwise forms the climax of the stanza. The effect is, of course, one of peri-

---

[4] Uría Maqua, Isabel, "El *Libro de Alexandre* y la Universidad de Palencia," *Actas del I Congreso de Historia de Palencia*, tomo IV, *Edad media latina y humanismo renacentista en Palencia, lengua y literatura, historia de América* (Palencia, Diputación Provincial de Palencia, 1985), pp. 431-442.

[5] Uría Maqua, Isabel, "Sobre la unidad del Mester de Clerecía del siglo XIII. Hacia un replanteamiento de la cuestión," *Actas de las III Jornadas de Estudios Berceanos* (Logroño, Diputación Provincial, 1981), pp. 179-188.

odic composition, something on the face of it alien to long sequences of clauses with little subordination.

I observe finally that Uría's splendid introduction to her edition of Berceo's *Vida de santa Oria*[6] is a thorough presentation of her views about Berceo and *clerecía* poetry.

As I say, I believe that I share interests with Marcos and Uría. I would add that I in no way duplicate their work. In general terms, the sort of analysis their essays imply would be finer and of smaller scale than mine; they are concerned with the play between syntax and other aspects of discourse, whereas my focus is on the way story, or fable (in the formalist sense), is presented and distributed over the text, and how story is mixed with other elements, commentary, evaluation. It is in any case worthwhile to set forth their views, not only because of their great interest absolutely, but because they genuinely complement mine.

The theme of my study is the debt of the *Libro de Alexandre* to ancient poetry. My object is not so much to shed light on the design of the poem as to show the persistence of certain formal patterns in narrative verse over long periods of time. I must, of course, emphasize the word "formal." I have had to work in isolation; I cannot say that I have found much guidance in the writings of others. But on the other hand, I have no wish to ignore the work of investigators who, like me, have also reflected about the formal aspect of early *clerecía* poetry. And, of course, the one area where I must acknowledge a genuine debt is not to formalists and critics, but to the scholars who have explored the Latinity and learning of the *clerecía* poets; I have in mind especially Brian Dutton and Francisco Rico.[7]

---

[6] Gonzalo de Berceo, *Poema de santa Oria*, edición, introducción y notas de Isabel Uría Maqua (Madrid, Castalia, 1981), especially pp. 28-35.

[7] Dutton, Brian, "French Influences in the Spanish Mester de Clerecía," *Medieval Studies in Honor of Robert White Linker* (Valencia, Castalia, c. 1973), pp. 73-93, and Rico, Francisco, "La clerecía del mester," *Hispanic Review* 53 (1985), pp. 1-23. I will mention two more formal studies of the *Alexandre*, Thalmann, Betty Cheney, *'El libro de Alexandre': a Stylistic Approach*, PhD dissertation, Ohio State University, 1966, and Goldberg, Harriet, "The Voice of the Author in the Works of Gonzalo de Berceo and in the *Libro de Alexandre* and the *Poema de Fernán González*," *La Corónica* 8 (1980), pp. 100-112. Thalmann's is a style study of the sort common in the years she wrote; it is not greatly different from Carmelo Gariano's *Análisis estilístico de 'Los milagros de nuestra Señora'* (Madrid, Gredos, 1965), or from Joaquín Artiles, *Los recursos literarios de Berceo* (Madrid, Gredos, 1968). Like other stylists who study older texts, she draws heavily from classical rhetoric, especially its classification of figures of speech and thought. Goldberg's essay is an at-

tempt to shed light on the question of the *Alexandre*'s authorship. Her starting point is Dana Nelson's hypothesis that the *Libro* should be attributed to Berceo. She examines the authorial interventions in her texts with a view to finding some solidarity in practice between the writings of Berceo and the *Alexandre* over against the *Fernán González*; such an agreement and contrast would count as evidence for Nelson's view. Things in fact do not work out that way: she can find no such binary opposition, and therefore is inclined to vote against the Berceo authorship.

## CHAPTER I

## THE *LIBRO DE ALEXANDRE* ITSELF

1) THE PROJECT

Mr. Peter T. Such in his dissertation on the influence of school rhetoric on the *Libro de Alexandre* makes the following observation: "It is, I believe, reasonable to suggest that our poet's study of the curriculum authors could well have been accompanied by some practical training at the hands of grammarians in the art of literary composition."[1] Some pages later (p. 75). Such quotes with approval some lines from Douglas Kelly's article on "The Scope and Treatment of Composition in Twelfth and Thirteenth Century Poetry":

> some important areas of medieval instruction in composition may have been lost to us or never even committed to writing, perhaps because much of it was based on the study and imitation of the works of literature themselves rather than on the type of formal presentation found in the arts of poetry.[2]

The effectiveness of this method of "study and imitation" is of course clearly evident to any reader of twelfth century Latin literature. The number of poets of this time who captured much of the apparatus of ancient Latin in their writings is not small, and in this sense the validity of Kelly's hypothesis is beyond question. Something of this same training would surely have had an influence on certain kinds of vernacular poetry also: this is, obviously, what Such

---

[1] Such, Peter T., *The Origins and Use of the School Rhetoric in the 'Libro de Alexandre'*, PhD dissertation, Cambridge University, 1979, p. 20.
[2] *Speculum*, XLI (1966), p. 276.

is suggesting. In general terms the study which follows is on one segment of the rhetorical practice of the *Alexandre*-poet which might have been influenced directly by his instruction in the *auctores*. We will, of course, be working under the disability Kelly speaks of, the fact that we know so little about the details of that instruction. It is not that the figures under scrutiny are unknown to the poetries or to the handbooks of rhetoric: the devices in themselves are among the most common. But our focus is to be more on the distribution of these figures over bits of text than on their mere presence there, and on such fine points of art the handbooks have little to say.

Our principal and fundamental concern in these pages will be the influence of ancient poetry on the composer of the *Alexandre*. My perspective will be very specialized: I am of course thinking of the *auctores* not as a fund of themes, or of narrative or descriptive motives, but as formal models, as exemplars to be studied and imitated. Our main body of evidence for this discussion will be the *Alexandre*-poet's practice itself. We of course know a great deal about this practice, not only in the trivial sense that his text is before us to analyze in as much detail as we wish, but also because we have a control text, a term of contrast: we know many of his sources and can see in full detail exactly what initiatives he takes with respect to them. These departures cannot but be a clear index to the poet's art and preferences, and for this reason they give us a fair notion of what he might share in a formal or stylistic sense with Ovid or Lucan. But here a note of caution. These distinctive features of the *Alexandre* text are not necessarily more interesting from our point of view than the details of his sources that he preserves. Our poet is a free agent: he can keep what he likes, change what he likes, or suppress what he likes. Everything that he does is significant: if he tells a particular story much the way his source Gautier does, that conveys as much to us as if he had made drastic changes of focus and style there. If, for example, we find traits in the poem which seem Lucanesque (something I indeed hope to show), we might expect to find those traits quite as often in the verses in which the poet is following Gautier as those in which he is not.

Which are the models which, as I claim, exert such an influence on the texture and structure of the *Alexandre*? My answer to this question may seem arbitrary and short. But the list of ancient poets known and studied in the early thirteenth century is not endless, and if we cut it down to narrative poets, it is still smaller. Let us take as a start the following: Virgil, Ovid, Lucan and Statius. These along with Claudian are the narrative poets known to Gautier:[3] in any case these are the ones drawn upon in the *Alexandreis*. There are obviously many ways of making up such a list, but I suspect that any method would most probably yield very similar results. To the four texts we have mentioned we must of course add one more, the *Ilias latina*, certainly known to the *Alexandre*-poet. At this point one issue should be kept very clear. Mine is meant to be a skeptic's argument. Exceptional cases aside, it would be very foolish to argue on the basis of formal and stylistic things that our poet knew certain particular works of ancient poetry. In such and such a passage in the *Alexandre* the narrative flow has something of Ovid about it. It may be very likely that the poet actually knew Ovid, but his text does not tell us that with any certainty: the narrative pattern may be very distinctive, but it may very well come to the poet second-hand, from Ovid-like strains in other poets, or, as Kelly might have put it, from the teaching of a grammarian versed in Ovid. In a word, this study is not about the details of our poet's literary culture, or about which *auctores* he read or did not read. One may want to say on the basis of independent evidence that he was indeed a fine humanist, or that his years at Palencia, let us say, took him on the world tour of literature, but that consideration is not immediately part of this study. What will concern us here is the state of the art, the way the craft of narrative poetry was taught in the schools at a certain moment in time. This craft was influenced *globally* by the study of the *auctores*. That much seems certain, and that is the subject of our study, and in particular it is the profile, the distinctive shape this craft had at the time, and as reflected in the verses of the *Alexandre* that interests us.

We must utter a further warning. The project at hand is in some sense a style-study. Style has many faces, and examinations of style can be put to many different uses. Not many years ago the study of style was generally understood to lead to an understanding of what was distinctive to a particular work of literature, or perhaps more characteristically, to the individual author. It should be obvious from what we have said to date that we are here up to no such busi-

---

[3] Christensen, Heinrich, *Das Alexanderlied von Wilhelm von Châtillon* (Halle, Verlag der Buchhandlung des Waisenhauses, 1905), pp. 195-204, *passim*.

ness. The high art and the elegance of execution manifest in the broad design and in the detail of the *Libro de Alexandre* seem to me to need no special proof, and as in the case of other great works of literature it is plain that there is much in it that is unique. But that singularity is not our quarry. In our approach the very special practice of our poet will on the contrary end up telling us a great deal about what he shares with other poets, and more immediately, what he owes to other poets; we are, after all, in search of traces in his work of Ovid and Lucan. I would go further and say that the *Alexandre* is by no means the end of the line. It is a conviction of mine which underlies much of what I will be saying that the influence in particular of Silver Latin on medieval and Renaissance literature is deep and wide. This persuasion may seem unremarkable to some: I might find that likelihood reassuring. But such a broad proposition, if it has any truth in it, must not be allowed to float like an advertising blimp there for thousands to admire. It needs to be proved, in one instance, and in another and another. This study of the *Alexandre* is meant to be one step in this global demonstration. Indeed, I hope to show that the work is in some decent sense typical. It should thus be obvious from the start that nearly everything I have to say about the *Libro* is wholly applicable to most *cuaderna vía* narrative poems of the first generation, those of Berceo, for example, or the *Apolonio* or the *Fernán González*; in this sense the *Alexandre* is interesting mainly because it is the longest of the group and the most varied. But far beyond that, it might be very profitable to point out what our poem has in common with works written many years after its time, texts in no way influenced by it. Thus, if we could find the same significant features in the *Alexandre* and in certain narrative poems of the sixteenth century, our case for the influence of Silver Latin might be very strong. This breadth is generally speaking what we are after: we will try to show that our great text is in no way unique in its relationship to its past, that the prestige of Silver Latin makes itself felt in much the same way in the thirteenth century as in later times.

The announced subject of this study is the rhetoric, the rhetorical art, displayed in the composition of the *Libro de Alexandre*. That is putting the matter too broadly. We are in fact going to concentrate on a single figure of rhetoric, one that goes under several names, but which Quintilian calls *evidentia*. Descriptions of the device vary, and it will be convenient for my purposes to give a very simple account of it, under two headings. In the first place, the essence of the figure is the presenting of an event to one's hearer in such a way that he can visualize it, as though it were before his eyes. As we will see, some texts on the subject tell us no more than this, but others explain to us how this vividness is achieved. Hence the second aspect. The figure is one in which a main event is recounted along with many of its attendant circumstances: if one wants to bring an account of an action to life, one must add details, fill in gaps, or, so to speak, leave little to the hearer's imagination. Here are some of the classic *loci*. The *Ad Herennium* has two texts, pretty much matching our two aspects. The first is one of the anonymous author's accounts of a figure of thought, this one being called simply *descriptio*: "Vivid Description [Caplan's translation for *descriptio*] is the name for the figure which contains a clear, lucid, and impressive exposition of the consequences of an act"; "Descriptio nominatur quae rerum consequentium continet perspicuam et dilucidam cum gravitate expositionem" (IV 51). The second text is his account of one of the commonplaces at the service of *amplificatio*, meant to stir the audience's emotions in the *peroratio*:

> By the tenth commonplace we shall examine sharply, incriminatingly, and precisely, everything that took place in the actual execution of the deed and all the circumstances that usually attend such an act, so that by the enumeration of the attendant circumstances (quaeque rem consequi solent) the crime may seem to be taking place and the action to unfold before our eyes.
>
> Decimus locus est per quem omnia quae in negotio gerundo acta sunt quaeque rem consequi solent exputamus acriter et criminose et diligenter, ut agi res et geri negotium videatur rerum consequentium enumeratione.[4]

Cicero's *De inventione* brings our two motives together in a single text. Here is his account of one of the topics for the *peroratio*, a passage which parallels the one we have quoted from the *Ad Herennium*:

---

[4] *Ad Herennium*, edited and translated by Harry Caplan (Cambridge, MA, Harvard University Press, and London, Wm. Heinemann Ltd., 1954), Book II, paragraph 49. I will henceforth refer to ancient texts by Book and paragraph.

> The tenth topic is that in which we bring together all the circumstances (omnia quae in negotio gerundo acta sunt), both what was done during the performance of the deed and what followed after it, accompanying the narration with reproaches and violent denunciations of each act, and by our language bring the action as vividly as possible before the eyes of the judge before whom we are pleading, so that a shameful act may seem as shameful as if he had himself been present and seen it in person.
>
> Decimus locus est per quem omnia quae in negiotio gerundo acta sunt quaeque post negotium consecuta sunt, cum unius cuiusque indignatione et criminatione colligimus et rem verbis quam maxime ante oculos eius apud quem dicitur ponimus, ut id quod indignum est proinde illi videatur indignum ac si ipse interfuerit ac praesens viderit.[5]

Quintilian devotes several passages of the *Institutio* to *evidentia*, stressing largely what I call the first aspect. But in at least one text he gives us both:

> For though, as I have already said, the sack of a city includes all these things [Quintilian's example of vivid description], it is less effective to tell the whole news at once than to recount it detail by detail.
>
> Licet enim haec omnia, ut dixi, complectatur eversio, minus est tamen totum dicere quam omnia.[6]

As we have seen from the texts quoted, *evidentia* is bound up with affect: we do vivid descriptions in our speech to move our audience, to arouse its indignation as it contemplates the unpleasant details of the crime. We will have more to say on this subject. But our all-important figure can be made to serve at least one other purpose. In his discussion of *narratio* Quintilian tells us that *evidentia* is a great resource, if we wish to bring clarity to our narrative account: "Evidentia in narratione, quantum ego intelligo, est quidem magna virtus, cum quid veri non dicendum, sed quodammodo eti-

---

[5] *De inventione, De optimo genere oratoris, Topica*, edited and translated by H. A. Hubbel (Cambridge, MA, Harvard University Press, and London, Wm. Heinemann Ltd., 1949); the passage from *De inventione* is in I 104.

[6] *The Institutes of Oratory of Quintilian*, edited and translated by H. E. Butler (Cambridge, MA, Harvard University Press, and London, Wm. Heinemann Ltd. 1920-1922, four volumes), VIII iii 70.

am ostendendum est; sed subiici perspicuitati potest"; "*Evidentia* in narration, as far as I understand the matter, is indeed a great virtue when a truth needs to be not only said, but in some sense displayed, but it may be placed under the heading 'clarity' [for Quintilian one of the virtues of narrative]" (IV ii 64; in this one case the translation is mine, which I supply because I find Butler's at this point misleading). Quintilian's remark is eloquent, for very special reasons. *Narratio* in a judicial speech is expected to be brief and clear: the facts are supposed to be placed before the judge as simply and effectively as possible. *Evidentia* would thus seem to be out of place in this setting: the piling up of details slows things down, so it would seem. But, says Quintilian in effect, the figure pays its way: the loss in speed is more than made up in clarity. At this point we must make two observations. First, the *evidentia* we will be studying in the *Alexandre* and in other texts is not necessarily tied up to the arousing of emotions or to any other special purpose. By connecting it, as I have, to more than one end I mean to free it from any particular one. Second, the kind of *evidentia* we will be concentrating on is precisely the sort that is an intimate and essential part of narrative. We must distinguish. Description may invade narrative, admittedly enriching it, but also interrupting its flow. Let us suppose that the story we wish to tell could be summed up "John drove to New Haven." We could begin, "It was a brilliant day; the sun beat down on the bright red of the tiny sports car, and the chromium hubcaps were like stars." The descriptive elements here are not necessarily inappropriate, but in this instance they are in no way narrative: they are something else, something added to narrative. What is distinctive about them is that they are simultaneous; they do not succeed each other in time. Let us make another try: "John got in behind the wheel of his car, took out the key, turned on the ignition, backed onto the street, and in a moment he was a block distant, on his way to New Haven." We must overlook the last remark, "on his way": this is a vulgar authorial intervention and has nothing to do with *evidentia*. But the rest fall under both rubrics. In contrast to "John went to New Haven" there is a gain in vividness, in particularity. And the motives are indeed successive. We have an accumulation of circumstances which are an integral and essential part of the narrative. It does not pay to be over-precise about these matters, as some theorists perhaps have been. I would generalize as follows. In a given narrative the collection of motives which are successive, that is to say genuinely narrative, are not necessarily of the same level of importance for the over-all story: some details of plot belong much more to the basic logic of the exposition than others. Matters are of course complicated by the fact that not all narratives are equally logical overall: relevance is not always easy to determine. But in any case there are degrees. In an effective and well-constructed text motives on the low end of the scale are obviously never idle: they may lend clarity in some sense, they may arouse emotions in the hearers, or they may simply convey an impression of reality – we may get Barthes' notorious "effet du réel."[7] In relatively modern texts they often evoke and connote. They are in any case not alien to high literature (or low, for that matter). Now, the narrative text which is biased towards the low end of our range of possibilities, particularly when the details it presents can be visualized, is our concern of the moment.

These distinctions of mine do not claim to be original. But for the purposes of this study their point is not at all trivial. In the first place, it should be clear that in the case of *narratio-cum-evidentia* we are dealing with one of the most fundamental and essential modalities of narrative, one register in the story-telling of all times and places. I would suggest cautiously that much of what we think of as "realism" in literature can be reduced to procedures like the one we have outlined. What is more pertinent to the matter at hand, narrative *evidentia* is a capitally important ingredient in epic poetry. Homer rarely tells us simply that A killed B; he specifies that A threw his spear, that it entered B's body at such a place, that the point emerged from his back in such a way, and that B fell backward or forward or sideways. A large proportion of the verses of the *Iliad* and the *Odyssey* are given over to exposition of this sort. I would put it that the principal narratives in Homer, Apollonius of Rhodes and Virgil are almost invariably *evidential*; in all of their narrative texts the main kernels of the story have sandwiched between them a multitude of secondary, "catalytic" motives which lend a variety and color to the story, a texture which one might think of as typically epic. The *Iliad*, the *Argonautica* and the *Aeneid* are very different poems in their conception, in the sensibility each embodies, and in countless other ways, but locally, in the flow of

---

[7] *Communications* 11 (1968), pp. 84-89.

the text one page after another, the three works have certain formal and structural features in common. We have a mix, a checkerboard of elements which are narrative along with those that are not. Thus, the story flow gets interrupted in various ways, by direct discourse and dialogue, by descriptions, usually brief, by stretches of text identifying persons and things, passages sometimes involving narratives of their own, by epic similes, and occasionally by comments, judgments and interpretative remarks of the narrator about the events he is recounting. The bulk of all these interruptions is relatively small; the story is the thing, and it moves swiftly. And as I have suggested, the story is full of narrative detail. We could specify further: broadly speaking the events recounted, large and small, important and unimportant, are the ones someone on the scene could actually witness. The wealth of detail in the main conveys precisely this first-hand quality, this apparent lack of mediation, which seems to characterize epic exposition. To be sure, this immediacy is not universal. There are moments in which the narrator advances the plot by telling us certain things on his own authority, this rather than simply displaying them to us. Occasionally, for example, he will inform us about the characters' emotions, or about what one of them thinks or intends. Often, more simply, he reveals facts our hypothetical witness could not possibly know. Finally, of course, there is the poet's argument as a whole: Homer knows, as a witness does not, that the Trojan war will last ten years, and Virgil likewise knows that Aeneas is going to found Rome. But once again, all these particulars notwithstanding, the preponderance of what I call evidential narrative in our three poems is overwhelming.[8] I remark

---

[8] This account is mine. It does not claim to be original; I would suppose that any reader might reach more or less the same conclusions. The classic treatment of Virgil's style of exposition is that of Richard Heinze in *Virgils epische Technik* (Leipzig and Berlin, Teubner, 1908), especially pp. 353-395; my analysis is in no way meant to reflect his very special views on the relationship between Virgil and Homer. Erasmus points to the passage in the *Iliad* telling of Hector's meeting with Andromache and Astyanax as an example of *evidentia* (*De duplici copia verborum ac rerum commentaria duo*, in *Desiderii Erasmi Rotterdami opera omnia*, ed. J. Leclerc, Leiden 1702-1706, 10 vols, vol. I, p. 108c). Erasmus throughout the *De copia* praises Homer for his vividness. Graham Zanker, in *Realism in Alexandrian Poetry: a Literature and its Audience* (London, Sydney and Wolfboro, New Hampshire, Croom Helm, 1987) has a collection of ancient witnesses associating the figure *enargeia* (*evidentia*) with poetry particularly, and affirms generally that the usage belonged to poetry first before it passed into oratory. Such, for example, is the testimony of the *Ars rhetorica* attributed to Dionysius of Halicarnassus (10:17, 11:372.9). Cicero

in commentary that my use of twentieth century concepts and terminology is not an accident. Modern narrative theory and ancient rhetoric have many interests in common, and it is surely not stretching things to assimilate the accumulation of narrative detail which makes up *evidentia* and the secondary functions Barthes and others speak of.[9] I will not hesitate to use either old or new language as it suits me.

## 2) THE NARRATIVE STYLE OF THE *LIBRO DE ALEXANDRE*

What I have tried to describe in the preceding lines is an epic norm, something identifiable as a constant in ancient heroic poetry. In considering the literary background the *Libro de Alexandre*, the issue is of course the influence of Virgil: Homer and Apollonius do not figure in the twelfth-century canon of *auctores*. And what to my mind is highly significant in this matter is that the epic norm, as I call it, has very little authority over the *Alexandre*-poet: as far as formal matters are concerned Virgil is simply not his model. For a contrast let us look at a long narrative of a sort wholly unlike the one we have been speaking of, one that might remind us that stories can be told in many different ways. The passage is from a well-known speech of Cicero:

> Publius Clodius was determined to use the post of praetor to convulse the government by every sort of evil-doing. But the elections of the previous year had dragged on so protractedly that he saw his own praetorship would be restricted to a period of no longer than a few months. Advancement in rank, which appeals to other men, was not his object at all. One of the purposes that carried more weight in his mind was a strong desire to avoid

---

thought vividness a particular beauty in Homer (*Tusculan Disputations* V 39:11 ff.). Quintilian (VI 2:29 ff.) draws extensively on Virgil to illustrate *enargeia*. As early a text as Philodemos' on poetry records the opinion that *enargeia* (so called) is the very essence of poetry. All these references are on pages 40 and 41 of Zanker's book.

[9] V. Barthes, Roland, "Introduction à l'analyse structurale des récits," *Communications* 8 (1966). The present study is not meant to be an essay in systematic narratology in the modern manner, but as will become obvious, I do find it convenient to borrow terms and concepts from certain contemporary theorists. The finest array of these notions is of course found in Gérard Genette's "Discours du récit," in *Figures* III (Paris, Seuil, 1972).

having an excellent man like Lucius Paulus as his colleague. But Clodius' main ambition was to have an entire year to devote to the disruption of our state. And so he suddenly abandoned the idea of being praetor in the earliest year to which he was entitled, and transferred his candidature to the following year instead. His motive in so doing was very far from involving the religious scruples which sometimes cause people to take such a step. On the contrary – as he himself admitted – what he wanted was to have a full and continuous year for the exercise of his praetorship: that is to say, for the subversion of the Republic.

All the same, in regard to the latter year as well, a worrying thought continued to nag him. This was the consideration that if Milo was elected to the consulate for that year his own praetorship would once again be hampered and paralysed. Indeed, as Clodius clearly appreciated, there was every likelihood of Milo becoming consul, and by the unanimous vote of the Roman people at that. In this situation he attached himself to Milo's competitors, and did so in such a way that he himself should have complete control of their electoral campaigns – whether they liked it or not. That is to say, as he himself frequently expressed it, his intention was to carry the entire election upon his own shoulders. And so he proceeded to marshal the tribes, acting as a go-between in every negotiation and mobilizing disreputable toughs who virtually amounted to a new Colline tribe in themselves.

And yet the more flagrantly Clodius' disturbances raged, the stronger waxed Milo's position every day, until finally it became evident to Clodius, through the unmistakable voice of public opinion expressing itself in a series of popular votes, that this courageous man, his inveterate enemy, was certain to become consul. And so Clodius, who was ready to stop at nothing, now began to operate openly: and he declared straight out that Milo must be killed.

Clodius had a gang of rustic and barbarous slaves whom he had recruited to ravage the national forests and harass the Etrurian countryside. These he now brought down from the Apennines – and you have seen the creatures yourselves. There was not the slightest concealment, for he himself asserted repeatedly and publicly that even if the consulate could not be taken away from Milo, the same could not be said about his life. Clodius frequently gave indications to this effect in the Senate, and he said it at mass meetings too. Moreover, when the gallant Marcus Favonius asked him what purpose all this violence could possibly serve while Milo was alive to resist it, Clodius replied that within three, or, at most, four days Milo would be dead. And Favonius promptly reported this remark to Marcus Cato here.

Meanwhile Clodius became aware (and it was an easy enough fact to discover) that on 18 January Milo was under an obligation, prescribed by ritual and law, to proceed to Lanuvium. He held the local office of dictator and it was his duty to make a nomination to the priesthood of the town. Equipped with this knowledge, Clodius left Rome without notice on the previous day. As subsequent events demonstrated, his plan was to take up a position in front of his own country manor, and set an ambush for Milo on that spot. Clodius' departure from Rome meant that he had to absent himself from a turbulent public gathering on that same day. His usual violent contributions were greatly missed at the meeting, and he would certainly never have failed to play his part had he not formed the deliberate intention to be punctually in the locality set for the ambush at the appropriate time.

Meanwhile Milo, on the other hand, attended the Senate on that day, until the meeting was concluded. Then he proceeded to his home, changed his shoes and his clothes, waited for the usual period while his wife got ready, and then started off at just about the time when Clodius could have got back to Rome if it had been his intention to return at all on the day in question. But instead he encountered Clodius in the country. The man was lightly equipped, not seated in a coach but riding on horseback, unimpeded by any baggage, with none of his usual Greek companions, and even without his wife who nearly always travelled with him. Milo, on the other hand, was sitting in a coach with his wife, wearing a heavy travelling cloak and accompanied by a substantial, heavily laden, feminine, unwarlike retinue of maids and pages. And this was our so-called waylayer, the man who had allegedly planned the expedition with the explicit purpose of committing a murder!

And so at about five in the afternoon, or thereabouts, he found himself confronted by Clodius before the gates of the latter's house. Milo was instantly set upon by a crowd of armed men who charged down from higher ground; while, simultaneously, others rushed up from in front and killed the driver of the coach. Milo flung back his cloak, leapt out of the vehicle, and defended himself with energy. But meanwhile the people with Clodius were brandishing their drawn swords, and while some of them ran towards the coach in order to fall upon Milo from the rear, others believed he was already slain and began to attack his slaves who had been following behind him. A number of these slaves of Milo's lost their lives defending their master with loyal determination. Others, however, who could see the fight round the coach but were unable to get to their master's help, heard from Clodius' own lips that Milo was slain, and believed the report. And so these slaves, without the orders or knowledge or presence of their master – and I am going to speak quite frankly, not with any aim of denying the charge but just exactly as the situation developed – did what every man would have wished his own slaves to do in similar circumstances.

The incident, gentlemen, took place precisely as I have described it. The attacker was defeated. Force was frustrated by force; or, to put the matter more accurately, evil was overcome by good.[10]

The preceding is a text the *Alexandre*-poet almost certainly never saw: as our argument unfolds it is important to keep this fact in mind. It is, as some will recognize, the entire *narratio* from Cicero's oration in defense of Titus Annius Milo (paragraphs 24 to 29). The strong moral judgments expressed here are, as we would expect, in line with the general purpose and argument of the whole speech, proving that Milo, undeniably the cause of Clodius' death, in fact acted in self-defense. One temptation at this point might be to say that if the above piece of story-telling seems wholly unlike that practiced by the ancient epic poets, it might be that the latter's purpose and the orator's were completely different. The *Pro Milone* is, after all, a utilitarian text framed with a practical end in mind, whereas the *Aeneid*, let us say, is poetry, and as such not in any way obliged to pay its way. But a little bit of literary history tells us that this distinction is not a very fundamental one. Oratory, for one thing, was almost from the first accustomed to proclaim its affinity to poetry. And on the other hand, poetry in antiquity was not thought to be as divorced from the rest of life as some in latter days would have it. And as we shall see presently, the large differences between poetic narrative as we have defined it and the sort of profile presented by Cicero's account of events here have much less to do with utility or the lack of it than one might guess.

---

[10] Cicero, *Select Political Speeches*, translated by Michael Grant (Hammersmith, Penguin, 1969), pp. 230-234.

Different Cicero and Virgil certainly are. The account of Clodius' death and the events leading up to it seems to violate every norm which in our view we must associate with older epic. *Evidentia* in our *narratio* seems to be largely evaded. It obviously is not suppressed entirely: Cicero is brilliant in what we could call his great scenes, and at the appropriate moment in our story he does show his hand. But in this passage *evidentia* seems to be a resource which is held in reserve: it is an occasional effect drawn upon when the orator especially needs it. But what fills the breach? If the bulk of this passage does not have vividness or immediacy, what are we given instead? The question is certainly not idle. It is surely far from useless to have before our minds, informally, at least, some of the many ways there are of telling a story, and in order to discover some of these we must follow Cicero step by step and see what he in particular is up to. If we are to map the territory, we can do no less: the difference between Cicero and Virgil or Apollonius is rooted in particulars, and it is up to us to list some of these.

What strikes us about the first few lines of our quotation is that it is given over almost entirely to Clodius' thoughts, motives and intentions. This is the first factor. Thus, the first sentence (in our translation) tells us broadly about his determination to become praetor and to disrupt the state. A little further down we learn that it was a matter of importance to him not to have Lucius Paulus as his colleague. The plain statement of fact that "the elections... had dragged on" serves only to give the reason for Clodius' first action, the postponing of his candidacy: he wanted to be an active praetor for an entire year. With two exceptions, then, the slowness of the elections and Clodius' withdrawal, everything recounted here takes place within Clodius' head. A second strain in this passage is the thinly disguised intervention of the orator. Cicero at certain points is ostensibly telling us about Clodius' intentions, but is really inviting judgment on him. The opening, once again, is a striking instance. It does double duty. It is conceivably about Clodius' real motive, but as presented in the speech the notion that he meant "to convulse the government by every sort of evil-doing" is so broad and comprehensive that it sounds less like information about his mind than it does like a global condemnation. It makes more sense as a judgment on the part of the speaker himself than as an account of Clodius' project. Much the same could be said of the proposition "Advancement in rank, which appeals to other men, was not his object at all." This could be read as a genuine consideration in Clodius' mind, but it is more convincing as an observation of Cicero about the other man's impatience to seize power.

That leaves the factual residue, the two visible, palpable events narrated, the slowness of the elections and Clodius' postponement of his candidacy. Motives aside, the second is stated baldly: we are in no way invited to visualize it, nor, indeed, do we need to. The first is a special case. It is a global happening, reducible to many particulars: it is in a class with "the Industrial Revolution" or "the decline of French influence in the Middle East," a long chain of events and circumstances belonging together more or less, and all put under a single heading. Speaking informally we could put it that everything narrated in this short section of the speech is mediated. We must take the speaker's word for it when he tells us what Clodius thought or what he meant to do. In addition, the speaker invites us to see these determinations from a certain moral viewpoint. Finally, the purely external events are narrated in a simple and abstract way, far removed from the particulars that attended them.

The next segment of the speech has a slightly different profile. Here Milo, the accused, finally makes his appearance. We begin, once again, inside the mind of Clodius, distressed as he is at the imminent consulship of his enemy. Milo's election was virtually certain, says Cicero; Clodius knew this as everyone else did. The statement about this strong likelihood is an intervention of the orator, his judgment about the state of things at a particular time. That this common knowledge was shared by Clodius is, once more, information based on the speaker's authority, as though he had access to Clodius' thoughts. The two factors together, the prospect of Milo's accession to the consulate and Clodius' distress, are presented as the motivation for the latter's next move, his alliance with Milo's rivals and his strong intervention in their politics. In this case we again have a portmanteau event, like the end of slavery or the rise of the middle class. Clodius' intervention as narrated could have been reduced to a long series of mini-events, conferences with one personage or with another, conceivably bribes or threats. But unlike the account of the slowness of elections as we spoke of it, this move of Clodius is indeed associated with some of its particulars, the negotiations, the recruitment of the "disreputable toughs." Cicero's list is short, however, and the account is still weighted heavily on the global side.

The next block of narrative begins with a large contrast: the more active Clodius became, the closer Milo came to the consulship. This is plainly meant to be a summary, another portmanteau. And again, one of the generalities is partly specified: Milo's success is measured by a series of election victories. This last declaration, needless to say, remains quite general: more particular than its predecessor, it is still fairly abstract. Then, once again, we enter Clodius' brain, though trivially: the popular votes were no secret to him. At this point we have the motivation for his next large resolve, which is to do away with Milo.

In this case the speaker does not need to draw on a secret source of information to tell us what Clodius intended. The prospective murderer speaks openly of his plans. Here we have an interesting series of contrasting statements. All report what Clodius is supposed to have said: in other words, all are indirect discourse. But the three utterances are progressively closer to the particular. "He declared straight out that Milo must be killed" lacks all specifics. The speaker could be referring to one declaration or possibly several; we know nothing whatever about settings or audiences. The next allusion to Clodius' words is in some ways indeterminate: "he himself asserted repeatedly" aside from its obvious sense leaves many possibilities open. But the style of the utterance is telling: "Even if the consulate could not be taken from Milo, the same could not be said of his life." This sounds like a quotation: the words in Cicero's mouth are surely meant to be damaging because they have every appearance of being Milo's own. Finally we have a piece of reported dialogue, uttered on a particular occasion, with both speakers identified, Marcus Favonius and Clodius himself.

Our narrative finally starts to touch the ground. Our last bit of narrative can certainly be called evidential: brief as it is, it is a genuine scene, displayed without comment. Even the indirect discourse is hardly a difficulty: we can easily translate it into direct. At this point in the text we come to the actual account of the attempt on Milo's life and of his assailant's violent end. The passage is of great interest because of its approach to our key figure, *evidentia*. Unlike earlier portions of the narrative, the facts recounted here are nearly all external, and not mental, and yet the density of narrative detail varies widely: some passages simply report, whereas others present and display. We begin on fairly familiar ground, with a mixture of motive, intention and action. Milo leaves Rome to fulfill a religious and civic duty; Clodius knows of his departure and he himself goes to the country meaning to lay ambush in front of his own farm. Cicero also mentions Clodius' absence from an assembly he was supposed to attend. The fact is cited as evidence: Clodius would surely never have missed the meeting, had he not from the first intended to confront Milo and destroy him on the way to Lanuvium. The orator's intentions are again in the foreground: the meeting and Clodius' absence are brought in to help argue the case. Milo's leisurely departure from Rome is displayed to us in homely detail: he changes his shoes and his clothes and waits for his wife to ready herself. This is not a purely literary exercise. Cicero is once again arguing: he dramatizes the easy style of the departure in order to convince the judges that Milo, accused of murder, in fact left Rome foreseeing no emergency, or violence. The same argument is sustained as the orator contrasts Milo's large train, including women and boys, his travel by carriage, the company of his wife, with Clodius' arrival, on horseback, wifeless, and with a small following. Cicero actually points to the anomaly: Milo, the supposed plotter, comes on the scene heavily encumbered, little equipped for action, hardly looking like a murderer, or a plotter.

The arrival of Clodius on the scene is marked in Cicero's text by a very significant linguistic feature, a change of tense. Though our English translation does not reflect as much, the Latin at this point shifts to the present tense, and the rest of the narrative to the very end is told in the present. One does not have to be trained in rhetoric to know that the historical present is supposed to give narrated events immediacy, to make them present in every sense. We need be in no doubt that this is the orator's intention here. We have only to look at his account under other aspects. The narrative from here on is full of detail and circumstance. We are told of the position of the principals at various moments, on the higher ground, in front of the carriage, behind it. The actual sequence of events is explicit and clear, and includes small matters as well as large, Milo throwing off his cloak, the attack on the driver, the rumor that Milo was dead. The whole episode is a sustained close-up.

Showing and telling, this is the all-important polarity.[11] Cicero

---

[11] I believe that my contrast "showing-telling" will be a useful one within this study, and that it will be quite adequate for my purposes. The sense of what I have to say in relation to the pair should prove coherent; the reader, of course, will have

in the great part of his narrative tells: he informs us about what goes on in Clodius' mind, and reports events globally, without details. And in the main, when he is not telling, he is judging. The showing, what there is of it, he saves for the climactic end, and this, indeed, not merely for the excitement. He shows, displays, the encounter scene so as to give verisimilitude to the account of Clodius' death most favorable to his client, Milo set upon by his rival. *Evidentia* is not there for ornament; it is meant to serve argument.

Our reasons for discussing at length such an unlikely narrative as the one we have chosen will be clear in time. Let us for the moment hang it up for comparison alongside one of the most dramatic brief episodes of the *Libro de Alexandre*. Here is the passage:

> 169) Vn rico omne que pueda mal siglo alcançar
> ouos de la reyna fuerte a enamorar
> por nul seso del mundo non la pudo ganar
> que ella era buena e sabies bien guardar
>
> 170) Pausona le dizian al que Dios de mal poso
> ouolo fecho Pehilipo rico e poderoso
> mas por su ocasion enloqueçio el astroso
> armo vn consello malo e peligroso
>
> 171) Asmo que sy pudiese a Pehilipo matar
> casarie con la reyna a todo su pesar
> aurialo todo el regno por señor a catar
> non osarie el fillo nunca ally asomar
>
> 172) Boluio con el guerra por non seyer reptado
> andaua por el regno a todo mal su grado
> touos el rey Phelipo deso por desonrrado
> fue a lidiar con el leuolo y del pecado
>
> 173) Commo sobre el falso fuese arincando
> nol valdrie todo el mundo que no fues justiçiado
> bastio toda enemiga commo omne perjurado
> que Satanas andaua con el todo encarnado
>
> 174) Diol salto en vn puerto en vn lugar apartado
> commo lo tenia bien de ante el traydor asmado
> el logar fue estrecho & el apoderado
> fue el rey Pehelipo muy mal esbaratado

---

to judge. I do realize that, strictly speaking, the opposition has little theoretical dignity: "showing", so called, is obviously nothing other than one species of telling. On this matter see Genette, Gérard, *Narrative Discourse Revisited*, translated by Jane E. Lewin (Ithaca, Cornell University Press, 1988), pp. 96-102.

175) Golpes ouo de muerte finco espantado
fue quando esto vio Pausana esforçado
el que mal siglo aya fue tan alegrado
commo si lo ouiesen sus parientes ganado

176) Dexo el rey por muerto que tanto se valie
adeliño pora la villa do Olinfias jasie
mas el mal venturado agrimar non sabie
la su mala ventura tan çerca le vinie

177) Sy vino en las nuues o lo aduxo el viento
o lo aduxo la fada por su encantamiento
abes fue entrado con su pendon sangriento
sobrel vino el jnfante laso e soñoliento

178) Quando lo sopo Pausana touos por afollado
vio que lo auia traydo el pecado
pero misos en armas e caualgar priuado
yxio contra el jnfante vista le demandando

179) Asas traye conpañas asas bien aguisadas
mas fueron con el jnfante todas muy mal quexadas
tallauan les los braços e fuyan querelladas
temian lo que les vino que serian mal falladas

180) El jnfante quando los uio luego los fue ferir
enpeçolos afirmes luego a desordyr
Pausona sy pudies queries referyr
mas lo que meresçio ouo lo a pedir

181) Ouol por su ventura el jnfante a veyer
desque lo ovo visto nos pudo retener
auenturos con el ouolo a vençer
lo que busco el falso ouolo a prender

182) Asas fizo Pausona quanto que fer pudo
dio a Alixandre grañt colpe en el escudo
rajas fizo la lança que tenie en el puño
cuydo el desleal que lo auie abatudo

183) Golpolo el jnfante bien a guisa de varon
non lo açecho en al sy non al coraçon
nol presto migaja toda su guarniçion
por medio de las espaldas le echo el pendon

184) Mandolo luego prender fizolo enforcar
alli lo comieron aues non lo dexo enterrar
desy fiso los huesos en vn fuego echar
que non pudiesen del falso nunca señal trobar

185) Murio el traydor commo lo meresçie
por y pasaron todos quantos que el traye
nada non acabo de lo que el querie
las tierras al jnfante todas lo bendizien

186) Todos los traydores asy deuien moryr
nigunt auer del mundo non les deuie guaryr
todos commo a merçed deuien a ellos yr
nunca los deuie çielo nin tierra resçebir

187) Quando fue librado commo auedes oydo
el jnfante commo se estaua de sus armas guarnido
fue saber de su padre quel auie contenido
e fallo que yazie fascas amorteçido

188) Ia tornaua los ojos e pasar se queria
contendio con el alma que transido jazia
pero quando entendio que su fillo venia
vinol mano a mano la mejoria

189) Abrio luego los ojos començo a plorar
cato contra el jnfante e nol podie fablar
sygnol con los braços que lo fuese abraçar
obedesçiol el fillo non lo quiso tardar

190) Diol Dios mano a mano ya quanta meioria
recobro la palabra con la grañt alegria
dixol yo fiio mucho cobdiçie este dia
desaqui que yo muera vna nues non daria

191) Fiera meñt e en grañt sobirandat nos honrrastes
quando a Nicolao matastes y ad Armenia prisistes
mas todas vuestras bondades agora las cunplistes
quando a nos aca a acorer viñistes

192) Gualardon deste serviçio fillo Dios vos lo y rienda
fillo el vos resçiba en su santa encomienda
el vos sea pagado e guide vuestra fazienda
de mano de traydores fillo el vos defienda

193) Fillo yo vos bendigo sy faga el Criador
el vos de sobre Dario vitoria e onor
el vos faga del mundo seyer enperador
en tanto me despido vome a la corte mayor

194) El regno de Philipo fuera muy mal traydo
sy el jnfante non fuese por uentura venido
mas quando a el vieron çeso todo el ruydo
e quedo todo el feruor que era somouido

195) Murio a poca de ora el su padre honrrado
fue con los otros reyes a Corrintio lleuado
commo el meresçie asi fue soterrado
finco en poder del jnfante el regnado[12]

---

[12] *El Libro de Alexandre: Texts of the Paris and the Madrid Manuscripts*, edited by Raymond Willis (Princeton and Paris, Princeton University Press, Elliott Mono-

We must begin our commentary by observing that the verses we have quoted are a very free paraphrase of some lines in one of the recensions of the *Historia de preliis* (see preceding note). I do not believe it is necessary at this point to make a detailed comparison of the two texts, however interesting that might be. It is, however, important to note that the rhetoric of the passage in the *Libro*, the distribution of the figures in the text, the narrative presentation generally, is distinctive: not much of it comes from its source. It should be obvious that from the very first stanza we are on much the same turf as we were with Cicero. We begin with a moral judgment, "vn rico omne *que pueda mal siglo alcançar,*" a complicated event recounted simply and colorlessly, his falling in love with the queen, a portmanteau happening, his failure to win her, and the poet's explanation why, her ability to look after herself. We have two interventions of the narrator and two events told without details. The next quatrain names the rebel, and tells us that he had been favored by the king. In the light of what we are to learn about Pausona this is plainly a damning detail, strong witness to his bad character, particularly to his ingratitude: the poet is citing evidence for his case, just as Cicero does. This stanza and the next take one step further, carrying us inside the young man's mind: he lost his good sense and dreamed of a possible course of action, killing the king, marrying

---

graphs 32, 1934), stanzas (cc.) 169-195. All quotations of the *Alexandre* will henceforth be from Willis' edition of the P manuscript, which I have chosen simply because, of the three he edits, it is the most complete. I preferred his paleographic edition over bolder ones, like those of Nelson and Cañas, because I wished to bypass completely the question of the *Libro*'s author and original language. Willis' transcriptions set out to reproduce the great variety of characters in his manuscripts with his own set of printed characters, one printed character corresponding to one manuscript character. In my selections from his texts I have reduced the number of characters used, respecting, as far as I could, the graphemes involved: for example, the great variety of symbols Willis uses that are the equivalent of a single *s* I have represented by *s*, simply. I have, however, preserved the distinction between *u* and vocalic *v*, and have used *ñ* wherever it appears in Willis' text, even when it does not have the value it has in modern Castilian. I have also kept Willis' *ā* and *ō*. The *mn* combination appears as such in my text, however rendered in Willis; thus, all the versions of *omne* appear as omne. In general, I have tried to keep as much of Willis' version in my quotations as was practical. The passage quoted is based on recension J2 of the *Historia de preliis*, in A. Hilka, *Der altfranzösische Prosa-Alexanderroman* (Geneva, Slatkine Reprints, 1974 reproducing the Halle edition of 1920), pp. 47-54. Professor Ian Michael's assertion that stanzas 190-195 depend heavily on the Old French version (Hilka, same pages) seems to me to be without basis [*The Treatment of Classical Material in the 'Libro de Alexandre'* (Manchester, University of Manchester Press, 1970), p. 288].

the queen, and holding the heir at bay. There follows another portmanteau event, the outbreak of the rebellion, along with the king's response and its motive, the affront to the royal honor and estate. We then have some more moralizing, and it is not until after that set of comments that we are given something to visualize: Pausona attacks the king in an isolated spot, a mountain pass, a narrow defile, "en vn puerto en vn lugar apartado . . . el logar fue estrecho." The *evidentia* is saved for a critical moment in the story, the assault on Philip which is to cost him his life. But even here the moralizing orator intervenes: Pausona is called "traydor." Beyond that, we are also told that the attack in a mountain pass had been long since planned by the wicked man, "commo lo tenia bien de ante el traydor asmado." Pausona now believes that Philip has breathed his last, and is therefore euphoric: once again, we have the consciousness of a principal character, and once again he is given a negative epithet, "el que mal siglo aya." Pausona runs to Olympias' side little guessing that his own end is near: the narrator intervenes once more taking us ahead in the story. The line on the sudden encounter with Alexander is introduced by still more commentary: the poet wonders whether the meeting came about by chance or by a disposition of fate. Then comes one more inner reflection by Pausona as he thinks that surely the devil had brought him to this pass. The great battle scene ensues, a scene in every sense. The narrative becomes dense: the succession of events is close, livened with a glimpse of broken limbs. The climax is the death of Pausona, told in perfectly Homeric fashion. His armor availed him nothing, the weapon passed through his heart, and at the end the pennant was visible from his back: a reader of the *Iliad* could ask for nothing better. After these details this section of the story ends with two stanzas of solid moralizing, one on Pausona in particular and the other on traitors in general.

I return to my earlier point: I do not believe that for our purposes the contrast between a utilitarian text and a poetic is a useful one. In a word, Cicero's story about Clodius and the *Alexandre*-poet's about Pausanias are cut from the very same cloth. Both authors plead, both narrate from a distance, that is to say, report, both are privy to the thoughts and intentions of their characters and put great emphasis on these elements, both make judgments about the events themselves, and finally, both present, dramatize for maximum effect, only at the decisive moment. We could put the whole matter in different terms. Pausanias is not on trial, nor is Alexander. No judge is on the scene to pass a real nonfictional sentence on one or the other. But the *Alexandre*-poet nevertheless works up the case against the rebel quite as if he had actually been called to judgment. The same set of resources a genuine advocate would use are brought into play here, plain judgments openly expressed, a sharp focus on motives, factual information brought in as it is pertinent, and finally the purple patch, the scene, rich in details, brought to life, to dramatize the whole argument. Many of the historical reasons for the assimilation of poetry to oratory are well known, and there is no need to rehearse them all at this moment. In one sense, however, we must call our argument home. The *Libro de Alexandre* is a product of the early twelve hundreds; it was not written in Imperial times nor in the Renaissance, two great ages of rhetorical poetry. Our real focus in this study, as we recall, is the literary and rhetorical culture of the years just before the composition of our poem. I believe that the striking set of likenesses between our two texts, and the similarity in scope shown by the two, are a valuable, indeed fundamental, testimony as we shed light on our principal theme. I would further like to claim that an important part of the general argument of this essay has now been laid down.

In the rest of our selection from the *Libro* the object of the pleading is not Pausanias, but Alexander himself. The sequence is another brief scene, giving us this time the last moments of Philip. The pathos produced by the dramatic detail centers around the young prince and the pride and joy he awakens in his dying father. The narrative pace slows down, and the events seen at close range start unfolding. We begin with Philip in agony, his eyes averted. He rallies, however, the moment he hears that his son is present. He opens his eyes, weeps, looks at Alexander, and unable to speak, gestures with his arms, signaling to his son to embrace him. The young prince complies, and Philip's speech returns. It is then that we are given the centerpiece of the scene, Philip's words in praise of his son, expressing gratitude to him, and promising him a brilliant future; the king declares that he is content to die at that auspicious moment. The drama attending the praise of Alexander in the mouth of his dying father is surely not wasted: it brings focus and high relief to a text announcing Alexander's future greatness.

Let us take stock of our progress to date. This study of the *Libro de Alexandre* was meant to shed light on two problems, the formal and rhetorical aspect of the poem generally and the factors in its author's schooling that might have influenced it, and second, the place of *evidentia* in our text, and particularly the evasion of this figure in the course of the work. This latter question, as we have seen, has a great bearing on its partner. The relative infrequency of vivid narration in the *Libro* turns out to be highly revealing of the poet's background and training in two senses. In the first place, it tells us clearly how pervasive the influence of rhetoric on his text really is. What is true of our quotation is true of the poem as a whole. *Evidentia*, narrative and otherwise, is reserved for critical turns in the story: certain moments are dramatized, brought into relief, are given a vividness greater than that of their fellows. Now, this disposition plainly has to do with the theme we have already aired, the connection the rhetoricians make between *evidentia* and affect. We have seen that in the Cicero passage and in the *Alexandre* episode alike, the argument seems to demand that certain moments of the story be highlighted, made cinematographic. What we must emphasize is that this sharp focus, effective in the argument as a whole, is not in itself an appeal to the reason: the total conviction on the part of the audience that the orator is trying to produce at such moments has little to do with rational argument, but a great deal to do with the arousing of feelings. The hearer's emotions are certainly not the whole basis of the case, but they do enhance it significantly. All of this is strictly according to the text. As we recall, vividness is linked in the classic treatises with two factors in the oration, the clarity of the narrative, and the production of affect in the audience. Of the two, the latter element is by far the most heavily emphasized in these texts, and it should be obvious that the occasional appearance of a purple patch in the *Alexandre* and in other narrative texts reflects just this emphasis. In works in which narrative *evidentia* is more general one could think of Quintilianesque clarity as the decisive factor, but this surely is not the case here. Paradoxically, the prevalence of the plainer sorts of narrative in the *Libro* and in similar works could be viewed partly as the byproduct of just this bond between *evidentia* and the production of affect: the arousal of emotions is only one of the resources of the orator, and it would seem unreasonable to expect him to exploit no other.

The second sense in which the poem's local, non-universal *evidentia* is revealing is with respect to its literary models. What is at issue is exactly which of the ancient texts known to the author were, and which were not, effective in the final shaping of the poem. But before turning to this matter, we must be quite clear that the rhetorical patterning we have discovered in the Pausona episode is indeed general throughout the *Libro*; casual reading can confirm this, and later portions of this study will attempt to do so in some detail. It is important to bear this presumed uniformity in mind, but what we have actually shown to date is that the elements of style in our passage, and more important, the configuration of these elements, are shared: the same group of features appears in a much older text, a work that is totally unlike the *Alexandre* in either its overall layout or in its purpose. One has to posit some kind of tradition of long standing to account for the likeness. Thus far our argument. But over all of these discussions there hangs a cloud, a nagging doubt. It may seem to some that our commentaries are flirting dangerously with the trivial. Is it not natural to use a variety of approaches and techniques in telling a story? Why stick to *evidentia*? What is so remarkable about a narrative that airs the motivation of its characters, in which the author intervenes with judgments and explanations, or in which some points in the story are told summarily and others in detail? This latter description might fit 75 per cent of the narrative texts any one of us has read in the last decade, works of fiction and others. Over most of this century this literary mode has more and more been brought into question, but it nevertheless survives, in journalism, in history to some extent, in popular fiction, and even in high literature. Art has become Nature: Virgil is archaic, exceptional. One object of the present study is to show that this commoner mode, this new nature, has a history, that it did not simply spring out of the ground. This is, or should be, one of the issues raised by an examination of the *Alexandre* and the currents that formed it. As we suggested before, this study is not greatly concerned with what is unique in the *Libro*. Our poem is in many ways very typical, and for this very reason it will be, as I hope, a perfect instance with which to illustrate this history, this process of naturalization.

3) TWO KINDS OF NARRATIVE

Not many pages back we spoke of a basic polarity in narrative, a pair of terms in opposition: showing and telling. One may of course think of these as two modalities available to any narrator to draw upon as he sees fit: the same piece of fiction or history might at one moment display events to its readers and at another recount them. For contrast let us imagine instead another pattern in which there existed two different whole species of narrative text in which one each of these two tendencies dominated. Thus, in one kind of story the narrator, present inevitably, might be scarcely visible or audible. In such a text we might have a great deal of direct discourse and dialogue, though such would not be entirely necessary. In any case, all the responsibility would lie with the reader. The narrator would not generalize, nor explain, nor analyze, nor would he sum up; he would not form judgments, nor would he list in principle the qualities which defined each of his characters. Absolutely none of this implies that his text is indeterminate, or that the reader was free to complete it as he liked. On the contrary, his hand is guided at every turn: the narrator offers him such a wealth of detail in his story that the audience can be left in little doubt about what is going on. He does not need to be told that "it was a splendid wedding," if it is conveyed to him that "the count attended, as did nobles from the whole county," or that "dozens of minstrels entertained, old men played chess, the young tilted, much food and wine was consumed, the festivities went on for nine days." In the other kind of narrative the teller of the story is at the center of the stage. We hear his voice constantly, as he does everything the other kind of narrator never did, explain, analyze, generalize, pass judgment, define character. Now, we hardly need to be reminded that neither kind of story exists in the world in its pure state. The most austere piece of fiction by Hemingway, made up almost entirely of dialogue, at some point guides the reader with a bit of information, or adds "he said," "Nick answered." And on the other hand, the most "classic," the most narrator-dominated novels of the eighteenth or nineteenth centuries, by Fielding, Dickens or Balzac, have some dialogue, and some bits of story brought in detail before the imaginations of its readers.

In antiquity these two modes of narrative belonged to different literary genres, the evidential, the showing kind, to older epic, and the more explanatory to oratory to the extent that storytelling was in its range, and to history. In time this picture gets complicated by contaminations and crossovers, but whenever the two styles appear they keep their identities, and latter-day readers have no difficulty spotting them. Epic texts up to and including Virgil belong to our first mode. We must of course recall that the expository approach in these works is mixed. Dialogue and direct discourse aside, the narrative gets interrupted by identifications of persons and places, by descriptions, usually brief, and by commentary of various sorts. What is distinctive about this poetry, however, is that the residue, the storytelling itself, is, as I would call it, evidential, almost exclusively, and that this narrative mode makes up a large percentage of the whole text. Our selection from the *Pro Milone* of course gives us the orator's version of our second mode. One might fairly say of this *narratio* that the years have not dimmed its luster. I mean, of course, that those lines have little in them that seems remote or archaic: events are presented in a way that is perfectly familiar to us. The reasons for this, which we need not detail at the moment, have perhaps less to do with the genius of Cicero than with the continuity of a tradition. As for the writing of history we should remember that the contact between this genre and oratory was always thought to be close. A classic locus from the *De oratore* is the most famous witness in his respect (II 62). And in fact, historians of the Hellenistic and Roman periods, very different as they sometimes were, all or nearly all produce narratives whose structural features are more or less those of our passage from the *De Milone*. It is not stretching things to say that this *narratio* could with the slightest changes be part of a historical work: the kinship between oratory and history is not less close.

Rhetoric invades every literary genre; so it is often said, with different emphasis relative to different periods and different kinds of texts. Rhetorical history is a recognized category, and the influence of rhetoric on the poetry of the Silver Age is a commonplace. But for our purposes the term "rhetorical" is too broad. Rhetoric itself recommends everything: there is no style in existence that is not in some sense rhetorical. More particularly, in periods in which training in rhetoric was universal among certain classes it is hard to imagine a literary text which could be wholly free from rhetorical influence. But on the other hand, there are clear boundaries. The storytelling in Cicero's *Pro Milone* is simply not of the same kind as that of any stretch of the *Aeneid*. But we gain little by declaring Virgil unrhetorical. It may make much better sense to speak of a text as distinctively oratorical. As we have kept saying, the style of narrative employed by legitimate orators seems to be not very different in kind from that employed by other men of letters, historians, perhaps even certain poets. Now, oratorical narrative, if we may coin such an ungainly term,[13] is certainly the modality of the *Libro de Alexandre*. The pattern is certainly an inheritance from antiquity. The *auctores* generally known to students of grammar in the twelfth and thirteenth centuries could have offered our poet more than enough models and examples for him to form his own style: the link to the past is visible. Our immediate task, however, is to examine the *Libro de Alexandre* itself, and to try to determine in detail what kind of rhetorical practices it realizes. We have taken a close look at one episode in the poem with an eye to these matters. I do not believe that it is rash to call these verses typical: a casual reader at large in the *Libro* could surely confirm this notion. But guesswork is not quite enough: we must explore the territory and see its detail first hand.

4) Virgil in the *Libro de Alexandre*

There is a prior question. Did our poet have the other model before him? One eminent and exemplary student of the *Alexandre*, Professor Willis, has suggested that its author was unacquainted with Virgil.[14] In the light of our argument to date this possibility is an interesting one. If the *Aeneid* cannot be considered a model, the practice of its author as we have described it seems the more explainable: the first mode was simply not on his radar screen. But if Virgil was part of his repertory, we have to look for more complicated reasons for this general procedure. Now, although the general study of sources and models belongs to a later portion of this essay, it may be fitting to explore here this small and local problem, Virgil's place in the canon of our poet.[15] We begin with Gautier. In book V of the *Alexandreis* we are shown Darius in defeat. As the

---

[13] A. J. Woodman speaks of "oratorical historiography," in *Rhetoric in Classical Historiography* (London and Sydney, Croom Helm, and Portland, Oregon, Areopagitica Press, 1988), pp. 83-88.

[14] Willis, Raymond " 'Mester de clereçia', a Definition in the *Libro de Alexandre*," *Romance Philology* (1956-1957), p. 218.

[15] I am here drawing on my own article, "Repetition, Old and New: the *Libro de Alexandre*," in *Studies in Honor of Sumner M. Greenfield*, edited by Harold L. Boudreau and Luis González del Valle (Lincoln, Nebraska, Society of Spanish and Spanish-American Studies, 1985), pp. 95-106.

battle of Arbela is coming to an end most of the Persians are in disorganized flight. The king is surrounded by a small group of his men; he,

> mournful and distraught, consulted those whom flight had united with him, and discussed with them the critical situation. After checking the sighs from his plaintive heart, and regarding with tearful eyes the remnant of the Persians who had escaped the Macedonians, he spoke these words
> lugibris et amens
> Consulit et pariter duro de tempore tractat.
> Cumque repressisset queruli suspiria cordis,
> Relliquias Macedum lacrimoso lumine spectans,
> ... inquit[16]

There follows Darius' speech urging conformity with fortune and promising better days. The paraphrase the *Alexandre*-poet makes of these lines is unremarkable, although it does add a few motives of its own:

> 1440) Dario con la rrencura daua grandes sospiros
> querrie seyer mas muerto que seyer con los biuos
> 1441) Encubrio su desyerro quando fueron llegados
> rrefirio los sospiros que tenie muy granados
> començo de fablar con los ojos mudados
> ca entendie que todos estauan deserrados

Distinctive to the Romance text here are the observation that Darius repressed his sighs just at the moment his men approached, and the attribution of a motive, his realization that they were themselves deeply distressed. Summing up, we could say that a character in low spirits disguises his feelings in order to speak cheerful words. Readers could object that in neither version does Darius hide his feelings entirely, and that the speech, though meant to encourage, is

---

[16] Walter of Châtillon, *The Alexandreis*, translated with introduction and notes by R. Telfryn Pritchard (Toronto, Pontifical Institute of Mediaeval Studies, 1986), Book V, verses 382-386 (the verses of the Latin are numbered in this translation). All of my quotations in English from the *Alexandreis* will be from this version, and references to the Latin original and quotations from it will be from *Galterii de Castelione Alexandreis*, edidit Marvin L. Colker (Patavii, in aedibus Antenoreis, 1978).

scarcely joyful. But my abstraction, or if you will, distortion, is deliberate. The *Libro* offers us several parallels to the situation at Arbela, in passages that have no analogue in Gautier. Darius' general Memnon has just been defeated. To make matters worse, the battle is accompanied by a terrible omen: the sun is in eclipse. The Persian king is hardly in the best of spirits, but he makes the best of things: "Dario por esto todo non quiso esmayar / commo que mejor pudo encubrio su pesar" (827). There follows a genuinely cheering speech saying that things are sure to change for the better. In a passage a few lines further along we read that Alexander makes a daring forced march which brings him closer than ever to the Persian. Darius is not pleased: "Supolo luego Dario commo eran pasados / nol pudieran venir mensajes mas pesados" (844). He addresses his men nevertheless, telling them that victory will be easy, that the Greeks are less powerful than they, and that Alexander has become overconfident. The troops begin their march, but the king's anxiety does not leave him: "non podie de sy partir el baticor." Some pages later we have one more scene on the same pattern. Darius has been mistakenly informed that Alexander is in retreat. The Persian is taken by surprise: the unhappy moment comes when he realizes that his enemy is about to attack. His distress and anger are high; he inquires after the false messenger. But the speech that he makes to his men moments later is entirely optimistic: "Dixoles grañt esfuerço quando fueron plegados / varones tengamosnos por omes venturados" (983); the addresss goes on for six lines more. As I stated above, these passages are all original. The prevailing source through all of them is the *Alexandreis* of Gautier, but in every instance the speech spoken by Darius is invented by the vernacular poet, as are the lines describing the king's mood. The result is something completely foreign to Gautier's text, a narrative motif, a cliché repeated: the character in low spirits who disguises his feelings and utters cheering words. This is surely a remarkable initiative in itself: the pattern in question would seem to be more typical of a *chanson de geste* than of a learned *cuaderna vía* poem. But its interest, as I believe, goes further. One cannot help remembering a passage in the first book of the *Aeneid* which presents a situation exactly like the one that so seems to fascinate our poet. During the storm off Libya the Trojan ships are scattered, and once on land, Aeneas is convinced that a great part of his band of men is lost forever. His grief at that terrible moment is what one would expect, but he nevertheless puts on a cheerful face and addresses encouraging words to his remnant. Did the *Alexandre*-poet have this scene in mind when he invented his motif? Is this a good humanist's imitation of a venerable *auctor*? One can never be certain. There are in any case two arguments for the affirmative. In the first place, of all the narrative details that he could have found in Gautier this is the one he selected to repeat, that is, to turn into a migrant motif. He need not have chosen any, but he in fact chose this one. One possible reason for this strange move might have been his memory of and veneration for the lines in *Aeneid* I. But more important, Gautier here passes on to the later poet nothing whatever that can be called Virgilian. We recall that of all of the four appearances of the motif in the *Alexandre* the one which is undoubtedly taken from the *Alexandreis* must add the distinctively Virgilian element on its own: Gautier does not specify that the speaker hides his sadness (*Alexandre* 1440-1441, based on Gautier, V 382-386, our first quotation from him). In other words, the passage in the *Alexandreis* was almost certainly not intended as an imitation of Virgil, and the Virgilian calque would thus be a pure initiative on the part of the vernacular poet.

Here, then, for better or for worse, are the arguments favoring Virgil as a source for the *Libro de Alexandre*. The case is certainly not closed, but the dilemma of the one who wants to make its author a person trained in grammar and *auctores*, but wants to deny him access to Virgil is partially resolved.

## 5) THE MIXED STYLE: THE *LIBRO DE ALEXANDRE* AND ITS SOURCES

With Virgil more or less disposed of we may turn to our theme of the moment, the oratorical mode of narrative in the great Spanish poem. We may begin by affirming once again that the notes which characterized our first long quotation from the *Libro*, the sequence about Pausanias, are quite general throughout the work. One simple way to confirm this is to pick another passage and show that more or less the same rules apply there as in the Pausanias episode. Without risking the charge of great partiality we might choose the lines immediately following the Trojan War narrative. As we recall, Alexander tells the whole story to his men to inspire them to greatness and to raise their spirits. The troops indeed react as he had wished: they show themselves the more eager for battle and conquest. They in fact express their new zeal in a short speech. The young king then orders them into action; they respond conducting raids throughout the neighborhood and occupying new territory. Rumor, however, does her work, and soon word reaches Darius that his enemy is at hand. The first part of this passage is original on the part of the *Alexandre*-poet, and the rest is his usual free paraphrase of two sources, the *Alexandreis* and one of the versions of the *Historia de preliis*. Here are the lines immediately after the collective speech:

> 773) Quando entendio el rrey que estauan ardientes
> los cueres saborgados ençendidas las mientes
> fizo rrancar las tiendas mando mouer las gentes
> por yr buscar a Dario a las tierras calientes
>
> 774) Echaron las algaras a todas las partidas
> quando las vnas tornauan las otras eran ydas
> conquirien los castillos las villas enfortidas
> non fallauan contrasto onde fuesen enbaydas
>
> 775) Todo lo conquerien quanto nunca trobauan
> quanto mas yuan yendo mas se encarnauan
> mas la junta de Dario tanto la cobdiçiauan
> que toda la conquista nada non preçiauan
>
> 776) Tanto pudo la fama por las tierras correr
> fasta que ouo Dario las nueuas a saber
> enpeços el buen omne todo a contorçer
> pero dixo en cabo no lo puedo creyer
>
> 777) Dario era de dias de gerra desusado
> auie con la grañt pas el lidiar oluidado
> ca desque rrey fuera non auie gerreado
> sy entonçes fues muerto serie bien venturado
>
> 778) Sy quando era rrico e era poderoso
> sysquiere de vasallos sysquiere de thesoro
> asy fuese ligero e fuese venturoso
> non fuera Alixandre a Jndia tan gozoso
>
> 779) Pero que non touiesen que era rrecreyente
> enpesço de baldir menazas alta mente
> juraua con la yra del rrey omnipotente
> que lo farie colgar a el & a su gente

We are surely on familiar ground. The "quando" clause in the first quatrain has to do, trivially, with the mind of Alexander: the king understood that his men were well-disposed. The last two verses tell of his orders, indirect discourse, and of his motive for giving them: he sends his men on the march so that they can overtake Darius. The next six lines, on their military activities, are very rapid summary: the subject is an all-embracing "they," unexpressed in the Aragonese-Castilian, and the events recounted are referred to globally, also in the plural. The rest of stanza 775 gives us the state of mind of the triumphant soldiers, so intent on catching Darius that they count their immediate gains as nothing. The spread of the news is a portmanteau event, told as if it were a single happening, but in fact reducible to many particulars. The glimpse we catch of Darius in the lines following is a genuine closeup, the king writhing with anger, and then declaring his disbelief, in direct discourse. Stanza 777 gives us background, Darius weakened by long peace. This in turn becomes the springboard for a piece of editorializing: if the Persian were as full of vitality and as fortunate as he is rich, Alexander would not have become a world conqueror. We then go back to the king: to disguise his distress (another Virgilian cliché?) he begins to talk boastfully of hanging the lot of them, Alexander and all his people. The speech is reported; it is not in direct discourse.

There we have it, reported speech, summary, one small touch of *evidentia* saved for a critical moment, commentary, and, of course, reports on the thoughts of characters, particularly on their intentions. Here, for comparison, is the much leaner version of Gautier:

> Bearing news that Alexander, avenging his fatherland, was even now threatening destruction, Rumour, as she ran to and fro through the Persian cities, had struck with terrifying sound the ears of Darius who was sluggish with the paralysis of sloth and dissolute through luxury. In terms of empire, he was the greater, and he was better supported by arms and by kings who owed him allegiance. Also he was richer in costly bronze, and far stronger and riper in age than the new warrior. Nevertheless, the experience of fighting, to which he was unaccustomed, and long lasting peace had so influenced the wavering spirits of the king, that in all respects he was inferior to Alexander, to whom he could have been superior, if his bellicosity had only equalled his military resources. However, so that his royal majesty might not

appear to be downcast by terror or to have less firmness, from his proud lips Darius thundered forth threats &c.[17]

I can testify that I did not have to search long hours for the later version, the one in the *Alexandre*; it is perhaps significant that it comes early in the poem It is important to realize how consistent the Romance poet's practice actually is, how many times in the course of the work he forces his material into its distinctive mold. It is easy, after all, to see the artisan's hand at work. We have pretty thorough knowledge of the poet's sources, texts that he often follows closely: his departures from these sources are the more conspicuous and easy to spot. Nothing is more revealing than these initiatives. Let us take as an example a stretch of the Trojan War narrative, from the section based on the *Homerus latinus*, or the *Ilias latina*. We should note first that as far as style is concerned this text does not give the poet much support or guidance. Others of his sources of course do: the *Alexandreis*, for example, light years distant from the *Libro* in many respects, is close to it in its wealth of commentary, of summary, and of other approaches to storytelling that we have spoken of. But the *Ilias* is another matter. What sets it apart most notably from its companions in the *Libro* is the great speed of its narrative. It is, after all, a summary of the plot of the *Iliad* in less than eleven hundred verses; it covers very nearly every episode, and therefore cannot afford to be anything but rapid. The Spanish poet, generally pretty independent before his sources, is in many ways influenced by this unusual text: as we will see, he himself produces more than one instance of rapid narrative, in the Troy

---

[17] The Latin of this passage runs:
    Vltorem patriae Magnum iam fata minantem
    Nuncia Persarum discurrens fama per urbes
    Desidiae torpore grauis luxuque soluti
    Terrifico strepitu Darii concusserat aures.
    Qui licet imperio maior, munitior armis,
    Obsequiis regum, precioso ditior ere,
    Viribus excedens, euo maturior esset
    Bellatore nouo, tamen experientia Martis
    Qua dissuetus erat et pax diuturna labantes
    Impulerat regis animos ut in omnibus esset
    Inferior duce quo poterat prestantior esse
    Si mens tanta foret pugnandi quanta facultas.
    Ne depressa tamen terrore minusque rigoris
    Regia maiestas uideatur habere, superbo
    Intonat ore minas Darius. (*Alexandreis* II, verses 1-15)

episode and elsewhere. But the very bareness of the *Ilias* gives him every temptation to do his distinctive thing. The passage we must examine is the one on the hand-to-hand combat between Hector and Achilles, climax of the Latin poem as it is of its Greek model.[18] There are only two explicit references in the *Ilias* to the fear of Hector. At the beginning of the episode we are told that neither the fear of death nor the entreaties of his father kept him from going out to meet his enemy: "non durae timor undique mortis, / Non patriae tenuere preces, quin obvius iret / Et contra magnum contendere vellet Achillem" (verse 932-934). But immediately he sees Pallas fully armed, and runs in terror along the walls of the city. Juan de Mena renders the passage as follows: "fué vista ante los ojos de Hétor la tritonia Palas, et ovo miedo; y el sin ventura començó a fuyr en contorno de los sus adarves, et hallava las puertas cerradas."[19] Later, in the middle of the conflict, he suddenly realizes that Paris is not at hand, that his (false) appearance there had been a trick of Pallas. "What should he do? What divinity should he call upon?"; "quid agat? quae numina supplex/ Invocet?" (970-971). The *Alexandre*-poet does not hesitate to put his thumbprints on this text. In the first place, he suppresses entirely the flight before the walls of Troy; this is surely significant. But, more interesting for us, he refers over several verses to Hector's fear or the lack of it. Immediately before the great conflict we see him reflecting on the imminent danger:

672) Fue comediendo Etor añt que fuese entrado
asmo de todo en todo que era engañado
dixo entre su cuer yo so amortiguado
mas mas me valdrie seyer muerto & soterrado

---

[18] *Homerus latinus, id est, Baebii Italici Ilias latina*, in *Poetae latini minores*, post Aemilivm Baehrens iterum recensvit Fridericvs Vollmer, vol. II, fasc. III (Leipzig, Teubner, 1913); the final encounter between Hector and Achilles begins in verse 931.

[19] Juan de Mena, *La Yliada en romance* según la impresión de Arnao Guillén de Brocar (Valladolid, 1519), edición, prólogo y glosario por Martín de Riquer (Barcelona, Selecciones Bibliófilas, 1949), p. 185. Quotations from Mena's translation henceforth will be from this edition. Riquer has placed Vollmer's edition of the *Ilias* facing the Mena, but has omitted the numbering of the verses. The Latin of the passage runs:
[Ante oculos subito visa est Tritonia Pallas]
Pertimuit clausisque fugit sua moenia circum
Infelix portis. (936-938)

Five stanzas of prayer and soliloquy follow, and then we have,

> 678) Etor asmando esto perdio el mal espanto
> por lo que auie fecho tenieslo por quebranto
> acomendo su alma a Dios el padre santo
> torno contra Archiles esforçado ya quanto

The fear motif in the *Ilias* gets turned into an interior scene, comments on Hector's inner thoughts as well as a monologue. We should add that these are not the only additions to the material taken from the Latin. We have still more looks inside Hector's mind. There is his deception and undeception, his belief that Paris is at his side to help him, followed by his realization that he is fighting alone:

> 683) Cuydo que ferrie luego Paris del otro cabo
> quel farien con la priesa cuestas tornar priuado [Achilles]
> cato e non lo vio tovos por engañado
> quebrol el coraçon e paros deserrado

The hero's reflections on fate and Providence follow:

> 684) Entendie de su vida que era acabada
> la rrueda de su fado que era trastornada
> sopo que nol valdrie nin lança nin espada
> que quando Dios non quiere todo non vale nada

A second prayer follows. Still another ingrafting in the Hector-Achilles sequence has a familiar look to it. In the *Ilias*, as we know, it is the goddess Pallas who produces the false appearance of Paris. The Romance poet takes us inside her mind. We are party to her deliberations:

> 679) Pallas contendie sienpre nunca en al andaua
> por fer matar a Etor mas nos le aguisaua
> que entendie que Troya por el se enparaua
> sy non que serien todos caydos en la traua
>
> 680) Asmo la maledita vna grañt trauesura
> priso forma de Paris su misma figura
> armas quales las suyas e tal caualgadura
> e vino contra Etor a muy grand presura

A general reflection is appropriate here. It is a kind of topic, especially in older manuals and critical literature, that vernacular is livelier than Latin. Commentators on Old Spanish texts which are translations or paraphrases of material in Latin have at times been eager to stress the spontaneity and freshness of these versions: we are asked to admire the many fine touches produced by the later writer. Realism is sometimes an issue: the original texts are dry and abstract, but the vernacular writers bring a lifelikeness, a presence, a particularity to the matter they treat, qualities missing in the older texts. One could of course begin by objecting to a romantic prejudice which puts a premium on novelty and originality. Some might think that craftsmanship, rhetoric and in some cases *imitatio* were more pertinent categories in dealing with this literature. One would hope that this battle has already been fought and won. But poetics, general theory, is not the only problem. Did, in fact, the older critics observe correctly? The expressions "viveza del relato" (my own paraphrase, not a quotation), or the famous "realism native to Spanish literature and to the Spanish soul," if they refer to anything in the text, might suggest to sensible persons that Berceo's writings, the *Alexandre*, Alfonso's two histories, were all redolent with *evidentia*. But this is not my judgment at all. I cannot claim to remember every detail in all of those texts, but I do suggest that the verses we have just cited from the Trojan War episode of the *Alexandre* are a fair sample and are good evidence to the contrary. Not one of our additions or modifications brings a scene before the eyes of the reader/listener. All express some kind of inner state. One gives us the motive and purpose of Pallas, one, Hector's passage from fear to courage, and another, his shock facing the certainty of death. The reflections on Fortune and Providence do double duty: they tell us, literally, what Hector was thinking, but they also serve as commentary, a judgment about life and death generally, brought to bear on a particular situation. Our selection was ideal for our purposes. The *Ilias latina* tells its story very rapidly. Its narrative is normally sparing in its details, and this means that it is the perfect framework to hang new material on. The poet with a bent towards *evidentia* meets his great challenge in the *Ilias*: he may add to its bare account all the visual detail that he likes. But this assuredly is not the way or the taste of the *Alexandre*-poet. Some new details in the Troy episode are evidential, but many more are not. Let us round out our case by citing a few more artful additions our poet makes to his barebones original. In the *Ilias* version, before the Greeks march on Troy, Thersites, exemplary coward, pleads self-interest as a reason for not going to war; we labor, he says in effect, and others gain the rewards. The *Libro* follows *Homerus*, but adds, quite on its own, a general explanation for the reaction of the Greeks:

> 425) Commo diz la palabra que suelen rratraher
> que mas podie en vn conçeio vn malo cofonder
> que non podrien diez buenos asentar nin poner
> ouiera ally por poco asi a conteçer
> 426) Creyeron a Tresidas la mas mayor partida
> era pora tornarse toda la gente mouida

This is a fine piece of editorial intervention, a general rule, expressed in a *sententia*, with an application to a particular case. Some verses later we have the great Homeric catalogue of the Greek forces. Priam is deeply distressed at the arrival of so great an enemy, but is assured by his son Hector, who speaks to his father, then puts on his arms and takes to his horse. All the great of Troy fall in behind him. The poet gives us his judgment of such a splendid Trojan army:

> 461) Tanta de buena gente y era aplegada
> si non que era contra ellos la fada
> ouieran de los griegos a Troya enparada
> e non fuera su cosa atan mal agisada

Were not fate against them, the Trojans would surely have won the war. This is a contrary to fact condition, editorializing and not narration. The vainglorious Paris takes a daring stand in battle, and the *Libro* tells us why:

> 463) Paris por demostrarse de qual esfuerço era
> e por far pagamiento a la su conpañera
> partiose de los suyos priso la delantera
> commo si el ouiese a tener la frontera

As in Homer, the *Ilias* has the truce between Greeks and Trojans broken by Pandarus' arrow shot. The *Alexandre*-poet makes his explanation or commentary. He introduces the episode as follows:

497) commo Dios non quiere non val conpusiçion
pudo mas el diablo metie y diuision

As I have suggested, the *Ilias latina* is perhaps the one of the poet's *auctores* who leaves him the greatest freedom. Given his tendency to amplify and alter generally, the very bareness of the Latin text is an invitation to him to do what he is inclined to do. The resulting product is well within the range of the pattern we have described. The Trojan war episode is in some ways distinctive within the *Libro*; the rapidity of the narration in the *Ilias* sometimes speeds up considerably the pace of the paraphrase, but most of the characteristics of the exposition in the Pausona sequence are present here, commentary, motivations, accounts of emotions and other inner states, and the others. These lines based on the *Homerus* are a good test case, and on this basis I believe that we can call the narrative practice here as well as in the Pausona episode representative, and a good index to his concept of narrative generally.

## 6) SUMMARY

Our task is not yet completed. The storytelling in the *Libro de Alexandre* puts further problems and questions to us which need to be aired before we can move forward. The first of these is in a sense a non-problem, an issue we cannot avoid, but which winds up resolving itself. Summary as a narrative technique over and over again uses two procedures, putting under one heading the actions of many agents – the Trojans fought the Greeks –, and putting under one heading the repeated actions of a single agent – I lost my keys several times today. I need not say that these devices are familiar, or that we have already seen instances of them in our quotations. One can scarcely open one's mouth without using one or another of them. Our own interest in them is that they seem to be evasions of *evidentia*; using other language we could say that they had the look of mediation about them, that they do not work unless we have a conspicuous narrator taking all the responsibility. We must make distinctions. As we have seen, these two moves are indeed closely bound to summary. Summary can hardly do without them; for all practical purposes the pair, along with rapid narration, belong to the essence, to the definition, of summary. But that is only half the story. The two, the telling, all in a gulp, of many actions by many agents, or of multiple actions by one agent, do not inevitably belong to summary: summary perhaps cannot do without them, but they fare very well without it. Let us take the universal battle scene cliché, belonging to epic poetry of all periods, "On the field of Pharsalus (or Valencia, or wherever) one might see horses wandering without their riders, streams of water red with blood, one could hear the moans of the dying, the shouts of vengeance, the clash of swords." One could think of an instance which might be more obviously narrative: "The Greeks (or Romans) stormed the town, and one could hear the shouts of battle and almost immediately after their cry of victory, as the men streamed out, some by the main gate, others climbing over the walls like schoolboys." A summarizer would not permit himself all this luxury. Neither scene has the least savor of summary. What is more, if any text is evidential, these are (we do our best). There is no incompatibility here. Neither is there with the other pattern, multiple actions, one agent. One of the most memorable moments in Book IV of the *Aeneid* is the one showing Dido, already distraught with love for Aeneas, offering sacrifices and performing sacred rites of various sorts. This is a brilliantly evocative scene, and one that falls entirely within our pattern. Likewise, one of the glories of the *Pharsalia* is the passage on the priestess at Delphi, reluctant to prophesy, but finally doing so under duress. This magnificent scene may well be an imitation of the one in Virgil, and much the same can be said of it as of its predecessor.

In a word, the two patterns belong to summary but not vice versa, and, against expectations, there is nothing in either that is incompatible with *evidentia*. Needless to say, the pair appear frequently in the *Libro de Alexandre*, in both forms, as a part of summary and otherwise. Of the two the first, multiple agents, one account, is by far the more common. Vivid description is by no means alien to it in the poem; battle scenes much like the one I invented occur more than once, a perfect instance.

## 7) Description

The lengthy static descriptions in the *Libro* constitute a problem of another order. Any reader of the poem can supply examples of this figure, the *ecphrases*, of Darius' shield, of his mother's tomb, of

Achilles' shield, the simple descriptions, of Babylon, of the Persian army. In principle, the issues this device raises are many and complicated. But more than anything else it is simple extent that matters to us, the large proportion of the text of the *Libro de Alexandre* which is given over to static description. Other matters aside, the space taken up by description obviously has a great deal to do with the large architecture of the poem. Very generally we should reflect that the flow of the narrative, the speed or slowness with which events unfold in the course of the text, is far from uniform. As regards the story strictly speaking the pace is not always the same, as should be clear from some of our observations: certain events are told summarily, and others in detail. It is an important feature of the poem that in some episodes the pace varies even within the story-unit itself. But quite as significantly, the narrative at certain moments comes to a dead stop. We have already seen instances of this narrative arrest: the *sententiae* and the proverbs that decorate many episodes of the poem, the commentaries and explanations introduced in the poet's own voice, the dramatic apostrophes that occur from time to time, all bring the unfolding of events to a halt. One species of narrative interruption in the *Libro* is especially long, the static description; I have already mentioned some examples, the *ecphrases*, of Darius' shield, of his wife's tomb, of Achilles' shield, and the more informal descriptions of Babylon, and of the Persian army. These lengthy interruptions involve us in a paradox. The descriptive accounts taken as a group include all sorts of material. By no means is all of it of classical inspiration; some of it is blatantly medieval. This should hardly be a startling disclosure, but it is pertinent in an essay that sets out to be a study of humanism, the story of the influence of the *auctores* on a medieval text. There is no need to recall every bit of medievalia in the *Alexandre*; not least, Professor Michael has already done the job brilliantly, and there is little point in redoing his work. One striking account which is notoriously unclassical is the poet's topical description of the Wild Man, on the model of Raincourt in the *Song of William*, or of more than one odious Moor in the *Song of Roland*. The character in the *Libro* is the boastful Philistine, son of a black father and a giant mother, the soldier of Darius whose horrific description fills up several stanzas (1364ff). Curiously, he is not original with the the vernacular poet; he comes by direct line from the *Alexandreis*, proof, incidentally, that the classicist Gautier de Châtillon was not averse to borrowing from *chansons de geste*, when it suited him. The medieval matter is there, in both texts. Our paradox is the following; the fact that the stuff of our long descriptions, their themes, their character and origin, have no bearing at all on our argument. As we have stated, bulk is the only thing that interests us here. Our theme in time in this study is to be the influence on the *Alexandre*, direct and indirect, of Silver Latin. Precisely what is most conspicuous about Roman epic starting with Lucan is the slowness of its narrative: it is not uncommon for critics to say that the authors of these poems have little interest in narrative at all. And once again, the most grievous offender against speed in these texts is nothing other than description. It is therefore one gross aspect of the *Libro*, the length of its descriptions and the large space they occupy, which turns out to be distinctively imitative and humanistic, or, as it were, classicizing. This is true even when the material which actually fills up those accounts is neither Virgilian nor Lucanesque.

8) INDIRECT DISCOURSE

Indirect discourse is one more feature of the *Libro*'s narrative practice which we must look at closely. Its principal interest for us is that by its very nature it evades immediacy. As has been repeated since antiquity, speech reproduced or simulated is the imitation of nature in its fullest sense. The narrator does not have to report anything: we hear directly the voice of Achilles or Hector. But if instead we are told what Achilles said, we are at one remove from his words: a narrator has to intervene, become audible, to do the reporting. In the *Libro de Alexandre* indirect discourse is not extensive, but it is there, and its presence in the work is distinctive and significant. Here are some of its instances of reported speech. Alexander several times gives orders. Just before the first great battle with Darius he is disposing his forces: "mando que cada vno guardase su frontera / mando que non ouiese vagar la doladera" (976). His ambassadors are killed by the Tyrians, and he orders that the city be attacked: "mandolos conbatir" (1104). Earlier, he orders a march on Sidon: "mondo mouer sus pueblos de lazerio vsados / por çercar a Sidon" (1090). Babylon has surrendered peacefully, but Alexander, fearing treachery, tells the army to enter the city in battle order:

1535)  Mando todas sus gentes que fuesen allegadas
       al entrar de la villa fuesen hazes paradas
       commo para batalla fuesen todas paradas
       que por enemistad mala non fuesen engañadas

Still in Babylon Alexander lays down a new code of laws for his army. He orders his men to come together to hear its provisions: "Mando fincar las gentes en vn rico lugar" (1550). Other speech-acts get reported in the text. Prayer is an instance. The inhabitants of Jerusalem are fearful at Alexander's approach, and they have recourse to their God: "fizieron rrogationes por toda la santidat / que les fiziese Dios alguna piedat" (1136). At least once an oath is recorded. Outraged by the treachery of the people of Tyre, the Greek soldiers swear vengeance: "ende juraron todos por los suyos griñones / que pornien en ella todos sendos tisones" (1100). Reported speech, pure and simple, is not rare in the *Libro*, though most of the accounts in question are brief. One of the longer ones is the report of the spy who tells Alexander that Darius has fled the field at Arbela. The passage runs two stanzas long, and there is little need to quote it (1346-1347). We can also do without the many instances of "dixo" and "dixoles" which appear on many pages of the poem. Here is a small sample. Informed that Tyre would not surrender, Alexander expresses satisfaction:

1096)  dixo que los de Tiro grañt seruiçio le dauan
       ca ellos toda via mayor presçio sacauan
       quando por pura fuerça lo ageno ganauan

After his pilgrimage to the shrine of Ammon Alexander is informed that Darius was on the march:

1185)  Dixieronle que Dario era aparellado
       por batalla le dar estaua aguisado
       avñ que lo auie por la tierra buscado
       e retrayen que era por a Greçia tornado.

Bits of reported speech which are even shorter are perhaps the most typical. One instance will do. The Greeks for an unhappy moment are hard pressed at Arbela. They express their despair: "ya dizien los de Greçia que eran enollados / que la yra de Dios los auie deparados" (1430).

On the whole this is not a large representation, small bits of indirect discourse, sometimes turning on important matters, sometimes not. We recall that in the relatively short narration in the *Pro Milone* reported speech played an important part. It was in this mode that we were told that Clodius intended to kill Milo. More than that, in the ears of the intended audience the supposed utterances of Clodius would have been very damning. Given the relatively short extent of the *narratio,* the length of the passage is considerable. If oratory is our term of contrast, our lines from Cicero would seem to say that indirect discourse in the *Alexandre* is of small importance. Ancient historiography, as it would seem, also puts the *Libro* to shame. Broadly speaking, direct discourse is limited to the invented orations, while other bits of speech that are pertinent to the story are simply reported. In fact there is a great deal of the latter.

It should also be noted that there is a large proportion of direct discouse in the *Alexandre*. We are fortunate to have a fine study on the subject, an unpublished dissertation by Professor George Greenia.[20] Greenia points out that many pieces of indirect discourse in the sources of the *Libro* get changed there into direct; the proportion of direct to indirect in our text is, therefore, rather larger than it is in the *Alexandreis*. But the significant term of contrast here is the *Aeneid* itself, where indirect discourse is quite rare. In all of the last six books I can recall one instance of Aeneas giving an order: this is surely an index. The *Alexandre*-poet thus winds up somewhere in the middle; there is not a great deal of indirect discourse in the *Libro*, but the very presence of some is surely interesting, if we compare it in this respect to Virgil's poem.

9) THE PLAIN STYLE

The *Libro de Alexandre* is in many ways like a medieval historical compilation: different sections of it are based on different *auctores*, and each brings its own particular information to the story. Now, the *Alexandre*-poet is a conscious artist, and as we have seen,

---

[20] Greenia, George, *The 'Alexandreis' and the 'Libro de Alexandre'; Latin versus Vernacular Direct Discourse*, PhD dissertation in Romance Languages and Literatures, University of Michigan, 1984.

he takes great liberties with his sources as he tries to shape his material to his own purposes. It is easy in a way to exaggerate this independence. Modifications notwithstanding, the fact is that much that is distinctive about each of his sources survives intact in the *Alexandre*. This applies not only to matter, but to form: a good deal of the narrative layout of the *Libro* is inherited wholesale from the *Alexandreis*, from recensions of the *Historia de preliis*, and so on. The *Ilias latina*, which is a very extensive source, presents a special case of this influence, one which is especially pertinent to our argument. The focal point of these discussions has been the species of narrative that is particularized, that offers the reader sufficient detail so that he can visualize the events recounted. The *Ilias latina* and its version in the *Alexandre* are, as we shall see, an eminent case of the evasion of this figure. The plain style, as we might call it, is, first and last, an important ingredient in the mix of our poem: it is interesting in itself, and as one voice among many, and an examination of some of the passages in this work related to the *Ilias* is a practical first step towards getting the close look we need of this strain.

That the narrative mode of the anonymous *Homerus latinus* should be less than full or variegated should hardly come as a surprise. This short poem tells the whole story of the *Iliad* in exactly 1070 hexameter verses. It is by no means a failure: its poet is hardly a second Ovid, but his work has elegance, and a good sense of style and register. Its narrative pace is mostly rapid (how could it be other-wise?), inevitably plain and poor in detail. There are, however, bits of authorial commentary, and occasionally we are treated to fully developed scenes, some routine, but others far from contemptible. The turn in the story that tells of Thetis' flight to Olympus to intercede for her son is indeed splendid. Short of that, we are given bits of particularizing detail which bring life to otherwise unadorned stretches of narrative. One should add finally that the storytelling itself, rapid and simple as it is, is expert and craftsmanlike. With exceptions we will take note of, the same cluster of qualities that marks the *Ilias latina* survives in the related passages in the *Alexandre*, even, indeed, when it wanders away from the source. Here is the Spanish poet's Briseis episode, briefer than its model, and supplied with an ending that is entirely un-Homeric:

> 417) Auie vna amiga que el mucho querie
> teniela por fermosa qui quiere que la veye

pagose della el rrey Agamenon por que bien paresçie
tirola a Archiles que mal non meresçie
418) Pesol de voluntat touos por desonrrado
que lo auie el rey mala meñt aontado
non lo quiso sofryr partiose del yrado
començo darle gerra commo omne desesperado
419) Tañt denonada meñt lo pudo gerrear
tantos muchos vasallos le pudo matar
que commo dis Omero que non quiere bafar
tantos eran los muertos que non los podien contar
420) Asy jazien los muertos commo en rrestrojo
paja non los podien cobrir nin meter en mortalla
leualos commo lieua los pelos la naualla
ermarseye la hueste sy duras la baraja
421) Fizieron los varones conçejo general
dixeronle al rrey señor estate mal
la hueste es mal andante e a tu non tencal
si la dueña non rriendes tornaremos en mal
422) Rindio el rrey la dueña a todo su mal grado
quando la ouo Archiles fue todo amansado
torno en pas la gerra sy peso al pecado
fue de ally adelañt don Archiles dubdado

In some ways this selection has the look and profile of others we have quoted. The same repertory of devices is in evidence. There are editorial judgments, that the forces would be entirely cut down if the struggle continued, or that Achilles did not deserve to lose the girl. Motives are stressed: we are told that everyone thought Briseis beautiful, including Agamemnon, and that Achilles took violent measures, because his honor was sullied. Curiously, there is an appeal to authority, that of Homer. All of these touches are of course distinctive to the *Alexandre*: the whole passage is, indeed, very independent of its source. The details are fairly typical of what the poet adds to the *Ilias* in his adaptation. But even within them, this Briseis passage is bare bones, little more than an outline. The only particularizing detail is the number of the dead, matter which can hardly be said to alter seriously the profile of the story. Here, for comparison, is the account in the *Ilias*, first in Mena's version:

No empero se apartó de Agamenón el ardor de Crisida: antes por muchos días lloró los sus perdidos amores; et luego mandó privar al gran Achiles de Brisida, assí como Achiles avía hecho a él de Crisida, y consoló los fuegos de sus ardores con los ajenos. Y el fiero nieto de Achiles Eaco, luego con el espada desnuda se vino contra Agamenón, por saña de aqueste hecho; amenazándole muy cruelmente si le no diesse a Brisida; ni Agamenón se aparejó menos contra éste defenderse por espada. E si la casta mano de Palas tenido no oviesse a Achiles, el ciego amor le oviere hecho dexar turpe y desonesta fama en el siglo a las gentes argólicas. (pp. 59-61)

> Non tamen Atridae Chryseidos excidit ardor:
> Maeret et amissos deceptus luget amores.
> Mox rapta magnum Briseide privat Achillem
> Solaturque suos alienis ignibus ignes.
> At ferus Aeacides nudato protinus ense
> Tendit in Atriden et, ni sibi reddat honestae
> Munera militiae, letum crudele minatur
> Nec minus ille parat contra defendere se ense.
> Quod nisi casta manu Pallas tenuisset Achillem,
> Turpem caecus amor famam liquisset in aevum
> Gentibus Argolicis. (69-79)

The Thersites episode in the *Libro*, which follows immediately, is put together along much the same lines as is the Briseis passage. The narrative is simple and rapid and interrupted by only a few bits of moralizing. The story is largely the Homeric one, as preserved in the *Ilias*. The cowardly Thersites, "auol e mal lenguado" (423), urges the Greeks to abandon Troy and return home. Ulysses, enraged, strikes him and abuses him verbally. A mêlée follows, and not a few Greeks resolve to abandon the field. Only the wise words of Nestor can put down the disturbance and recall the mob to their purpose. The *Libro* tampers with this material only in minimal ways. Thus, though the *Ilias* does not give us Thersites' words to the Greeks, our poem does. And as we have seen, the narrator intervenes to generalize about evil counselors, and so explains why the coward's words have such an effect on his audience (425). Here, finally, are the *Alexandre*'s lines about Nestor:

> 428) Auie vn omne bueno vieio e de grañt seso
> era de grandes dias blanco commo queso
> do quier que vuiaua sienpre fue bien apreso
> era en los judicios tan leal commo el peso
> 429) Nastor era su nonbre auie mucho beuido
> escuchauanlo todos e era bien oydo

> pesol de voluntat quando vio el roydo
> metioseles en medio con vn baston bronido
> 430) Maltrayelos a firmes daua les bastonadas
> todos por su verguença escondien las espadas
> dizieles a las gentes que se ouiesen quedadas
> que fazien desaguisado eran mal acordadas
> 431) Maltraye a Trexidas que dixiera locura
> rebtaua a los otros que fazien desmesura
> dizieles ay amigos mal vos mienbra la jura
> que jurastes al rrey quando vos disia su rrencura

In these lines Nestor is dramatized, brought into focus. The poet creates this high relief by barely two particularizing details, a new strain in the passage. The first is the allusion to the old man's white hair, a touch alien to the *Ilias*. The second is also original, an un-Homeric turn of plot, absent from the Latin poem: Nestor's great prestige among the Greeks is shown to us as they shamefacedly put up their swords at his display of anger. The poet's treatment of Nestor is effective, a good index to his art and skill generally. What needs to be stressed is not simply the severe economy of means, but the fact that even these tiny particularizing details are exceptional. The episode manages nicely without them up to the old man's first appearance.[21]

As I have suggested, the plain style in the *Alexandre* is one mode among several, and is sometimes made to contrast with others. The Trojan War episode once again supplies the example. Here are the verses that come immediately after the Homeric catalogue of ships:

> 452) Avn ellos non eran del puerto leuantados
> al buen rrey de Troya llegaron los mandados

---

[21] Here is part of the Thersites episode in the *Ilias*:
> Hic tunc Thersites, quo non deformior alter
> Venerat ad Troiam nec lingua protervior ulli,
> Bella gerenda negat patrias hortatus ad oras
> Vertere iter; quem consiliis inlustris Vlixes
> Correptum dictis sceptro percussit eburno.
> Tum vero ardescit conceptis litibus ira:
> Vix telis caruere manus, ad sidera clamor
> Tollitur et cunctos pugnandi corripit ardor.
> Tandem sollertis prudentia Nestoris aevo
> Compressam miti sedavit pectore turbam
> Admonuitque duces dictis. (136-146)

# THE *LIBRO DE ALEXANDRE* ITSELF

        que auien grandes pueblos de Gresçia arribados
        que vinien sobre Troya sañosos e yrados
453)  Menbrol al rrey del sueño ouo miedo sobeio
        el grañt cuer que auia fisosle poquilleio
        mando feryr pregones que fisiesen conseio
        sobre tan grañt fazienda que prisiesen consejo
454)  Dixo don Etor al padre vos fincaduos en pas
        avedes buenos fillos e vasallos asas
        nos salrremos a ellos seremos les de fas
        nunca se encontraron con tan crudo agras
455)  Armose el buen cuerpo ardiente & muy leal
        vistiose a la carona vn ganbax de çendal
        de suso la loriga blanca commo vn cristal
        fijo dixo su padre Dios te curie de mal
456)  Calço sus brafoneras que eran bien obradas
        de sortillas de açero sobra bien enlasadas
        asi eran bien presas e tan bien asentadas
        que semejauan calças de la tienda sacadas

The arming of Hector goes on for two more strophes. As is obvious, we cross a boundary in our text immediately after Hector's speech: the pace of the narrative slows down noticeably as we see the Trojan hero putting on his armor. In stanzas 452-454 events unfold much as they do elsewhere in our Spanish Iliad, but thereafter we are suddenly given a wealth of particulars as one piece of armor goes on after another. The point of this slowdown is clear. On one hand, it calls attention to Hector himself, the greatest of the Trojan warriors, and on the other, it marks a turning point in the story: the arming is the first event in the war properly speaking. We should note that in isolation the arming sequence is not especially colorful. Its effectiveness lies rather in that it follows some lines of rather plain narrative, and that it comes after a text that over a long stretch has been generally poor in paticularizing details. I remark finally that the contrast in these verses between the arming sequence and what precedes it comes to the *Alexandre* whole from the *Ilias latina*. The lines in the Latin poem leading up to the arming are rather different from the ones in the *Libro*, but the scene itself contrasts with the preceding material in quite the same way in the two poems.

    There are degrees of plainness. Some important episodes in the life of Alexander are told in the *Libro* in a mode that can only be called summary. The conquest of Egypt is reported in three verses:

> 1166) entro para Egibto commo rrayo yrado
> el rrey fue de seso el pueblo acordado
> rresçibieron lo luego juraron su mandado

This account is, incidentally, succeeded by one of the most dramatic sequences in the *Libro*, the one on the pilgrimage to the shrine of Ammon; the story is told at length, with a full complement of details. Egypt and the pilgrimage are both in Gautier, the latter narrated fully, the former dismissed in a single verse: "Tendit in Egyptum. qua sub ditione redacta, / Ardet" &c. (III 371-2). Egypt is not the only whirlwind campaign in the *Alexandre*: Sidon is another, and is paired off with Tyre to form the same contrast of fast narrative with slow. Here is Sidon:

> 1090) Quando ouo Alixandre los averes donados
> los septenarios fechos los clamores pasados
> mondo mouer sus pueblos de lazerio vsados
> por çercar a Sidon que fuesen bien guisados
> 1091) Commo eran encarnados non dubdauan morir
> pensaron a porfidia en los muros sobir
> no tanto se pudieron los otros rreferir
> ouieron la por fuerça estonçe a conquerir
> 1092) Quando Sydon fue presa fueron Tiro çercar

Gautier again supplies the model, with a two-line Sidon and a lengthy Tyre (III 274-341). Here is Sidon: "tendit Sydona uetustam, / Phenicum gentem. quibus in sua iura redactis, / Ad Tyrios conuertit iter" (276-278). Gautier and the *Alexandre*-poet play the same script again when they give us the falls of Susa and Uxion. The *Libro*'s version is quite independent and covers two quatrains:

> 1561) Fueron çercar a Susa vna noble çibdat
> serie grañt exaramiello fablar de su bondat
> commo tierra syn rrey e syn abtoridat
> rresçibieron lo luego syn otra poridat
> 1562) Asas auie en Susa que pudiesen prender
> mas por que lo prisiesen non lo podrien traher
> ca en casas nin en callejas non podien mas caber
> auienlo a dexar mas non en su querer

Two motives are new here, the lawlessness of the inhabitants, and the Greeks' failure to take booty. The Latin has simply: "Susam tradentibus urbem / Ciuibus et multis hilarato milite gazis, / Agmen ad Vxias conuertit turbidus arces" (VI 64-66).

## 10) EVIDENTIA

Timing is everything in comedy, and pacing is everything in storytelling, at least in some kinds. The *Alexandre*-poet shows his art and skill as elsewhere in his pacing, as he contrasts rapid narrative with slow, with varying degrees of both. Thin also contrasts with fat in the *Libro*: passages poor in particularizing details are brought up next to others full of them, to the greater effectiveness of both. As we have often repeated, the scene, the fully realized bit of narrative, in which the accumulation of details allows the audience to be, as it were, witness to the event, is far from universal in our poem. Even some of the best narrated episodes are poor in such touches. When they are indeed present, their effect is greater, and when we are given fully developed scenes, these are striking indeed. These remarks pretty much tell the story of *evidentia* in the *Alexandre*. We need make only a few observations more. There are the battle scenes. These tend towards drama, color and the particular, not only in the *Alexandre* but in many other forms of narrative, poetical, historical, and indeed, novelistic. Things slow down, and the camera is brought up close when the fighting begins. One of the hardiest species of the whole class is the battle that is narrated as a series of hand-to-hand combats. Since Homer the requirement has been that we know the details, in what order the weapons were used, where each blow falls, and how each defeated warrior hits the ground. In the *Alexandre* as in other such texts, battle sequences tend to be fully realized as a matter of routine. Elsewhere in the work, ocular *evidentia* seems to be a special effect saved for moments in the story which are particularly interesting or significant. This is an old theme with us. Let us look at two notable examples. The taking of Uxion is the subject of one of the finest sequences in the *Libro*, and the climax of the episode is marked by a fine play of particulars. The hero of the day is, as we recall, Tauron, who is commissioned by Alexander to penetrate the stronghold. A comparison of the passage in our poem with its source is revealing. Gautier's account begins in a style that is abstract and explanatory, but it takes on life and color as the poet shows us Tauron appearing suddenly at the top of the citadel: this turn in the story is the first we are expected to visualize. The *Alexandre* follows a similar plan, as we shall see. But its composer adds dozens of details to Gautier's rapid account. There is more direct discourse. The informers, for example, who in the Latin poem are referred to hastily *in genere*, become speaking characters. At various moments in the story the narrator comments on the courage and other virtues of the principals. Thus, we are told in the poet's voice that Tauron, man of courage, is from the beginning prompt to try the walls of the city, but as the enterprise starts to seem hopeless, his determination becomes all the greater. Intentions count for a great deal in the passage, especially general ones like those of Tauron, and plain deliberations and plans on the part of Alexander. Oddly enough, the explanatory mode of Gautier not only survives in the parallel verses in the *Libro*, but actually comes off stronger, thanks to these additions and others. But all of this changes at a moment in the story just before it does in the *Alexandreis*. In the Latin poem Tauron is introduced very soberly indeed: "Alexander put Tauron of proved merit in charge of the picked horsemen who were to face this extremely perilous undertaking [the approach through the secret passage]"; "Delectis equitum tantum in discrimen ituris / Prefecit Macedo meriti Taurona probati" (VI 73-74). The vernacular work sets out with a fair paraphrase of these lines, but immediately adds a speech by Alexander, warning the young man of the danger to himself if the mission fails, and in the act the king hands him the all-important pennant:

> 1572) dixo sepas Tauron en ti so acordado
> que vayas con estos rrecabdar vn mandado
> 1573) Pero quiero que lieues de nuestra señal
> bien ten que so muerto e que so con grañt mal
> sy ante que tu seas en medio del real
> en medio de Vxion non fuere Buçifal

The next quatrain shows Tauron eagerly making preparations and setting off. But immediately things go badly for him: he is spotted by the enemy and cannot enter the city. At that point, Alexander creates a diversion to protect him:.

> 1576) Enpeçoles a dar vna lit apresada
> mas non querien por eso dexar le la entrada
> mager que auie preso mucha mala colpada

> commo querie morir non lo preçiaua nada
> 1577) El rrey Alixandre de la otra partida
> tenie bien la señal que auie prometida
> auie a parte echado mucha barba bellida
> mas non podie por eso entrar a la bastida
> 1578) Pero tanto los pudo ferir e acuytar
> que dieron a Tauron vn poco de vagar
> acreçiol el esfuerço ovo ad abiuar
> ouieronle sin grado la puerta a dexar

These lines bring matters down to earth. The diversion leaves the gate free, the gate, let us note, that is unknown to Gautier. Then comes the surprise. Without any preparation we are given Tauron not only in the citadel, but actually planting a pennant on its summit. The next touch is very nearly as elegant. The abstract and economical Latin verse "Quo semel aspecto Grais audacia creuit," (VI 104) gives way to a scene, Alexander looking up at Tauron high above him, making his men do the same:

> 1580) Estaua Alixandre que la cosa veye
> catando a las torres quando asomarie
> quando fue veyendo que ya aparesçie
> mostrolo a todos quantos çerca tenie
> 1581) Fueron los de Vxion todos mal desmayados
> quando el pendon veyeron fueron todos mal corasnados
> mas los griegos con el gozo fueron mas esforçados
> semejaua que eran nueua mente vuiados[22]

As we can see, both texts save the ocular *evidentia* for the turning point of the story, when a difficult battle suddenly promises victory for Alexander. We should note, incidentally, that in the *Alexandreis* Tauron is not mentioned once in between his introduction into the story and his moment at the top of the citadel; this in itself is a striking disposition of the narrative. But of the pair perhaps the *Libro* should carry off the prize for drama, thickening the plot generally, as it does, and focusing on the look up at the citadel, with Alexander and Tauron on different levels.

---

[22] The specifying of spatial relationships in early poetry is the subject of a whole book, Anderson, Theodore M., *Early Epic Scenery* (Ithaca, Cornell University Press, 1971).

The famous sequence in Tarsus, Alexander swimming in the river and taking a bad chill, is also by its nature a genuine scene, pointless without all its details. We might expect an Eisensteinian detail here, public, epical and monumental. The extras on the set have to be in the thousands, and as we know, the consequences opened up by the king's possible death are very wide. But the passage is not what one would expect. The focus is on the crisis in the health of one simple human being; the scale of things is narrow and particular. Here is the beginning of the sequence in the *Libro*. Parmenion has just entered the city, and put out the fire set by the retreating Persians. The king enters in haste:

880) El rrey con la priesa fue escalentado
era de la calor del fuego destenprado
e y prouo vna cosa que non auie prouado
que la salut non dura sienpre en vn estado

881) El mes era de jullio vn tienpo escalentado
quando en el leon aue el sol su grado
auia a lo de menos quinze dias andado
segunt esto paresçe que era bien mediado

882) El tienpo era fuerte e el sol calieñt
querie de calentura moryr toda la geñt
Çiliçia sobre todas aue ayre caliente
quel ardor del sol la aquexa fiera mente

883) Iua por medio la villa vna agua cabdal
que es seguñt la tierra buena vno con al
naçie en vna sierra deçiendie por vn val
paresçe so el agua crespo el arenal

884) Priso el rrey sabor de bañarse en ella
que corrie tan fermosa que era marauilla
ouiera y por poco contido tal mancilla
que ouiera del rio todo el mundo querella

885) Fizose desarmar e tollerse los paños
teniendo gelo a mal los suyos & los estraños
dio salto en el rio con anbos sus calcaños
paresçie bien que jugo pocas vezes en baños

886) Commo estaua el cuerpo caliente e sudoriento
era el agua fria e contrario el viento
priso en aquel vaño vn tal estrenpamiento
que cayo fascas muerto syn seso e syn tiento

The following quatrains give us his soldiers' distress, realized in wails and gestures. It is significant that nearly all the particularizing details in the lines I have quoted are absolutely necessary to the story, the heat of the day, the coldness of the river, its course through the center of the city, and so on. It should therefore come as no surprise that the same circumstances are mentioned in other accounts of the event, in Gautier (II 148-172), and in his source Quintus Curtius (III 5:1-3). What is further significant is that all three versions moralize the story. In the verses following the ones cited and in their analogue Gautier and the Spanish poet raise the question of Fortune. Quintus Curtius gives us much the same music in an elegant paradox, the greatest of all kings brought low, not by warfare, but by a brief swim. The *Libro* and the *Alexandreis* also speak of the helplessness of humans in matters of health: our poet is simply following his model here. Curtius goes down a different path. We have a genuine peripety, a sudden change of fortune. The king thinks that bathing in the nude before the eyes of all will win him the good will of his men: the display will, as he thinks, show his simplicity and lack of pretense. A great project is brought low by a piece of bad luck. The Macedonian overreaches himself by forgetting his vulnerability before Fortune. The point of this discussion is that the *Alexandre*-poet lets stand a narrative sequence that is at the same time a moralizing exemplum and a fully realized and particularized scene. In the nature of things the two genres might have a certain affinity: one might well want to dramatize the story that has some special significance. And in the economy of the *Libro* the Tarsus sequence and others similar in intention are differentiated from their neighbors by their greater vividness and color. This is indeed one of the functions of *evidentia* in the poem.

* * *

I conclude here my examination of some of the narrative devices which appear in our great Alexander-epic. It is important to remember that the materials from the *Libro* we have scrutinized are first and foremost meant to be document: I have summoned them as witnesses. The real quarry in this investigation is not the work's internal design, but its place in the history of narrative poetry. But since the history I am attempting is about formal matters, it is inevitable that my account should speak at length about the formal and rhetorical layout of my primary text. The real point of the whole discussion is that the set of devices that in my view mark the

*Alexandre* are in no way peculiar to it. I have already given some hint of which texts have formal characteristics in common with our poem, and my next project must be to make good on my promise and look in detail at the rest of our corpus. We will examine first the ancient poems that set an example to writers of latter days, and then the medieval texts that tell us something about the transmission of the old lore. This, as I would insist, is not the end of the journey. Although I will not have the space to explore the matter, I hope it will eventually be clear to readers familiar with Renaissance poetry that the *Libro de Alexandre* belongs to a still larger class of texts, many of which belong to much later times, works in many ways not at all like our poem. In simple terms, I would put it that our great poem is witness to a tradition, perhaps against expectations. Our next task, therefore, will be to try to say something about this tradition.

## CHAPTER II

## OVID, LUCAN AND OTHERS

1) ORATORICAL POETRY, OLD AND NEW

Why did the *Alexandre*-poet write as he did? If, as we believe, he learned his craft in part from grammarians and teachers of the *auctores*, then we would have to say that these lessons bore fruit in a very particular way. What characterizes the storytelling of the *Libro de Alexandre* is that cluster of narrative techniques we have termed oratorical, and this is not necessarily the manner one might think a thirteenth century poet would learn from the old authors. Ancient poetry is not uniformly oratorical. At certain periods, at least, the declamatory mode was more typical of prose genres than of poetry: the *narratio* sections of judicial speeches have this profile eminently, and so to a lesser degree do many important historical writings. How did this mode get into narrative poetry? And how, particularly, did it get into the *Alexandre*?

The first of these two questions is in one sense secondary to our main concern. It is an old one; much commentary and criticism has been written on the subject of oratory and poetry. At a certain moment in the history of Latin letters poetry gets to be rhetorical; so runs the commonplace. The account often speaks of the popularity of public declamation in the early years of the Empire, and of the indelible mark that strange institution left on non-oratorical literature. Our most extensive ancient testimony about declamation, Seneca the Elder's *Declamations,* actually mentions Ovid, referring to him as a student of the declaimer Porcius Latro; it also makes a point of the mutual influence between his activity as a declaimer and as a poet.[1] The link between the two genres in the person of Ovid is surely significant; it is certainly not the end of the story. Where exactly the shadow of declamation falls on Latin letters generally is a question we need not ask, but it is surely not unreasonable to affirm that, starting with Ovid, certain poets show characteristics which are recognizably declamational. What is also certain and indeed pertinent to this discussion is that, from the time of Ovid on, Latin poetry becomes rhetorical in the diffuse modern sense, and as a separate matter, that it displays certain features which belong to the repertory of the orator, all in ways that are generally alien to older poetry. That the new factor might be the influence of declamation is at the very least believable. The idea is after all no invention of mine: such a judgment has been made before.[2]

As to our second question of how the oratorical mode got into the *Alexandre*, we may propose two answers. The first is that an answer is hardly possible. How could we ever explain the taste and preferences of an age? How can we tell what impelled a poet to follow one path rather than another? The most that we can say is that the *Alexandre*'s mode of narrative was in no way unique in its time. Our second answer is at once narrower and more telling. The great majority of ancient poets in the twelfth century canon, the ones students of grammar would have studied, are of the so-called rhetorical kind, Juvenal, Persius, Ovid, Lucan, Statius and Claudian. The only poetic *auctores* outside this mode are Virgil, the Horace of the Satires and Epistles, and Terence.[3] If we stick to narrative poet-

---

[1] The Elder Seneca, *Declamations*, in two volumes, translated by M. Winterbottom (Cambridge, MA, Harvard University Press, and London, William Heinemann, Ltd., 1974), 2.2:8-12 (vol. I).

[2] Bonner, Stanley F., *Roman Declamation* (Liverpool, Uniuversity of Liverpool Press, 1949), pp. 149-167. As should be obvious to those who read this chapter, when I show a parallelism between the teaching of some rhetorical text and the practice of a particular poet, I do not mean to imply that there is a direct influence of the former on the latter: such would be absurd, in any case, with respect to Quintilian and Lucan. I do draw upon rhetorical handbooks as a testimony to a tradition, to a constant teaching, a perennial lore of rhetoric. Quintilian, for example, describes *comparatio* and Lucan fills his poem with *comparationes*; I do not think it rash to assert, therefore, that the poet's *comparationes* are primarily oratorical and do not belong to a distinctively poetic tradition.

[3] I am excluding Christian writers for the moment. My list of *auctores* is otherwise a little arbitrary; it represents what seems to me to be a general agreement of many sources. See Curtius, E. R., *European Literature and the Latin Middle Ages*, trans. Willard R. Trask (New York, Pantheon, 1953), pp. 48-54, 260-269. The col-

ry, we are pitting Virgil against Ovid, Lucan, Statius and Claudian. The verbal reminiscences of ancient poets in Gautier himself convey a very fair sense of this imbalance. On Christensens's listing (see note 2) the echoes of Virgil are many, 99, but he is exceeded by Ovid, who has 112. Lucan in fact contributes only 33, Statius, 22, and Claudian, 16. Thus, if we compare Virgil to the rest, the ratio is 99 to 193, barely over a third of the total. We should note that these five sources carry the day with Gautier; the other poets cited by Christensen, Horace, Juvenal and Silius Italicus, together contribute only 32 passages more (Christensen, pp. 195-211). I am not, incidentally, using these borrowings as an index of style; in their inner make-up and personality they tell us little about Gautier's taste for oratory one way or the other. The latter-day peruser of manuals might be tempted to say that this twelfth century repertory of authors gives a very distorted view of ancient poetry. It is in any case hardly strange that a poet trained in *auctores* should show a preference for what I would call oratorical patterns of narrative over others, when the oratorical mode, in narrative texts and elsewhere, is practically universal in his models.

Let us review quickly the ground we have covered to date. We begin with Virgil. In the *Aeneid* the primary narrative (excluding the bits of story that get into the explanatory passages) is uniformly evidential, in my term, that is, events are recounted in detail with a wealth of particulars. The narrative flow is interrupted by direct discourse and dialogue, by epic similes, by brief pieces identifying persons, things and places, by static descriptions, mostly short, and by occasional commentary. Speeches aside, the whole bulk of this material is not very great. In the main narrative itself, events mainly are seen from without. There is little retelling of the thoughts or motives of the several characters. Their emotions are sometimes specified, notoriously in the fourth book, but elsewhere they are

---

lection of *accessus ad auctores* published by R. B. C. Huygens (*Accessus ad auctores, Bernard d'Utrecht, Conrad d'Hirsau Dialogus super auctores*, Leiden, E. J. Brill, 1970), pp. 19-54, lists the following among the non-Christian poets: "Cato" (the *Disticha*), Ovid, Horace. The Conrad of Hirsau work in the same collection (pp. 71-131), has Cato, Lucan, Horace, Ovid, Juvenal, Homer, Persius, Statius and Virgil. The "Homerus" in both texts refers both to the original, known by reputation, and to the *Ilias latina*. Heinrich Christensen, in his study of the *Alexandreis* (*Das Alexanderlied Walters von Châtillon*, Halle, Verlag der Buchhandlung des Waisenhauses, 1905), pp. 195-215, lists the following as Gautier's poetic sources: Virgil, Ovid, Lucan, Claudian, Horace, Juvenal, and, curiously, Silius Italicus.

mostly reported in the simplest terms: we are told in a word or two that Aeneas is sad or that Turnus is angry. When we do come to understand how the characters feel, it is almost always because we can deduce this from what they say or do. In great part and with some notable exceptions the sense and meaning of events is either implicit in the action itself, or is a theme in the speech of one of the characters; in the former case, the reader/listener is left to discover this meaning on his own. Indirect discourse is not at all common. The narrative of the *Alexandre*, as we have seen, is quite another matter. It is a mixed media event. The storytelling itself is full of variety. Its speed changes: it can go all the way from the hastiest summary to the most detailed and vivid dramatic scene. The motives, thoughts and emotions of the characters are all recounted in the most explicit terms. Commentary and interpretation abound, and form an important part of the whole text. Descriptions can be lengthy. Indirect discourse is not extensive, but it is more so than in Virgil, and it is plain that our poet has no objection to it in principle. As a term of comparison to our Spanish poem we may consider the *narratio* section of a typical judicial speech. We have actually cited one from an oration of Cicero, and we found that it followed much the same literary code as the narration of the *Alexandre*. The point of this confrontation was twofold: it showed generally that the pattern and style of the *Libro* was not unique, and at the very least, that this common mode was not alien to oratory. We have gone one step further. As it would appear, certain poets in the twelfth century canon, probably accessible to our poet as the Cicero oration was not, might be the channel through which the oratorical manner could have reached our poet. What remains to be done is to look at some of these texts in detail to see exactly what elements in each were available to him, and what kind of resources and models they could offer him. There is obviously great variety here: each Roman poet would have been useful to the author of the *Alexandre* in a different way. But to my mind, the strain common to all, the factor which was most decisive in the formation of a thirteenth century poet, is the downplaying of evidential narrative, and its replacement by discourse, including narrative discourse, of other sorts.

I should emphasize that this exercise, the comparison of the practice of the *Alexandre*-poet with that of certain ancients, is not in the first place meant to be exegesis; the point was not primarily to try to describe or comment on the character or historical position of our medieval text. To be sure, the formal side of literature always has a history, just as do others of its aspects. It may indeed be interesting to reflect that the patterns in the *Libro* which we have been speaking of have a past, immediate or remote. But what is at issue here is the prevalence of a certain kind of taste: in a very partial and limited way I am trying to document the fact that the procedures and uses of post-Virgilian Latin poetry enjoyed great prestige over a long period. One could put the matter otherwise. The *Alexandre* is in a sense a reading of ancient poetry: one could view it as an index to how a cultivated person of the early thirteenth century thought the old poetic texts in his repertory were put together. The witness of the *Libro* is interesting, and as I think, especially eloquent, because it is in the vernacular and is not directed to a learned audience; a work like this one is where one would least expect to find traces of ancient practice, but as I will try to show, it is there nevertheless. But this reading of the *auctores,* this reception, if you will, is in no way unique. I hope it will also become clear that, particular circumstances aside, our poet's classicism, if we can call it that, is absolutely typical.

## 2) OVID

The number of old authors who left their mark on the *Alexandre* is perhaps not very large. Let us look first at Ovid, a poet of such spectacular variety and power as to give any poetic neophyte a great deal to think about. Even in the narrow range of our investigation we find that Ovid is a believable model for our latter-day poet. The layout of many of the episodes of the *Metamorphoses* should have a very familiar look for a reader of the *Libro*. Let us begin with the story of Phaëthon, a very Ovidian one in all its changes and turns. Towards the end of the first book we see the boy's brother taunting him by casting doubt on his divine origin. Phaëthon turns to his mother. The narrator gives us her reaction: "Clymene, moved (it is uncertain whether by the prayers of Phaëthon, or more by anger at the insult to herself), stretched out both arms to heaven"; "ambiguum Clymene precibus Phaethontis an ira / mota magis dicti sibi criminis utraque caelo / bracchia porrexit spectansque ad lumina solis."[4] These lines score on two separate points, as an account of Clymene's possible thoughts, and as an editorial intervention, offering a pair of alternate explanations for her act. Clymene of course advises Phaëthon to see Phoebus so that the god can assure the boy he truly is his father. There follow four lines of very rapid narrative telling of Phaëthon's journey to the court of the Sun God:

> Phaëthon leaps up in joy at his mother's words, already grasping the heavens in imagination; and after crossing his own Ethiopia and the land of Ind lying close beneath the sun, he quickly comes to his father's rising-place.
> emicat extemplo laetus post talia matris
> dicta suae Phaethon et concipit aethera mente
> Aethiopasque suos positosque sub ignibus Indos
> sidereis transit patriosque adit impiger ortus. (I 776-779)

Then, with a change of pace that is very Ovidian indeed, the narrative flow comes to a stop – at the beginning of Book II –, and we are given a splendid description, the famous account of the palace of the Sun. There is no need to quote it. Brilliant as it is, it is brief, eighteen lines. No one ever accused Ovid of being a poor storyteller, and indeed, the shortness of the description seems to testify to the sureness of his touch: the flow does not get dammed up for long. But this is a false impression. Later in the Phaëthon passage comes what surely is one of its glories, one of the most splendid bits of the whole poem, the account of the conflagration that threatens to destroy the globe when the solar chariot goes off course. The passage is anything but brief: it goes on for 62 verses (II 210-271). It conveys the illusion of narrative movement, because it tells of many separate things happening all at once. But, taken as a whole, it is static: the main story comes to a long halt as we are served up one horrible detail after another, disaster following disaster. As I suggested, the genius of Ovid keeps us from seeing this as an interruption. It is perhaps the management of the pace in the neighboring passages as well as the liveliness of the account itself that keeps us from chafing at the narrative pause. But in any case, it is not the

---

[4] Ovid, *Metamorphoses*, ed. with a translation by Frank Justus Miller (Cambridge, MA, and London, Harvard University Press, and Wm. Heinemann Ltd., originally published in 1916) two volumes, verses I 765-767; references to the *Metamorphoses* will henceforth be by verse and will be to this edition and translation.

modesty of the descriptive passages, or their brevity, that is notable, or for that matter admirable, in the *Metamorphoses*. Neither can we say that Ovid's great poem contrasts with the *Alexandre* in that the latter's descriptions are long and the former's short. Both have both.

Returning to the earlier part of our text, we come on a sequence that is also interesting from our viewpoint. The moment arrives when Phoebus makes his fateful offer: Ask me for anything you wish, says the god, and my granting of it will be a sign that I am indeed your father. Here is Phoebus' speech in Ovid:

> "Thou art both worthy to be called my son, and Clymene has told thee thy true origin. And, that thou mayst not doubt my word, ask what boon thou wilt, that thou mayst receive it from my hand. And may that Stygian pool whereby the gods swear, but which mine eyes have never seen, be witness of my promise."
> "nec tu meus esse negari
> dignus es, et Clymene veros 'ait' edidit ortus,
> quoque minus dubites, quodvis pete munus, ut illud
> me tribuente feras! promissi testis adesto
> dis iuranda palus, oculis incognita nostris!" (II 42-46)

Then comes the surprise: Phaëthon's request is presented very hastily in indirect discourse: "Scarce had he ceased when the boy asked for his father's chariot, and the right to drive his winged horses for a day"; "vix bene desierat, currus rogat ille paternos / inque diem alipedum ius et moderamen equorum." (II 47-48). The touch is of course very effective: to give the boy's answer in his own words would have slowed down the pace, and what Ovid wants here is to convey the suddenness of the response. There is assuredly nothing in the *Alexandre* quite as fine as this, but as we recall, the artful arrangement of successive bits of narrative of different speeds and kinds is one of the characteristics of the *Libro*'s narrative style. In a lengthy speech which follows, Phoebus tries to convince him not to drive the chariot. Phaëthon of course resists: "he fought against the words, and urged his first request, burning with desire to drive the chariot"; "dictis tamen ille repugnat / propositumque premit flagratque cupidine currus" (II 103-104). Ovid here supplies the motive for the refusal, a rebellious spirit, and tells of the boy's emotions, his eagerness to get on with the adventure. A few lines later we read that Phaëthon was "magnanimus" (II 111), that is, "ambitious" or "full of confidence in himself," a judgment about the boy's inner life. Phoebus rubs his son's face with ointment, "and made it proof against the devouring flames"; " rapidae fecit patientia flammae" (II 123); a motive is expressed. The god shows deep emotion, "heaving deep sighs ... presaging woe"; "praesagaque luctus / pectore sollicito repetens suspiria" (II 124-125); Apollo's foreknowledge is the motive for the sigh. Phaëthon, leaping into the chariot, "rejoices," "gaudet" (II 152), still another authorial judgment and interpretation, however rapidly recorded. The ill-fated journey begins, and we are introduced twice to the inner life, this time not of humans but of animals. First of all, "the weight [of the chariot] was light, not such as the horses of the sun could feel, and the yoke lacked its accustomed burden"; "sed leve pondus erat nec quod cognoscere possent / Solis equi, solitaque iugum gravitate carebat" (II 161-162). The chariot bounces: "When they feel this, the team run wild and leave the well-beaten track"; "Quod simulac sensere, ruunt tritumque relinquunt quadriiugi spatium" (II 167) Pages later, incidentally, we are given another equine inner scene: when Jove casts the thunderbolt at Phaëthon, "the *maddened* horses leap apart" (underscoring mine), "consternantur equi et saltu in contraria facto" (II 314). Early in the adventure Phaëthon bitterly regrets his decision. We are once again party to his mind: "And now he would prefer never to have touched his father's horses, and repents that he has discovered his true origin and prevailed in his prayer"; "et iam mallet equos numquam tetigisse paternos, / iam cognosse genus piget et valuisse rogando" (II 182-183). The inner process continues:

> What shall he do? Much of the sky is now behind him, but more is still in front! His thought measures both. And now he looks forward to the west, which he is destined never to reach, and at times back to the east. Dazed, he knows not what to do.
> quid faciat? multum caeli post terga relictum
> ante oculos plus est: animo metitur utrumque
> et modo, quod illi fatum contingere non est,
> prospicit occasus, interdum respicit ortus (II 187-190)

In time the conflagration comes and the king of gods is assailed with protests. He at last decides to take action, but not without first placing his good and solid reasons before his fellow gods, Phoebus included. This all-important speech is conveyed in indirect discourse:

> But the Almighty Father, calling on the gods to witness and him above all who had given the chariot, that unless he bring aid all things will perish by a grievous doom, mounts on high to the top of heaven &c.
> at pater omnipotens, superos testatus et ipsum,
> qui dederat currus, nisi opem ferat, omnia fato
> interitura gravi, summam petit arduus arcem (II 304-306)

A stretch of less than four hundred verses in Ovid, then, yields a good repertory of narrative devices of the sort that I believe we should consider distinctive, the long description, the report on the inner thoughts of the characters, the attribution of motives, the authorial judgment about the actions he relates, and indirect discourse. The familiarity of these procedures, taken individually and as a group, should not deceive us. It is not an exercise in triviality to point them out, this for two reasons: first, because there are other ways than that of Ovid of telling a story, Virgil's, for example; and second, because the very familiarity of the whole style is the point at issue. We have every right to inquire why we have naturalized one kind of storytelling among several. Ovid is inexhaustible. As we have suggested, a great part of his fame as a narrator undoubtedly has to do with the way he paces his story, the art with which he speeds it up and slows it down. This mastery is not pure caprice. Like other narrators many generations before and after, he is telling old stories, tales all too well-known to his audience, and he therefore feels no obligation to serve up every part of his account with the same wealth of detail.[5] He can bring a sharp focus onto some episodes, as he wishes, and dismiss others with a much hastier account. Circumstance, of course, turns into virtue. The resulting effect is always remarkable. One of the most daring essays in pacing in the *Metamorphoses* is its Argonautica. The story has its roots in the preceding narrative: Ovid, as we recall, grafts his Jason drama onto the end of the Boreas-Orithyia episode. The two sons of the

---

[5] See Wilkinson, L. P., *Ovid Surveyed* (Cambridge, Cambridge University Press, 1962), p. 65.

pair join Jason's expedition, as we are told in the last verses of Book VI:

> So these two youths, when boyhood was passed and they had grown to man's estate, went with the Minyans over an unknown sea in that first ship to seek the bright gleaming fleece of gold. And now the Minyans were plowing the deep in their Thessalian ship. They had seen Phineus, spending his last days helpless in perpetual night; and the sons of Boreas had driven the harpies from the presence of the unhappy king. Having experienced many adventures under their illustrious leader Jason, they reached at last the swift waters of muddy Phasis.
>
> ergo ubi concessit tempus puerile iuventae,
> vellera cum Minyis nitido radiantia villo
> per mare non notum prima petiere carina.
> Iamque fretum Minyae Pagasaea puppe secabant,
> perpetuaque trahens inopem sub nocte senectam
> Phineus visus erat, iuvenesque Aquilone creati
> virgineas volucres miseri senis ore fugarant,
> multaque perpessi claro sub Iasone tandem
> contigerant rapidas limosi Phasidos undas.
>
> (VI 719-721; VII 1-6)

This tiny handful of verses is remarkable on two counts. It is notable on one hand how much narrative information they manage to pack in, about the first ship in the world, about Phineus and the harpies and his rescue. On the other, the text gets in a few striking particularizing details, the "gleaming" Golden Fleece, Phineus' unhappy end, "spending his last days ... in perpetual night." We should add that passages like this, genuine summary livened by individualizing touches is an Ovidian trademark, something he does very well. The next large chunk of the Jason story is told in a pair of dependent clauses: "There, while they were approaching the king and demanding the fleece that Phrixus had given to him while the dreadful condition with its great tasks was being proposed to the Minyans"; "dumque adeunt regem Phrixeaque vellera poscunt / lexque datur Minyis magnorum horrenda laborum" (VII 7-8; we note that the Latin has two clauses dependent on "dumque"). The main clause introduces the heroine, and gets us into the story Ovid genuinely means to tell: "meanwhile the daughter of King Aeëtes conceived an overpowering passion"; "concipit interea validos Aeetias ignes" (verse 9). There follow a series of fully realized scenes, a long deliberative soliloquy at the end of which Medea resolves to remain loyal to her father, the chance encounter with Jason, which causes that resolution to fail, her offer of help, the sequence in which he performs all the prodigies the king had required of him, and finally, the actual taking of the Fleece. Then comes the great fillip: the journey back to Iolchos, which occupies hundreds of verses in Apollonius, is dispatched by Ovid in less than three. Here is the whole sentence: "Proud of this spoil and bearing with him the giver of his prize, another spoil, the victor and his wife in due time reached the harbour of Iolchos"; "spolioque superbus / muneris auctorem secum, spolia altera, portans / victor Iolciacos tetigit com coniuge portus" (VII 156-158). This is perhaps the smartest and most elegant touch of all. After this fine touch the pace slows down once again, and the episode is carried to the end, through the rejuvenation of Aeson and the murder of Pelias. The sequence, so it appears, runs fast, slow, very fast, and finally, slow; the abruptness of the changes of pace is what gives this narrative unit much of its drama. In this sense the Argonautica episode is entirely typical of the *Metamorphoses*. We must recall that this same variety and mixture of speeds is one of the great resources of the *Alexandre*-poet, and is one of the factors that gives his poem its special profile.

I should make it very clear at this point that I am not speaking here about what conventionally is called style, as in "the style of Montaigne" or "the style of Spenser." The *Alexandre*-poet does not write in the style of Ovid; the changes of narrative speed which are a feature of the works of both do not impart an Ovidian flavor to the latter-day poem. The two texts are in fifty obvious ways on wholly different planes: their manner and the level of accomplishment they represent are very unlike. What is to my mind very significant is that the Spanish poet, presumably a student of the *auctores*, had with respect to a very particular technique a splendid model in Ovid. Obviously, changing the pace of narrative is not an Ovidian monopoly: other ancient narrators work in the same vein. But as I suggested before, the Spanish poet's repertory of *auctores* is not unlimited, and the influence of any one of these separately has to be taken seriously.

Summary, as we have seen, is an important element in the narrative layout of the *Alexandre*. It sometimes stands by itself, but more frequently is made to contrast with bits of exposition where the pace is much slower. It is important to stress that the speedy passages in the Ovidian Argonautica are not unique within the *Metamorphoses*. The plain rapid style is a great resource for the Roman poet, as it is for the Spanish. The whole matter is worth dwelling upon, if we are going to keep looking to Ovid as one of the *Alexandre*-poet's possible models. The point is that Ovid here has a rival: one might be tempted to play down the likelihood of his influence as an exemplar of the plain style in the *Libro* by pointing out that one of its longest stretches of unadorned narration is simply an adaptation of an equally rapid and simple passage from the *Ilias latina*. Thus, on one hand it might seem that we needed no further explanation for the style of this particular bit in the Spanish work, and on the other, we could propose the *Ilias* as a formal model for the later poet generally. But neither of these considerations is very compelling. On the first count we could say that if the *Alexandre*-poet translated a plain text plainly, he did it by choice: he could have done otherwise. There are indeed instances in the *Alexandre* in which a bare piece of narrative in the source appears enriched in the definitive version. In some cases that plain source is the *Ilias* itself. But with regard to the second question, could we possibly think of the *Ilias* as a formal influence on the poem generally, that is, outside of the section actually based on it? One could answer broadly that the brief Latin work is formally a very strange text, and that, setting aside the Trojan War passage in the *Libro*, one might find it hard to see much likeness between either the older poem's large structure or its detail and those of the later work. The *Homerus* is assuredly not all bare bones: it has its lively moments. But the wide variety of narrative procedures typical of the *Libro* is quite beyond it. In particular, the contrast between plain and not plain is not as remarkable as in the Spanish work. The most that can be said about the *Ilias* in this context is that it might be one influence among several. And although it is not really necessary to trace the *Alexandre*'s plain style to any one source, rapid narrative, as we must stress, is not to be found absolutely everywhere in the ancient poets read in the thirteenth century; Ovid, first and last, has got to be an eminent model.

In any case, here is a fine bit of summary in the *Metamorphoses*, at the beginning of Book XII:

> Father Priam, not knowing that Aesacus was still alive in feathered form, mourned for his son. At an empty tomb also, in-

scribed with the lost one's name, Hector with his brothers had offered sacrifices in honour of the dead. Paris was not present at the sad rite, Paris, who a little later brought a long-continued war upon his country with his stolen wife. A thousand ships and the whole Pelasgian race, banded together, pursued him, nor would vengeance have been postponed had not stormy winds made the sea impassable, and had not the land of Boeotia kept the ships, though ready to set sail, in fish-haunted Aulis.

> Nescivs adsumptis Priamus pater Aesacon alis
> vivere lugebat: tumulo quoque, nomen habenti,
> inferias dederat cum fratribus Hector inani;
> defuit officio Paridis praesentia tristi,
> postmodo qui rapta longum cum coniuge bellum
> attulit in patriam: coniurataeque sequuntur
> mille rates gentisque simul commune Pelasgae;
> nec dilata foret vindicta, nisi aequora saevi
> invia fecissent venti, Boeotaque tellus
> Aulide piscosa puppes tenuisset ituras. (XII 1-10)

As we can see, this is in part a mixed media event. We have one bit of commentary, "nor would vengeance" etc., and some particularizing details, the "thousand ships," the "stormy winds," and an account of Priam's ignorance, "not knowing that Aesacus" etc. The rest is very rapid narration, none more than the "long-continued war" tucked away in a short dependent clause. Typically, the race through events gives way in a moment to a fully realized scene:

> When here, after their country's fashion, they had prepared to sacrifice to Jove, and just as the ancient altar was glowing with the lighted fires, the Greeks saw a dark-green serpent crawling up a plane-tree which stood near the place where they had begun their sacrifices. There was a nest with eight young birds in the top of the tree, and these, together with the mother, who was flying around her doomed nestlings, the serpent seized and swallowed in his greedy maw. They all looked on in amazement.

> hic patrio de more Iovi cum sacra parassent,
> ut vetus accensis incanduit ignibus ara,
> serpere caeruleum Danai videre draconem
> in platanum, coeptis quae stabat proxima sacris.
> nidus era volucrum bis quattuor arbore summa:
> quas simul et matrem circum sua damna volantem
> corripuit serpens avidoque recondidit ore,
> obstipuere omnes. (XII 11-18)

In Book XIV we are given a romp through several books of the *Aeneid*, all in some thirty-one verses. Things slow down only when the Trojan hero reaches Cumae. There is no need to quote the passage entire. Here is a portion of it:

> When the Trojan vessels had successfully passed this monster [Scylla] and greedy Charybdis too, and when they had almost reached the Ausonian shore, the wind bore them to the Libyan coast. There the Sidonian queen received Aeneas hospitably in heart and home, doomed ill to endure her Phrygian lord's departure. On a pyre, built under pretence of sacred rites, she fell upon his sword; and so, herself disappointed, she disappointed all. Leaving once more the new city built on the sandy shore, Aeneas returned to the land of Eryx and friendly Acestes, and there he made sacrifice and paid due honours to his father's tomb. &c.
>
> Hunc ubi Troianae remis avidamque Charybdin
> evicere rates, cum iam prope litus adessent
> Ausonium, Libycas vento referuntur ad oras.
> excipit Aenean illic animoque domoque
> non bene discidium Phrygii latura mariti
> Sidonis; inque pyra sacri sub imagine facta
> incubuit ferro deceptaque decipit omnes.
> rursus harenosae fugiens nova moenia terrae
> ad sedemque Erycis fidumque relatus Acesten
> sacrificat tumulumque sui genitoris honorat. (XIV 75-84)

Other instances of rapid narrative in Ovid are very easy to find. If the *Alexandre*-poet read him with attention, he would not be at a loss to find splendid examples.

The most important and significant feature of Ovid's narrative style is the one that needs the least commentary. Nowhere is the supreme poet's power more in evidence than when his story is particularized, when it is told with an accumulation of narrative circumstances. The book is called *Metamorphoses*, and as I believe, it is precisely the transformation scenes that are fullest and subtlest in detail, the accounts of those strange processes in which a human form is changed into animal or plant. Not infrequently the reactions of the person being transformed creep into the story. Phaëthon's sisters, mourning their brother, are changed into trees. One "complained that her ankles were encased in wood, another that her arms were changing to long branches"; "haec stipite crura teneri, /

illa dolet fieri longos sua bracchia ramos" (II 351-352). Actaeon, likewise, having become four-legged, marvelled "to find himself so swift of foot."; "et se tam celerem cursu miratur in ipso" (III 199). In another style there are Ovid's combat scenes. Some are genuinely Homeric: we know where every blow lands, and how each slain combatant hits the ground. There is the struggle between Achilles and Cygnus, epic in everything but its surprise ending. The match between Hercules and Acheloüs is told brilliantly. The attack on the Calydonian boar is remarkable in that the enemy is not human (or divine); in other ways it has a familiar look. But surely one of the most splendid battle scenes in all literature is the sequence narrated by Nestor in Book XIII, recounting the fight between the Lapiths and the Centaurs. In all of these passages narrative ocular *evidentia* dominates: everything is made visible, one particular and local circumstance giving way to the next. But what needs to be stressed is that these scenes, some of them quite long, are not universal: the poet holds them in reserve. One might want to say that Ovid is most himself in these purple patches, that his gifts come to full flower when he gives us these vivid bits of narrative. But within the *Metamorphoses* they are the mountain peaks, and the poem as a whole is a complex and varied landscape, with valleys, middle ground, rises and falls. What is most pertinent to our argument is the fact that in Ovid as in what I call oratorical narrative generally, ocular *evidentia* in narrative is reserved for special moments: it is not the normal or constant mode, as in other kinds of text. This economy, or reserve, is thus not exclusively Ovidian: it is Ciceronian, Tacitan, Livian, and it is also characteristic of the *Alexandre*. The special effectiveness of the procedure in Ovid should not disguise from us that he shares this very pattern with many other writers in prose and poetry, ancient and modern.

## 3) CONSECUTIO

Ovid is our master. He has carried us very far in our argument: a great many of the formal procedures used by our Spanish poet find their precedent in his work. But in one sense he leaves us out in the cold. What he fails to give us as we try to discover the prehistory of the *Alexandre* is the argumentative strain, the constant pleading that is such a prominent feature of so many episodes of the poem. The issue, the *point*, is always hurled at us as we read the stories in the *Libro;* It is hard to duck so much intention, so much desire to edify. We recall that the pride and folly of Pausanias and the vanity of ambition and lust generally is the focus of one typical episode, and that the confrontation we made of that passage with the narrative section of the *Pro Milone* was in great part to stress the strictly rhetorical and persuasive character of the *Alexandre*'s narratives. There is a useful term in Cicero's *De inventione, consecutio*, which I translate "significance."[6] *Consecutio* is one of the commonplaces set forth by Cicero for the discussions of events or actions, and in the broad sense it therefore belongs to narrative (I 43). The point is this: in a judicial speech the *narratio*, the setting forth of the pertinent facts, is not supposed to be a disinterested account. When the speaker gives his version of the crime, he is in no way trying to be impartial. On the contrary, his recital is supposed to incline the judge and jury towards a certain decision. Many different resources may be drawn upon for this purpose: the very selection of the events themselves, the emphasis on some in preference to others, the speaker's comments on them, the general principles invoked which the events are supposed to embody, all these materials and procedures shape the story so that it has a point, Clodius' probable guilt, or Milo's innocence. This "point of the story" is what is meant by *consecutio*. Ovid's narrative is not remarkable for this kind of focus or intention. In the Phaëthon narrative we are told of the boy's overconfidence, and of his rebellious spirit, but we are not asked to generalize. The rebelliousness is not the point, the *consecutio* of the story.

Ovid's case is a curious one. Rhetoric is everywhere in his work; by this I of course mean book rhetoric, coded rhetoric. This rhetoric is, however, distributed in a curious way. Seneca the Elder, as we

---

[6] I am oversimplifying. *Consecutio* in Cicero is a term which covers a number of sub-topics, what name can properly be given to the event in question, the moral and social standing of the agents in the affair and of those who approve or disapprove of it, whether it conforms to the *honestum* or to the *utile*, &c. It is striking, however, that Boethius, in a passage based on *De inventione* I 43, puts all of the modalities of *consecutio* within the range of *judicio* and *testimonium* (*De topicis differentiis*, in Migne, J. P., *Patrologia latina*, vol. 64, Paris, published by the editor and his successors, 1891, column 1214). A medieval commentator on Cicero, Thierry of Chartres, equates *consecutio* with *opinio* (*The Rhetorical Commentaries of Thierry of Chartres*, ed. Karin M. Fredborg, Toronto, Pontifical Institute of Mediaeval Studies, 1988, p. 146).

recall, speaks of him, and his remarks are revealing. He speaks of the future poet's preference for *suasoriae* over *declamationes*, that is, for simulated deliberative speeches over judicial (*Controversiae* II 2:12). The point of this was supposed to be Ovid's dislike for argument: Seneca suggests that the need for it was less in the *suasoria*. And yet, this observation is in the long run misleading. One might conclude from it that there was not much argument in Ovid. This is of course wholly untrue. The *Metamorphoses* is in fact full of pleading, arguing, persuading. But what is significant is that virtually none of this material belongs to the discourse of the poem itself: superficially at least, neither the text of the *Metamorphoses* as a whole, nor any part of it which is in the poet's own voice seems to incline us, persuade us or try to argue with us about anything. But by contrast, the characters in the *Metamorphoses* do argue and plead a great deal. One of the ways in which the influence of declamation is most visible in the poem is in certain of its speeches. The debate between Ulysses and Ajax over the arms of Achilles is the textbook case, and is in fact cited in just this connection (Bonner, *op. cit.* p. 151), but the instances of arguing and pleading in declamatory style by other characters are legion. These parts of the text all belong to the fiction, to the narrative level, the *récit*. The poem itself, the utterance of the narrator, is, as it would seem, pure luxury. The point of the *Metamorphoses*, if it has one, is so diffuse and general that it is hard to see traces of it in the actual practice of the poet, line by line.

4) LUCAN: CONSECUTIO

It is important to understand what we are looking for. In oratory, in historical literature, and in philosophical texts, there are many, many narratives that plead explicitly, that have a point, a *consecutio*. Their influence could conceivably come to the *Alexandre*-poet direct. But what about poetic texts? Can we think of any that also have this special profile? We may seem to be speaking in anomalies here, asking that a piece of high narrative poetry be designed to persuade or convince, just as a deliberative speech would. Spontaneously one might think that such a work, if it could be found, would violate boundaries, that somehow the laws of genre would be flouted. And yet this is our requirement. Any narrative might have a focus or thematic center, but the *Alexandre* carries its message like a flag: the point or *consecutio* of one episode after another is spelled out very plain. What would suit us would be an ancient model, accessible to our poet, a work that also deals heavily in *consecutio*. That anomalous text does actually exist, a splendid narrative poem in ten books written in the first century, a consecrated text in the twelfth and thirteenth, among other things a living set of contradictions. I of course mean the *Pharsalia* of Lucan.[7] The paradoxical character of this strange work is no discovery of mine. Servius thought it closer to history than to poetry.[8] Quintilian declared it a fitter model for orators than for poets (*Institutio* X 1:90). The very division of opinion about it, the large number of its readers who, merits notwithstanding, simply do not like it, may well reflect its anomalous personality. Let us start with Quintilian, or with the equivalence poetry-oratory. His remarks have always been read as though they were a piece of negative criticism: the *Pharsalia* is less poetry than public harangue and is therefore bad. Quintilian's intentions aside, one could remark that his judgment might have a different meaning in an age in which oratory was prized, and the texts of the great orators were known and admired. What is more, it is especially easy to misread Quintilian in an age like our own which despises rhetoric and at the same time knows practically nothing about it. What is there in fact, good or bad, that is oratorical about the *Pharsalia*? Let us consider first one of its bits of direct discourse, a long speech uttered by one of its characters. In Book II an unnamed aged Roman gives us a lengthy recital of

---

[7] To my mind, the wisest modern reader of Lucan is undoubtedly Berthe Marti. I am proud to say that some of my observations about the *Pharsalia*, notions I developed independently, coincide with some of hers, especially those in her classic article, "Lucan's Narrative Technique," *La parola del passato* 30 (1976), pp. 82-89. The comparisons she makes between the *Pharsalia* and the *Aeneid* are especially suggestive, and are not wholly unlike my own views about the way the two works contrast with each other.

[8] Servius makes the remark in his gloss on *Aeneid* I 382. The affinity of the *Pharsalia* to historiography has been noted by others. Arnulf of Orléans remarks that while Terence is a pure comic and Juvenal a pure satirist, Lucan is not pure, but a mixture of poet and historian (*Arnulfi aurelianensis glosule super Lucanum*, ed. Berthe Marti, Rome, American Academy in Rome, *American Academy in Rome Papers and Monographs* 18, 1958), p. 2. Charles Martindale, in *John Milton and the Transformation of Ancient Epic* (London and Sydney, Croom Helm, 1986), pp. 205-206, quotes Sir William Davenant to the effect that Lucan is more historian than poet.

events in the days of Marius and Sulla, particularly the widespread bloodshed that marked those years. He speaks as the Civil War is barely under way, and concludes by looking forward to even worse times, affirming that the ambitions of Julius Caesar and Pompey are far beyond those of their two predecessors. The old man's speech poses problems on several fronts. It sets out in the form of a digression, that species so hated by Lucan's detractors. The immediate context of the lines is the passage that tells of the earliest reaction in Rome to the outbreak of civil war: Lucan tells of the citizens' grief, and of their recourse to the gods in prayer and sacrifice. One utterance, also in direct discourse, calls the gods to account, and implores Zeus to strike down both leaders. At just that moment the old man's account begins, and the narrator makes not the least attempt to justify its lack of connection with the surrounding material. Pure caprice? Neoclassic critics may dislike digressions, but ancient teachers of rhetoric had no objections to them at all. On the contrary, they recommended them, and what is more, provided for their ingrafting into the main trunk of the oration: the end of the passage was supposed to be a sort of bridge to the main body of the text. This last disposition matches perfectly Lucan's practice in the old man's speech: the final comparison hangs up the horrors of the past next to the greater ones at hand, and so gets us back into the primary narrative. I must emphasize that the poet is here making use of an orator's procedure. In laying down the rules for the digression the old handbooks of rhetoric were trying to guide the practicing public speaker in his craft, and not the composer of epic verse. Lucan in applying the formula is therefore assuredly more orator than poet.

This final flowing of the digression in Book II into the mainstream of the discourse is significant in another sense. It tells us that the narrator himself takes full responsibility for the content of the whole speech: the fictional speaker speaks for him. Direct discourse is, after all, a mode that can stand in many different relationships with the main text: a quoted speech can convey a message which is also that of the work as a whole, or one which is at odds with this global sense. The principal narrator may speak through his characters, but he need not: he may give them a life and a will of their own. The point is trivial: the Bible says, "there is no God," but this is not the message of the Bible. In the Marius-Sulla speech, however, the old man is entirely the spokesman for the principal narrator. The final comparison tells us that, for reasons that should be clear. Even at this early stage in the poem the audience knows very well what its message is, that the present civil war is the worst of ills; that this theme should be articulated at the point at which the digression touches ground makes it clear that the intention of the speaker is also that of the poet.

The identity of message is telling in more ways than one. There is a second rhetorical figure involved, *comparatio,* a comparison between unequals. The figure has the following form: A is great, and therefore B which is greater must be indeed important. The sense of the passage in the *Pharsalia* is that if the times of Marius and Sulla were horrible, those of the Civil War which promise to be worse will be bad indeed. This is an orator's trick, a figure of amplification, described by Quintilian (VIII 4:9-15). Its use is hardly uncommon; not least, it appears in the most familiar judicial speech in the world, Cicero's first against Catiline (*In Catilinam* I 1). We are told there that Scipio, a private citizen, felt personally justified in killing a man he considered a threat to the public good. But, says Cicero, the danger to the state posed by Catiline's activities is greater, just as the Senate's authority is weightier than Scipio's; therefore, we the consuls and senators are more than justified in putting Catiline to death, and so, incidentally, is our inaction the more damnable because we do not. Since, as I have pointed out, the theme of the speech in Lucan belongs both to the fictional speaker and to the poem as a whole, so does the *comparatio,* and thus the force of the figure is that it highlights the message underlying the whole represented action: the Civil War is the worst that could happen, in itself and in its consequences.

We repeat: Lucan's procedure here has little to do with poetic traditions and a great deal to do with oratory. The whole pattern in the Marius-Sulla text gets duplicated in another great *digressio* which is also a *comparatio,* the speech in Book IV, telling the story of Antaeus. Curio travels to a part of Libya which bears the name of the mythical personage. Once arrived the Roman general asks a native to tell him of Hercules' victory over this monster. The man complies, adding hastily at the end that a greater yet than Hercules hallowed the spot: Scipio, the conqueror of Hannibal and Carthage, had encamped there. First we are given Hercules, the bringer of civilization, hoary, legendary, sacred. But he is succeeded by Scipio, wholly human and historical, still greater and thus great indeed.

Thus far the *comparatio*. But the chain does not end there. Lucan leaves it to his audience to reflect that Scipio, a warrior, struggled to bring greatness to Rome, whereas the Caesarian Curio, also a warrior, is fighting to its detriment. And one must of course add that the implication unexpressed is also a figure of amplification, called *ratiocinatio* (Quintilian VIII 4:15). The orator in Lucan never sleeps.

I am not attempting to form a judgment about the *Pharsalia* as a whole, as poetry, or as some sort of poetic oratory. The question is really not our concern. A recent book by Charles Martindale, *John Milton and the Transformation of Ancient Epic* (London, Sydney, Croom Helm, 1986) gives us an effective defense of Lucan as poet, strictly speaking, drawing on ancient and Renaissance texts in poetics for his proof. But since the scope of this study is purely local, there is little need to take these views into account, which have to do with the global character of the poem and not much with its details. The orator's tricks are there, plainly to be seen; the least we can say about Lucan as an example for orators is that Quintilian's judgment is not wholly ridiculous. A separate question arises, whether the rhetorical fireworks we have considered have anything at all to do with the relatively simple practice of the *Alexandre*-poet. Our answer is twofold. Initially we must say the obvious: the gap between the two poems is immense. Our Alexander text is splendid, a masterpiece of its kind. But the technical power and suppleness of the Latin poet is greater and broader by a large factor. The conventions of Romance narrative of the thirteenth century by themselves exclude many of the virtuoso leaps we expect to find in Lucan. In any case, the devices we have pointed out in his text are beyond anything the younger poet attempts. The *Alexandre* is assuredly a much plainer poem than the *Pharsalia*. But in our second sense the affinity between the older poem and the newer is strong and visible. It is clear that the two poets are after the same quarry. *Consecutio* wins the day. In both works the narrative is in one way or another slanted so as to convince the audience of certain propositions the poets think important. The gap between the two poems is thus not as dramatic as one might guess. What is more, there are ways of realizing *consecutio* which are wholly within the range of both authors: there are many such, as we have implied. One of them is the exemplary narrative, the heavily moralized story. Let us refresh our memories of the *Alexandre* and its focus by citing one brief example of such a passage, the account of the defeat of Darius' general

Memnon. The Persian king is at the banks of the Euphrates, uncertain of what move to make next against Alexander:

> 822) Mas ante que mouiese vinoles mal mandado
> que auie Alixandre a Menona matado
> de quantos que el lleuaua non auie rren fincado
> el juego dixo Dario en veras es tornado
>
> 823) Menona era de Media vn mortal cauallero
> non auie en su corte Dario mejor braçero
> gabose que a los griegos el querie yr frontero
> que cuydaua dar treynta por vn dinero
>
> 824) Diole el rrey Dario quantas quiso de gentes
> seys mill cavalleros de nobles conbatientes
> todos de grañt esfuerço todos omnes valientes
> deurien vençer vn mundo sola meñt a dientes
>
> 825) Maguer que tantos eran & tan bien adobados
> vençiolos Alixandre fueron desbaratados
> el cabdello fue muerto los otros desbalçados
> pardios dizen los barbaros mal somos enprimados

This short narrative is, by the way, virtually original: its only basis in the source is a phrase in Gautier which simply informs us of the king's dejection on hearing that his general had been defeated and killed. Out of this scrap the *Alexandre*-poet constructs a complete story of an exemplary fall. In the short run, of course, what he has given us is a peripety, a reversal of fortune: Memnon's fall is against expectations. The notion of peripety, let us observe, belongs to rhetoric with full title. Both the *Ad Herennium* and the *De inventione* recommend the pattern in narratives which focus on persons rather then on things (*De inv.* I 27; *Ad Her.* I 13). In other words, its appearance in the *Alexandre* is neither an accident nor a piece of pure creation. The terms of contrast in the passage are extreme. Not only is Darius' formidable lieutenant dead, but his large and valiant force is utterly routed: there is not a single man left to fight. The sense of disaster is confirmed by the utterances of the two principals, Darius and Memnon. "Play has turned earnest," says the king. His initial contempt for his young enemy and his overconfidence generally give way to bitter undeceit. Memnon also shows his hand. At the head of his splendid force he boasts: "gabose." The design of the short passage is quite clear. Memnon, and secondarily Darius himself, are presented as overreachers, or perhaps more modestly, as men too secure in their great power, and therefore destined to fall. The episode is brief and told with little commentary. But the pattern, decline-and-fall, is a basic one in the *Libro*. The story of Memnon is in time and in much greater detail also that of Darius himself, prodigious in power and wealth, defeated by a smaller force than his. It is the story of Porus, and ultimately of Alexander himself. The poet plainly expects us to generalize, about greatness and its cost.

This mode, the narrative built around an intention, is almost omnipresent in Lucan's great poem. It is hardly necessary to cite examples. There is hardly a page in the work in which the story does not point a moral, either by its inner shape and make-up, or by some sort of intervention by the narrator. Let us recall briefly the passage telling us of Caesar's attempt to cross the Adriatic in a small boat, and of his encounter with the boatman Amyclas. The large role given in the drama to the latter character plainly brings everything else in the story into focus. Caesar's arrogance and foolhardiness are of course emphasized generously, in his own speech, in the thoughts the narrator attributes to him, and later on, in the remarks of his men. But the real significance of the episode comes to light in the description of Amyclas, morally self-sufficient, content with his lot:

> No thought of the war had he: he knew that poor men's huts are not plundered in time of civil war. How safe and easy the poor man's life and his humble dwelling! How blind men still are to Heaven's gifts! What temple, what fortified town, could say as much – that it thrills with no alarm when Caesar knocks?[9]

The syntax of the English here is totally unlike that of the Latin. The "securus belli" in what follows is the end of a preceding clause. The Latin runs:

> Securus belli; praedam civilibus armis
> Scit non esse casas. O vitae tuta facultas
> Pauperis angustique lares! o munera nondum
> Intellecta deum! Quibus hoc contingere templis
> Aut potuit muris, nullo trepidare tumultu
> Caesarea pulsante manu?

---

[9] *Lucan*, ed. and translated by J. D. Duff (Cambridge, MA, and London, Harvard University Press, and Wm Heinemann Ltd., first published 1928), verses V 526-531; quotations from Lucan will henceforth be from this edition.

In the light of these lines the point of the story becomes nothing other than the folly of greatness itself. There are, after all, two sides to Caesar's strange resolve. On one hand, there is the gratuitous risk-taking, the tempting of fate. The narrator tells us that Caesar thought the gods more faithful to him than he to them, "se desse deis ac non sibi numina credit" (V 499). But the other factor is perhaps more important, the fact that the crossing of the Adriatic answered to a perfectly rational and practical end, albeit a perverse one. Caesar knows that he must establish contact with his forces in Italy, and since Antony is reluctant to take on the mission, he feels impelled to go himself. The motif of the attempted crossing is among other things one more link in the story. That Caesar's enterprise here should be played against Amyclas' serenity forces us to hold up to judgment not only the particular folly of defying a hostile nature, but the larger one of the war itself, and of the aspirations of both leaders (not only Caesar's). Caesar and Amyclas are thus both high examples. We could add that it is no accident that the Middle Ages turned the episode into a topic, an edifying *locus* known to all.[10] As we have noted, it is not unique in the *Pharsalia*. We need only remember the account of Cato's journey across the Syrtes in Libya, or the fraternization scene in the Spanish episode, the first a lesson in Stoic self-sufficiency, the second on the folly of civil war. The list goes on.

There is an even simpler way of articulating *consecutio*, to do so plainly and in a continuous text, or in other words, to play the role of Lewis Carroll's Duchess and point out the moral of the story. The *Alexandre*-poet does this over and over again, as is well known.

We recall the narrator's judgment on the treachery of Pausanias:

> 186) Todos los traydores asy deuien moryr
> niguñt auer del mundo non los deuie guaryr
> todos commo a merçed deuien a ellos yr
> nunca les deuie çielo nin tierra resçebir

Bessus and Narbazanes are plotting to kill Darius; the king had raised these two men from slavery to very high station. The moral is pointed in an apostrophe to Darius. It is folly to put confidence in the base-born:

---

[10] Currie, H. MacL., *Silver Latin Epic* (Bristol, Bristol Classical Press, 1985), p. 34.

1650)  Libraronte los fados de los tus enemigos
       dieronte a matar a los tus amigos
       sy quisieses creer los prouerbios antiguos
       non daries tal poder a villanos mendigos

The wicked pair take the king prisoner. The narrator comments in a series of paradoxes:

1716)  El buen rey en su casa auie cabtiuidat
       el justo de los falsos auia grañt crueldat
       al omne piadoso falleçiel piedat
       en lugar de justiçia regnaua falsedat

Then he generalizes, speaking of the obscure ways of God:

1718)  Los juizios de Dios asy suelen correr
       quiere dar a los malos e a los buenos toller
       lieva todas las cosas segund de su plazer
       por mostrar que ha sobre todos poder
1719)  A los buenos da cueyta que biuan en pobreza
       a los malos da fuerça averes e rriqueza
       al fol da el meollo al cuerdo la corteza
       los que non lo entienden tienen lo a fereça

After describing Darius' death and his tomb, the poet gives us some stanzas on mutability. The passage begins:

1805)  Nunca en esti siglo deurie omne fiar
       que sabe a sus cosas tan mala çaga dar
       a baxos nin a altos non sabe perdonar
       non deuriemos por esto el otro oluidar
1806)  Anda commo rrueda que non quiere aturar
       el omne mal astrugo non se sabe guardar
       trahe buenos falagos sabenos engañar
       nunca en vn estado puede aturar

There is no need to multiply examples. The great author of the *Pharsalia* also gives us his judgments about the actors and their deeds. Some of these are annexed to what is surely one of the most admirable passages in the poem and one of the finest battle scenes anywhere, the lines on the glorious end of the military hero of Dyrrachium, Scaeva. Brilliant verse paragraphs go to recounting the last hours of this courageous, resourceful, and unfailingly energetic soldier, destructive of his enemy to his own last breath. Alas, he was a Caesarian. Here is the narrator's comment:

> Happy had he been in this title to fame, had he routed hardy Iberians or Cantabrians with their targets or Teutons with their long shields. But Scaeva can never deck the Thunderer's temple with his trophies nor shout for joy in the triumph. Unhappy wretch, how bravely you fought that a tyrant might rule over you!
>
>     felix hoc nomine famae,
> Si tibi durus Hiber aut si tibi terga dedisset
> Cantaber exiguis aut longis Teutonus armis.
> Non tu bellorum spoliis ornare Tonantis
> Templa potes, non tu laetis ululare triumphis.
> Infelix, quanta dominum virtute parasti! (VI 257-262)

Pompey of course prevails at Dyrrachium, and true to his finest self, hating bloodshed, he restrains his soldiers at the end, meaning to spare Roman lives. But the humanity and decency of the great general prove to be the undoing of Rome. The poet remarks:

> Civil war might then have shed its last drop of blood, and peace might even have followed; but Pompey himself kept back his furious soldiers. Rome might have been saved, free from tyrants and mistress of her own actions, if a Sulla had won that victory for her. Grievous alas! is it, and ever will be, that Caesar profited by his worst crime – his fighting against a kinsman who had scruples. Out upon cruel destiny! Libya and Spain would not have lamented the disasters at Utica and Munda; the Nile, defiled by horrid bloodshed, would not have borne a corpse nobler than the King of Egypt; the naked body of Juba would never have fallen on African sands; Scipio would not have bled to appease the Carthaginian dead, nor would the land of the living have lost the stainless Cato – that day might have ended Rome's agony, and Pharsalia might have been blotted out from the central scroll of destiny.
>
>     Totus mitti civilibus armis
> Usque vel in pacem potuit cruor: ipse furentes
> Dux tenuit gladios. Felix ac libera regum,
> Roma, fores iurisque tui, vicisset in illo
> Si tibi Sulla loco. Dolet heu semperque dolebit,

> Quod scelerum, Caesar, prodest tibi summa tuorum,
> Cum genero pugnasse pio. Pro tristia fata!
> Non Uticae Libye clades, Hispania Mundae
> Flesset et infando pollutus sanguine Nilus
> Nobilius Phario gestasset rege cadaver,
> Nec Iuba Marmaricas nudus pressisset harenas
> Poenorumque umbras placasset sanguine fuso
> Scipio, nec sancto caruisset vita Catone.
> Ultimus esse dies potuit tibi, Roma, malorum,
> Exire e mediis potuit Pharsalia fatis. (VI 299-313)

I offer one more piece of Lucanesque editorializing. The decisive battle of the civil war has just begun: Pharsalus is to witness the struggle which is to place power forever in the wrong hands, to the destruction of Rome and its liberties. The dreadful consequences of this bloody and tragic scene are far-reaching. Here is a part of the poet's long comment:

> These hands [of the combatants on both sides] will bring it to pass that, whatever the ninth century [Lucan's own] unfolds, it shall be free from warfare. This battle will destroy nations yet unborn; it will deprive of their birthtime and sweep away the men of the generation coming into the world. Then all the Latin race will be a legend; dust-covered ruins will scarce be able to indicate the site of Gabii and Veii and Cora, the houses of Alba and the dwellings of Laurentum – a depopulated country, where no man dwells except the senators who are forced to spend one night there by Numa's law which they resent. &c.
>
> Hae facient dextrae, quidquid nona explicat aetas,
> Ut vacet a ferro. Gentes Mars iste futuras
> Obruet et populos aevi venientis in orbem
> Erepto natale feret. Tunc omne Latinum
> Fabula nomen erit; Gabios Veiosque Coramque
> Pulvere vix tectae poterunt monstrare ruinae
> Albanosque lares Laurentinosque penates,
> Rus vacuum, quod non habitet nisi nocte coacta
> Invitus questustque Numam iussisse senator. (VII 387-396)

I return to an old argument of mine. My remarks about some of the narrative patterns shared by the two poems are not trivial. We have to see things in context. To some it may seem less than exciting to be reminded that the *Pharsalia* points morals and tells exemplary tales and that the *Alexandre* follows suit. One might object especially that such obvious parallels do not shed much light on the special personality of either poem. Both objections miss the real point, raised by the common features, which is that they are distinctive. Not all narrative texts behave the way our two poems do. The matter is a simple one. There are many storytellers who ply their craft without pointing morals, or offering broad judgments on the action and the actors; there are others who do so sparingly. There are many likewise who frame narrative episodes from which it is hard to draw generalities. Speaking more broadly, we may observe that the element of *consecutio* in some narrative texts is weak; in some it is diffuse. The *Pharsalia,* along with the *Alexandre*, and as I think a whole set of medieval and Renaissance works which are influenced by Lucan's work, stand out notably from their fellows for the great extent to which the point of the story is driven home: they plead and argue vehemently as other narratives do not. If with respect to the *Libro* we wish to trace this element of commentary, this clear focus on the theme of the moment, to a source other than Lucan, the task before us is far from easy. The list of possible models among the *auctores* is after all not endless. If we take the *Aeneid,* for example, we must observe that the comments on the action in the narrator's own voice are rare; when they do occur, they are usually quite brief. Moreover, Virgil's great poem, assuredly heavy with meaning and intention generally, does not convey that great sense in any way similar to that in which the *Pharsalia* expresses its own meaning. Certain episodes aside, the message or messages of the older poem are global. Comtemporary Rome as the end and purpose of Aeneas' labors, his *pietas,* the *furor* embodied in Juno and later in Turnus, all belong to the poem as a whole, or to large parts of it; the single narrative unit designed to dramatize some theme, the ruthlessness of the powerful, or the folly of civil war, is alien to Virgil's work. Ovid poses problems of a different kind, but as I have already suggested, his influence does not account for everything that is in the *Alexandre.* The *Pharsalia* is simply not one poem among many. In the respects that interest us it is not like the *Aeneid,* not like the *Metamorphoses,* and in spite of certain similarities, not much like the *Thebaid.* Lucan is a unique model, and the shape and organization of the *Alexandre* should therefore tell us something about the special standing of his remarkable poem in those latter years.

## 5) Lucan: Explanation

We pass on now to another orator's procedure that invades the narrative of the *Pharsalia,* a pattern which to my mind is especially interesting because it is anti-visual: it is the eminent case of ocular witness or *evidentia* evaded. I am referring to explanation, simply, to the text that specifies causes and motives. We have examined this strain in the *Alexandre* in some detail, and we must now study its role in Lucan's poem, particularly because explanation and the specifying of causes and motives are so pervasive there, and so fundamental to its whole conception. The evasion of *evidentia* which I spoke of can be thought of as the reverse of the same coin. Although explanation and visual evocation can coexist in a single passage, they are more often alternatives: normally, when you explain, you do not have to evoke, and vice versa. Lucan's great poem is remarkable on both sides: it avoids the visual over long stretches of its text, and it does a great deal of explaining. We should at this point issue a warning: we are not dealing here with a narrative that is simply well-motivated, in which the chain of cause and effect is clear to the reader from the very fabric of the story. This is, after all, a broad category. A logical narrative structure of this sort is, for example, perfectly compatible with much visualization or with little. The narrative flow in the *Aeneid,* for example, is surely coherent and logical, but as has often been observed, it is also elliptical: the logical and causal connectives often have to be reconstructed by the reader. Kenneth Quinn devotes eloquent pages to this subject,[11] and in a sense we also have ancient witnesses: the commentaries of Tiberius Donatus and Servius frequently point out motives and causes in the story which Virgil leaves unexpressed. One could further assert that in contrast to the *Pharsalia,* it evokes, because it does not explain: frequently enough the concrete detail draws the reader into the narrative so that he can perceive intuitively the sense of the story. But in any case, Lucan's is not that kind of text. The poet wishes us not only to witness events, but to understand them, and at certain points in the poem the latter motive is exclusive. A comparison of the openings of the *Aeneid* and the *Pharsalia* is very instructive. Vir-

---

[11] Quinn, Kenneth, *Latin Explorations* (London, Routledge and Kegan Paul, 1963), pp. 203-211.

gil's poem winds up the clock by telling of the wrath of Juno and its causes, all in a very few verses. But the action of the *Pharsalia* does not begin until verse 83 of the first book, and the greater part of this long introduction is given over to the immediate and remote causes of the civil war. We are given a piece on the cosmic process, one on the mutual jealousy and suspicion of the two principals, we are told how the hatred was made ineffective by the mediation of Julia and Crassus, and that their deaths hastened the outbreak of the conflict. Finally we have a fine section on the decay of the civic spirit in Rome, a general cause for the war. An impressive display of reasons, unparallelled, as I believe, in earlier epic poetry. The poet shows his hand out of hand.

Narration supported by explanation is an orator's procedure. The theme should be familiar to us. In a judicial speech the *narratio* is functional and utilitarian: judge and jury are supposed to understand the events in question, to comprehend them to the point of being able to make a judgment about them, and explanation leads them to this goal. Naturally, each advocate recounts and explains in a way that will favor his case: his recital, however logical, is not expected to be impartial. Explanation, in any case, is entirely at home in the *narratio*. The classic handbooks of rhetoric leave us in no doubt on this subject. *Narratio*, as we know, should be brief, clear, and plausible, or verisimilar. Explanation comes under this last heading, the plausible. The *Ad Herennium* has the following:

> Our Statement of Facts will have plausibility (veri similis narratio erit) if it answers the requirements of the usual, the expected, and the natural; if account is strictly kept of the length of time, the standing of the persons involved, the motives in the planning, and the advantages offered by the scene of action, so as to obviate the argument in refutation that the time was too short, or that there was no motive, or that the place was unsuitable, or that the persons themselves could not have acted or been treated so.
>
> Veri similis narratio erit si ut mos, ut opinio, ut natura postulat dicemus; si spatia temporum, personarum dignitates, consiliorum rationes, locorum opportunitates constabunt, ne refelli possit aut temporis parum fuisse, aut causam nullam, aut locum idoneum non fuisse, aut homines ipsos facere aut pati non potuisse. (I 16)

Cicero's *De inventione* has a passage in much the same vein (I 29). Quintilian has: "The *statement of fact* will be credible, ... if we assign reasons and motives for the facts on which the inquiry turns"; "Credibilis autem erit narratio ... si causas ac rationes factis praeposuerimus" (IV ii 52). A few lines further along he adds significantly: "It will also be useful to scatter some hints of our proofs here and there, but in such a way that it is never forgotten that we are making a *statement of facts (narratio)* and not a proof"; "Ne illud quidem fuerit inutile, semina quaedam probationum spargere, verum sic ut narrationem esse meminerimus non probationem" (IV ii 54). Earlier on Quintilian complains of the over-subtlety of earlier writers on *narratio:*

> For they demand an explanation dealing not only with the facts of the case which is before the court, but with the person involved ..., or of the place where an incident occurred, ... or of the time at which something occurred..., or of the causes of an occurrence, such as the historians are so fond of setting forth, when they explain the origin of a war, a rebellion, or a pestilence.
>
> Non enim solam volunt esse illam negotii, de quo apud iudices quaeritur, expositionem, sed personae, ... loci, ... temporis; ... causarum, quibus historici frequentissime utuntur, cum exponunt, unde bellum, seditio, pestilentia. (IV ii 2)

Quintilian here seems to be alluding to nothing more complicated than a doctrine like that of the *Ad herennium*. We observe that the broader view rejected by him, but affirmed in the other texts, leaves wide scope for explanatory discourse, admitting as it does other factors besides the motives and dispositions of the principal actors. In this context Quintilian's allusion to history and historians is of course very significant. We must remember that the ancients often declared that history was closely akin to oratory, and we must recall also that critics in antiquity and since have complained that the *Pharsalia* has more in it of history than of poetry. Explanation in narrative, whether grounded in the character and motives of the characters, or in other circumstances, time, place, the past, the order of nature, or fortune, is indeed at the heart of the historical text, in antiquity and to a great extent since. If, then, my judgment about the large role of explanation in Lucan is accurate, the accusation thrust at him seems at least partly fair. This point will become still more obvious when we start looking at his text in detail.

The anomaly here, obviously, is the invasion of the explanatory mode into narrative verse: what originally belonged to oratory passed easily into history, but at the eleventh hour established a beachhead in poetry. Ovid, who, as we have seen, speaks plainly about the motives of his characters, is already one of the invaders. But Lucan, as we shall see, goes much farther. In fact, long stretches of his poem remind us of historical texts precisely because of their wealth of explanations of all kinds. Martindale and others may wish to save the *Pharsalia* for poetry, but in portions of the work the features that make it seem oratorical also give it the look of history. The least we can say about this historical personality is that it is highly unusual in ancient poetry, and that with the possible exception of Silius Italicus, whose narrative style is more or less Lucanesque, the older poet has to wait many years before he has many imitators.[12]

Lucan's great poem plays the harlot; so one would one conclude. Bound initially to epic poetry, it consorts with other genres, other modes. Let us look at a passage I consider typical for just this promiscuity. The piece will give us on a small scale elements which we may later study on a larger. We return to Caesar's attempt to cross the Adriatic. The great general, recently arrived in Greece, meets Pompey for the first time as an enemy. He implores his ally Mark Antony to establish contact with the Caesarian troops still in Italy, but his entreaty is in vain. Lucan gives us Caesar's speech at this point, but the lines that lead up to it are pertinent to our theme:

> Though Caesar was frantic to join battle, he was forced to endure a postponement of wicked war by the partisans he had left in Italy. Bold Antony, who commanded all those forces, thus early, during the civil war, was plotting an Actium. Again and again Caesar urged him to haste with threats and entreaties. (V 476-481)

---

[12] There of course did exist a large body of Latin historical epic before Virgil. Ugo Piacentini, in *Osservazione sulla tecnica epica di Lucano* (Berlin, Akademie-Verlag, 1963), p. 11, affirms that Virgil, under the strong influence of Hellenistic poetry, intended in the *Aeneid* to part company decisively with the epic mode of Ennius and Naevius, with its dry annalistic style. I have never heard it suggested that Lucan was trying to recover something of the older manner. The fragments of Ennius and Naevius do not convey to a non-specialist like me any special affinity to Lucan.

Duff's version conveys little of the tautness and elegance of the original. Here is the Latin:

> Caesaris attonitam miscenda ad proelia mentem
> Ferre moras scelerum partes iussere relictae.
> Ductor erat cunctis audax Antonius armis
> Iam tum civili meditatus Leucada bello.
> Illum saepe minis Caesar precibusque morantem
> Evocat.

Before we dismiss these lines as a hasty formula of transition, we must take a close look at what they contain. We begin with an account of Caesar's moral disposition, his *furor*, as one might say, his impatience for battle. One should note that this inner quality is not an element that in any way particularizes this scene. Caesar's restlessness and love of violence is a constant throughout the poem: by the time we reach this point in Book V we have been informed about the strain many times. The motive we are given for Caesar's action is global and generalized: the poet is in effect saying "that is the way Caesar is." The second narrative element here, a matter of place, is the dispersion of the Caesarian troops: some are with their leader in Greece, but others are still in Italy. This fact, along with Caesar's *furor*, is what impels him to action, first to speak to Antony, and eventually to try to get back to Italy himself. Are these two motives, the impatience of Caesar and the scattering of the troops, characteristic of epic? It is generally risky to try to answer questions of this sort, but in this case the contrasts and parallels are strong enough to keep danger to a minimum. Caesar's restlessness and love of battle seem to me to be well within the tradition, of a piece with Aeneas' *pietas* and Turnus' *furor*. The only jarring note here is the explicit reference Lucan makes to this disposition, but this is a separate matter. We must understand. His rage and impatience is assuredly a thing of the moment: he is frustrated by the state of things at one particular moment in time. But as I have suggested, it is a fact that his emotion is one permanently connected with him, and this feature seems to me to be hardly distinctive. But what are we to make of the disposition of the Caesarian forces? Does this motif have a Homeric or Virgilian personality? We may look at this reference in two ways, as an authentic narrative element, a state of affairs in the external world, and as a consideration in Caesar's mind. In the first mode we can say that Lucan has presented here a genuine military problem, a serious obstacle to any strategy Caesar may want to execute. He wishes to confront his enemy, but is at a disadvantage, because his forces are scattered. Our first large point of interest is that Lucan does not realize this situation as a scene: he does not ask us to visualize it. One might wish to go further and say that the turn of plot he has given us is unrealizable, impossible to visualize – the troops scattered abroad, the difficulties of the general. This is plainly not true. We could imagine two perfectly Lucanesque scenarios built around the incident which might be executed in a highly visual style. If, for example, we wished to dramatize the play of fortune in the affairs of Caesar, we could show Antony's forces champing at the bit, restless, eager to meet the enemy, but unable to. The mood of impatience could be conveyed by speeches, by describing the physical attitudes of the men, by recording significant incidents. If we chose this path, we would be presenting a unity of wills, Caesar's and his followers', frustrated by an unhappy circumstance. Alternately, if we wished to emphasize the irony of the whole situation, we could show Caesar impatient for battle and his men in Italy, idle, with thoughts far from the war, lazy, failing in all military discipline, all for the want of a present enemy. And in turn, we could give character to this scene, as we did to its rival, by inventing details and anecdotes analogous to those of its fellow. The poet is a free agent. If Lucan is simply reporting Caesar's difficulties, rather than trying to dramatize them, that was his choice. He simply does not poetize this detail. Instead he is offering us a set of circumstances of place that make Caesar's decisions plausible. In other words, he is fulfilling the precept of texts like the *Ad Herennium* to the letter. The plain conclusion would seem to be that we have a gross incursion of rhetoric, oratory – and perhaps also history – into narrative poetry; exposition and explanation displace evocation.

When we speak of Caesar's intentions, properly speaking, his inner resolutions, we are on even firmer ground. His two decisions, first to try to persuade Antony and then to travel to Italy himself, are serious tactical moves. They deal with remote matters, remote in place, the soldiers across the sea, far from where they are needed, and remote in time, since the forces cannot be reunited in any short period. Let us be very clear that what we are here considering is something going on inside Julius Caesar's head. Complex inner scenes like this are not very characteristic of epic song: this is already an old subject with us. But as we have seen, the airing and specifying of motives is enjoined by the handbooks of rhetoric: indeed, the sort of text that Quintilian attacks as over-subtle favors just such quasi-historical accounts as this one. Once again, in Lucan's practice oratory and kindred forms prevail over poetry. We return now to the element of passion, the impatience shown by the general. We remarked above that this strain could be thought of as akin to Aeneas' *pietas* or Turnus' *furor*, but that perhaps Lucan protested too much, that the plain labelling of Caesar's impatience might seem un-epic or un-Virgilian. But once again, this violation, if that is what it is, is in conformity with the rules set forth in many rhetorical texts: the action is verisimilar, if it is traced to a permanent disposition in the actor. In a judicial speech one would indeed expect these constants to be talked about explicitly, so that the judge and jury could be in no doubt about their effect on the person's deeds. In this kind of setting the fine indirection of poetry would surely not be the general rule.

Caesar's two acts, the futile attempt to persuade Antony, and his equally vain one to cross the Adriatic, are explained on the basis of three factors, the facts on the ground, his apprehension of them along with his resolve to act on them, and in the case of the sea-adventure, his restless disposition. This full and logical account of the affair makes up what we could call an orator's text, or perhaps with equal force an historian's. The passage we have been examining is indeed a very short one, but as I have suggested, it gives us the fabric and design of long stretches of the *Pharsalia* in little. Explanation, the specifying of causes, motives and practical circumstances, is an essential part of the work's narrative throughout. It accompanies the opening, as we have seen, and is at hand at every important stage in the story. The assimilation to history, made by Servius and others, is in this sense fully justified: the poet clearly wishes us to understand the events he is talking about and not merely to witness them. The assimilation to oratory is also justified on many different grounds, to be sure, but particularly because of the same bias towards explanation that we have been considering.

What is at issue here is perhaps less the actual character of this or that explanatory passage than the strategic position some of them occupy, as well as the actual function they have in the argument of the poem. Thus, the two great battles between Julius Caesar and Pompey are the centerpiece of the surviving *Pharsalia,* and would surely have been high points in the completed work, but the drama one would expect in such central episodes is not in fact their prevailing mode. As Lucan presents them the encounters are matters to be grasped and comprehended, but not primarily to be visualized. Strategy is paramount. As the two generals make the moves preparatory to the first of the pair of battles, we are asked to view the whole affair in a very special light. Things get under way as Caesar tries to outflank his rival by rushing to Dyrrachium. Pompey counters by taking the great stronghold Petra. In a descriptive passage we are told of the security of the place, its great height, its inaccessibility from the sea. These circumstances, along with the fact that Pompey's huge forces were ensconced over a large piece of territory, fully explains Caesar's daring response, a prodigious set of fortifications. These works, which are also commented on at length, are meant to surround the whole extent of Pompey's troops, an extreme measure in the face of a serious disadvantage. We should be quite clear what the poet is up to at this point. In the account of the natural situation of Petra, and eminently in that of the impressive line of defenses, we are once again given generously of those circumstances of place which rhetoric speaks of. In the latter instance the physical features of place are man-made, but they are quite as much a part of the landscape as though they were natural. The works, extensive as they are, give plausibility to Pompey's eventual next move, which is to put pressure on Caesar along a broad front.

This is a fair sample of Lucanesque narrative in the first of the two battle sequences. Intention plays a great role in these accounts. The tactical shrewdness of both generals is at the center of our attention, the race towards Dyrrachium, the taking of Petra, the building of the wall. We are far removed from the focus on simply strength and courage, and on single combat, in a word, from all the things that seem authentically epical. Deliberation and the long view are what count. The Pharsalus sequence, for its part, is perhaps told with less logic than that of Dyrrachium, but in any case, tactical elegance is still a large issue. Under a withering attack of the Caesarians, Pompey's men, less bloodthirsty than their enemy, close ranks and stand phalanx-fashion, with overlapping shields. The Caesarians, logically enough, concentrate their fire on this one formation, and manage to break the line. Moments later, the Pompeian horse, apparently in front of the troops, divide into two long wings, freeing the hordes of lightly armed men to harass Caesar over a long front. He, "fearing that his front line might be shaken by their attack" (VII 521-22), releases a column from behind this very line, a force that puts large segments of the enemy to flight; many fall in the process. These men, as it turns out, are non-Romans, prone to retreat. The Roman remnant of course stands fast, and is the next object of attack; the end of the sequence is very bloody. This whole chain of events is unthinkable without a wise guiding hand on either side, and as we have seen, Caesar's deliberation is actually mentioned once. But even here it is unnecessary: the rhetoricians' requirement that the actors' intentions be clear is more than satisfied. Equally rhetorical in this scene, as we have observed, are the explicit allusions to the personalities of the actors: the barbarians are untrustworthy, the Romans firm, and the Pompeians less bloodthirsty than their rivals. We recall Quintilian and the *Ad Herennium* on the significance of character in narration. Broadly speaking, then, the important arguments in the sixth and seventh books are directed towards our understanding. The logic of events, the reasons for them, remote and proximate, human and otherwise, are what dominate the story. In the course of things we are also given the dramatic account of the last hours of Scaeva, and other texts of very different character. But this latter mode is by no means exclusive, and it would not be incautious to say that it was not dominant.

Books Six and Seven tell of the chain of events leading to Pompey's final defeat, and the demise of Republican hopes. This is hardly a peripheral episode, and the wealth of explanation here by itself launches this feature of the text into high prominence. The explanatory mode also prevails in other important places in the poem. Several of the ten books open with a recital of causes. Book Two starts with the cosmic background. In a debate with himself the narrator asks if the war was written in the stars or was a product of simple chance:

> Why didst thou, Ruler of Olympus, see fit to lay on suffering mortals this additional burden, that they should learn the approach of calamity by awful portents? Whether the author of the universe, when the fire gave place and he first took in hand the shapeless realm of raw matter, established the chain of causes for all eternity, and bound himself as well by universal law, and portioned out the universe, which endures the ages prescribed for it,

by a fixed line of destiny; or whether nothing is ordained and Fortune, moving at random, brings round the cycle of events, and chance is master of mankind – in either case, let thy purpose, whatever it be, be sudden; let the mind of man be blind to coming doom; he fears, but leave him hope.

> Cur hanc tibi, rector Olympi,
> Sollicitis visum mortalibus addere curam,
> Noscant venturas ut dira per omina clades?
> Sive parens rerum, cum primum informia regna
> Materiamque rudem flamma cedente recepit,
> Fixit in aeternum causas, qua cuncta coercet
> Se quoque lege tenens, et saecula iussa ferentem
> Fatorum inmoto divisit limite mundum;
> Sive nihil positum est sed fors incerta vagatur
> Fertque refertque vices, et habet mortalia casus:
> Sit subitum, quodcumque paras; sit caeca futuri
> Mens hominum fati; liceat sperare timenti. (II 4-15)

At line eleven of Book IV there begins a description of Ilerda and its river:

> The fertile land rises in a hill of moderate height and ascends with easy slope; and on this stands Ilerda, founded by hands of old. The Sicoris, not least among western rivers, flows by with quiet waters; and a stone bridge, fit to withstand the winter floods, spans the river with mighty arch. A steep hill close by was occupied by the army of Magnus; and Caesar pitched his camp aloft on another hill as high; the river flowed between and divided the camps. Beyond, the level land spreads out in plains whose limit the eye can scarce embrace; but the rushing Cinga bounds the plains –- Cinga, whose own swift waters may never smite the shore and the sea; for the Hiberus, which gives its name to the country, mixes its flood with the Cinga and steals its name from it.

> Colle tumet modico lenique excrevit in altum
> Pingue solum tumulo; super hunc fundata vetusta
> Surgit Ilerda manu; placidis praelabitur undis
> Hesperios inter Sicoris non ultimus amnes,
> Saxeus ingenti quem pons amplectitur arcu
> Hibernas passurus aquas. At proxima rupes
> Signa tenet Magni; nec Caesar colle minore
> Castra levat; medius dirimit tentoria gurges.
> Explicat hinc tellus campos effusa patentes
> Vix oculo prendente modum, camposque coerces,

> Cinga rapax, vetitus fluctus et litora cursu
> Oceani pepulisse tuo; nam gurgite mixto
> Qui preastat terris aufert tibi nomen Hiberus. (IV 11-23)

Lucan is here not being picturesque: every one of the features mentioned has a bearing on the military action about to be recounted. Near the beginning of Book VIII we are given a general motive for Pompey's behavior after the disaster at Pharsalus:

> Though fallen from his lofty eminence, he knows that the price of his blood is still high; and, mindful of his career, he believes that his death can still earn as great a reward as he himself would give for the severed head of Caesar. Though he seeks solitude, his known features suffer him not to hide his disaster in safe concealment.
>
>   Quamvis summo de culmine lapsus
> Nondum vile sui pretium scit sanguinis esse,
> Seque, memor fati, tantae mercedis habere
> Credit adhuc iugulum, quantam pro Caesaris ipse
> Avolsa cervice daret. Deserta sequentem
> Non patitur tutis fatum celare latebris
> Clara viri facies. (VIII 8-14)

The cause here specified has two faces, the facts on the ground and Pompey's perception of them. Book IX, after a warm-up, starts with an account of Cato's mind about the war. Initially contemptuous of both Caesar and Pompey, after Pharsalus the venerable hero and Stoic saint embraces fully the cause of the latter and of the Republic; he sees himself as the possible savior of the Roman world at its critical hour. The rest of the book is given over to Cato's deeds, and the lines at the beginning of the Book tell us generally why he acts as he does. Book X begins inside the mind of Caesar, lately arrived in Egypt. His position there is anomalous. The murder of Pompey places the young king squarely on his side, so it would seem, but resentment of the Roman presence in the land of the Ptolemys also puts him on his guard. This is the disposition with which the general begins his activities there.

Many of the important episodes in the poem are accompanied by explanations. In Book V we are given the reasons why Caesar's weary troops are at the point of revolt. Later in the same book we are told why Pompey saw fit to leave his wife at Lesbos. In Book VI we learn why the weak and cowardly Sextus Pompeius consults the old woman of Thessaly. Caesar's first move at Ilerda is told in a logical way. Intentions and circumstances of place are kept clear. Night is approaching on the first day of the campaign:

> But when the sky was westering towards night, Caesar surrounded his army with a trench dug in haste, while his front rank kept their ground; thus he deceived the enemy, screening his camp with a line of troops drawn up near at hand. At dawn he ordered his men to move with speed and climb the hill, which lay between Ilerda and the camp and protected the town. Fear and shame alike drove the enemy to this point: with flying march they reached the hill first and occupied it. Their courage and their swords promised possession of the ground to Caesar's men; but the foe relied on actual possession. &c.
>
>         prono cum Caesar Olympo
> In noctem subita circumdedit agmina fossa,
> Dum primae perstant acies, hostemque fefellit
> Et prope consertis obduxit castra maniplis.
> Luce nova collem subito conscendere cursu,
> Qui medius tutam castris dirimebat Ilerdam,
> Imperat. Huc hostem pariter terrorque pudorque
> Inpulit, et rapto tumulum prior agmine cepit.
> His virtus ferrumque locum promittit, at illis
> Ipse locus. (IV 28-37)

Perhaps the most brilliant of all the well-explained episodes is the story of Curio's disastrous campaign in Africa and his defeat at the hands of Juba. The narrator's commentary guides us effectively through the whole passage. Juba is powerful, the ruler of an immense kingdom:

> No ruler possessed a broader realm than he: at its greatest length his kingdom is bounded on its western point by Atlas, neighbour of Gades, and on the East by Ammon, bordering on the Syrtes; and on the line of its breadth, the hot region of his huge domain separates the Ocean from the burnt-up torrid zone.
>
>         Non fusior ulli
> Terra fuit domino: qua sunt longissima, regna
> Cardine ab occiduo vicinus Gadibus Atlas
> Terminat, a medio confinis Syrtibus Hammon;
> At, qua lata iacet, vasti plaga fervida regni
> Distinet Oceanum zonaeque exusta calentis. (IV 670-675)

The next few lines are a catalogue of the peoples subject to the great king. Juba had been an ally of the Pompeian general Varus and is therefore hostile to Curio, but he has his own reasons for hating him:

> For Curio, in that year during which he outraged heaven and earth, had also tried to dislodge Juba from his ancestral throne by means of a tribune's law – he sought, at the same time, to take Africa from its rightful king and to set up a king at Rome!
> Hunc quoque, quo superos humanaque polluit anno,
> Lege tribunicia solio depellere avorum
> Curio temptarat, Libyamque auferre tyranno
> Dum regnum te, Roma, facit. (IV 689-92)

Varus is of course defeated. Paradoxically, this is welcome news to Juba: "But when Juba heard of the lost battle of conquered Varus, he rejoiced that the glory of the campaign was reserved for his arms"; "Tristia sed postquam superati proelia Vari / Sunt audita Iubae, laetus, quod gloria belli / Sit rebus servata suis" (IV 715-717). The rest of the narrative is given over to the brilliant tactics of the African, who in a series of deceitful moves convinces Curio that he is in retreat. Geography plays a part in the final disaster:

> Along a perilous path he [Curio] led his men, over high rocks and cliffs, and then the enemy was sighted far away from the top of the hills. They, with their native craft, drew back a little, till he should leave the height and trust his army in loose array to the open fields. Curio, ignorant of their treacherous device, believed that they were fleeing, and, as if victorious, marched his army down to the fields below. &c.
> Super ardua ducit
> Saxa, super cautes abrupto limite signa,
> Cum procul e summis conspecti collibus hostes
> Fraude sua cessere parum, dum colle relicto
> Effusam patulis aciem committeret arvis.
> Ille fugam credens simulatae nescius artis,
> Ut victor, mersos aciem deiecit in agros. (739-745)

Verisimilitude, the wealth of explanation, is at the heart of the great poem's conception. One reason why this strain is particularly interesting to the student of the *Alexandre* is the obvious one. Explanation plays a large role here as well. This is plain from much of what we have said to date, and as I have pointed out elsewhere,[13] many of the etiologies of the *Libro* are distinctive: they are not to be found in the sources, but are added by the later poet. Our text tells us that Darius' wife, a captive of Alexander, dies from anxiety over an imminent battle between the two kings (copla 1235). In the Trojan War episode Paris answers the reproaches of Helen by blaming his defeat on Pallas, angry because he denied her the golden apple (copla 494). Both of these motives are new: the respective sources, Gautier and the *Ilias latina* know nothing of them. These are examples among many. At least part of the verisimilitude of the *Libro* is of the poet's own making, and this distinctive strain brings it closer to the *Pharsalia*. But we must also emphasize that our *Libro* also inherits many of its etiologies from Gautier. This, as I have insisted before, does not take away any of their force within the text: they also belong to the *Libro* by full right, just as do the original ones.

There is a second, more general reason why Lucan's many explanations are interesting to the student of the *Alexandre*. As we have obeseved so often, one of the main characteristics of our medieval poem is the fact that it contains so much that is not simple narrative, that the thread of the story is curled and wrinkled by evaluations, bits of commentary, and indeed of explanation; in some instances, as we know, these elements actually break up the narrative line with passages which are non-progressive. As I keep insisting, this style of exposition is distinctive. If, as seems reasonable, we are going to look for classical models for the origins of this broad feature, our easiest targets are Ovid and Lucan, especially the latter, all for reasons that we have aired. Explanation is significant in our whole argument about the *Pharsalia*, because it tells us more plainly than anything else that the poet does not wish to be a simple story-teller. His text is a mixture of epic, judicial oratory, treatise, special pleading and more; explanation, as I have stressed, is perhaps the most important part of this complicated scheme, and in any case is surely the feature least characteristic of epic poetry. But surprisingly, this notorious example of a mixed media event, unique in its time, is actually a prestige text in the years when the *Alexandre* is written, and it is for this reason that its own mixture of dis-

---

[13] Fraker, Charles F., "Aetiologia in the *Libro de Alexandre*" (*Hispanic Review*, 55 (1987), pp. 277-299.

courses might well be thought of as traceable to Lucan more than to anyone else. We must add, by the way, that this whole matter is greatly complicated by the fact that the mix itself seems so natural to us. It is everywhere: journalism, historiography, the style and design of the classic novel, all give us this very same potpourri of story, supporting information, etiologies, interpretation, evaluation, and other commentary. We, of course, make a great mistake, if we think that this style simply sprang out of nothing, or that nature guides the hand of every true-born writer to do this kind of text and no other. The mixed media story is distinctive and has a history; we seriously misread the *Alexandre* and many other older works of literature, if we ever overlook this fact.

6) VERISIMILITUDE AND EVIDENTIA

The exposition in Lucan's poem is full of variety, quite as much as in Ovid or in a fine piece of historiography. Earlier I suggested that in the *Pharsalia* and in general, verisimilitude, plausibility tends to work to the exclusion of *evidentia*. In Lucan's poem they in fact compete: some passages are addressed to the understanding, while others, like the Scaeva episode, are aimed at the imagination. In my judgment, this mix of the two modes is a major factor in the broad influence of Lucan on medieval and Renaissance narrative poetry; I am convinced, indeed, that often it is the very mark of that influence. The *Alexandre* is to my mind an eminent case. Our two terms, verisimilitude and *evidentia*, for this very reason deserve a close look. Are we drawing the line between them too sharply? As a practical matter the distinction between the verisimilar and the evidential in the *Pharsalia* is plain enough, but even so, is it not possible that our contrast has more in it of modern theory than of ancient? The opposition "showing-telling," familiar to readers of modern criticism, might seem to be intruding here. How do things stand in this regard? Now, no one ever accused Lucan of being uninformed about rhetoric, and it might therefore make sense to look at the rhetorical tradition itself for some kind of light on our problem. The difficulty with our opposition verisimilar/evidential is that these two rhetorical concepts at times seem to fade into each other. One modern commentator, Lausberg, actually says that *evidentia* contributes to verisimilitude,[14] and there is a passage in Cicero's *De oratore* which seems to link the pair explicitly. The text is about the figure *commoratio* (*De oratore* III 202). The techniques for producing *evidentia* and verisimilitude seem to be virtually the same: the text must specify the circumstances surrounding the event being recounted. The all-important *Ad Herennium*, alas, manages to keep things muddy, in one text at least. The example of *demonstratio* given in IV 68 is mostly a lively, visualizable narrative (significantly), but it begins by telling of the motives and reactions of the principal characters:

> As soon as Gracchus saw that the people were wavering, in their fear that he might, by the Senate's decree, be moved to change his mind, he ordered a convocation of the Assembly. In the meanwhile, this fellow, filled with wicked and criminal designs, bounds out of the temple of Jupiter.
>
> Quod simul atque Graccus prospexit fluctuare populum, verentem ne ipse auctoritate senatus commotus sententia desisteret, iubet advocari contionem. Iste interea scelere et malis cogitationibus redundans evolat e templo Iovis.

One must indeed admit that the old manuals are not very systematic and that the definitions they draw are not always very elegant. But this annoying overlap between our two terms should not fool us: the verisimilar and *evidentia* and its equivalents in fact belong to two wholly different strains in rhetoric. Versimilitude is one of the virtues of the *narratio*: in a judicial oration it is essential that the speaker so present the facts of the case that his hearers find his account plausible. But vivid, ocular description or narrative is generally assigned to the *peroratio,* and is supposed to produce affect: the orator may wish to inflame the audience's emotions by painting the crime in vivid colors. Alternately, *evidentia* lends clarity. Clarity is another virtue of *narratio,* along with verisimilitude, and Quintilian explicitly connects *evidentia* not with the latter, but with the former. In his conception, then, the two function quite differently. One could remark that at least one late text in poetics, that of Cascales,[15] follows Quintilian in assigning *evidentia* to clarity in narra-

---

[14] Lausberg, H., *Manual de retórica literaria*, trans. José Pérez Riesco (Madrid, Gredos, 1975), vol. I p. 282.

[15] Cascales, Francisco, *Tablas Poéticas*, edición y notas de Benito Brancaforte (Madrid, Espasa Calpe, 1975), p. 149.

tive, and making verisimilitude fall under a different heading. Finally, the example of *demonstratio* in the *Ad Herennium*, which is plainly narrative and progressive, is in fact indistinguishable from the livelier parts of the *narrationes* of existing speeches. Cicero's account of the actual attack of Clodius on Milo and of the ensuing struggle is obviously of the same kind of exposition as the one in the anonymous handbook. Its author, who also makes verisimilitude one of the virtues of *narratio,* discusses *demonstratio* many pages later under a totally different heading, and makes no show whatever at linking the two. Lucan, therefore, as a poet deeply immersed in the traditions of rhetoric, has the full sanction of that art, when he narrates some events advancing reasons and causes, and other quite different ones accumulating visual details.

This segregation of modes is no small matter; the wealth of explanation in the *Pharsalia* is, after all, an effective violation of the conventions of epic poetry, loaded heavily, so it would seem, on the side of the ocular and visual. And yet, it is the Lucanesque mix that counts: its influence on medieval and Renaissance narrative poetry is incalculable. For our purposes what is significant about the verisimilar strain in the *Pharsalia* is not only the parallel to the *Alexandre* itself, but its very strong echoes in the Latin poetry of a generation or two earlier. This latter fact is hardly irrelevant to the study of the *Libro.* The importance for us of Lucan's influence on the poetic texts of the middle and late twelfth century is twofold. In the first place, these texts are the perfect index to what is supposed to be the immediate literary background of the *Alexandre.* It is a commonplace by now that the culture of the author of the *Alexandre* and of other *cuaderna vía* poets was that of the humanists and grammarians of that time and before. We have heard frequently enough of the appointment of two *auctoristae* to the faculty of the University of Palencia, and are reminded often of the influence these men may have had on the formation of vernacular literature in Castile in the early thirteenth century.[16] But if we wish to know

---

[16] For the literary culture of the *Alexandre*-poet and others like him, see, for example, Rico, F., "La clerecía del mester", *Hispanic Review* 53 (1985), pp. 1-23, *passim.* For humanism in Castile, see Rico, F., *Alfonso X y la "General estoria," tres lecciones* (Barcelona, Ediciones Ariel, 1972), pp. 174-178, Díaz y Díaz, M. C., "Tres notas sobre cultura latina medieval en la región palentina," *Actas del I Congreso de Historia de Palencia,* tomo IV, *Edad media latina y humanismo renacentista en Palencia, lengua y literatura, historia de América* (Palencia, Diputación Provincial de Palencia, 1985), pp. 9-28, the Dutton article mentioned in note 7 of the Foreword of

what that culture actually was like, what better witness than the Latin poetry actually produced by men trained in just such schools, or by teachers like the ones at Palencia? If Romance poetry is supposed to show some influence of the schools, how much more will the Latin. We are hardly in the dark about the style and character of this latter material: we possess at least two splendid classicizing Latin epics of the period, works which tell us a great deal about the poetic practice of that period. They are the *Bellum troianum* of Joseph of Exeter, and the *Alexandreis* of Gautier of Châtillon.[17] But as it happens, both works are exceedingly Lucanesque, never more so than when they exploit verisimilitude. At the very least, one might judge that the Lucanesque mode was not out of fashion in our poet's day. My second point backs up the first: Gautier's work is actually the principal source of the *Alexandre*. This is hardly a negligible detail. We can scarcely be in doubt about the kind of Latinity that was familiar to the *Alexandre*-poet as long as we ourselves can study an ambitious Latin poem of more than five thousand verses which we know was the basis of his own. In general terms, what the Lucanesque character of these two works, Gautier's and Joseph's, tells us is that the strong bias in favor of Silver Latin which we seem to find in the *Libro* was not in any way peculiar to it: it was common and shared. The two works, after all, could be considered readings of ancient poetry. As archaizing texts they tell us what their authors thought was typical or important in the formal aspect of their models. Practically this means that the two poets have made a selection of certain poetic narrative patterns and styles over others. It is on this basis clear that none of the features of the *Alexandre* which seem to ally it to later Latin are special initiatives of its author. The tradition, the body of conventions, is already in place. The testimony of our two Latin poems is especially eloquent, because in some ways they follow their ancient models so closely. The vernacular *Alexandre*, after all, poses a special sort of problem. For dozens of reasons, the state of the written Romance in the early

---

this study, Faulhaber, Charles, "Latin Poems from Palencia," *Romance Philology* 43 (1989), pp. 59-69, and Pérez Rodríguez, Estrella, "Un tratado de gramática dedicado a Tello Téllez de Meneses," *Actas del I Congreso de Historia de Palencia*, tomo IV, *Edad media latina y humanismo renacentista en Palencia, lengua y literatura, historia de América* (Palencia, Diputación Provincial de Palencia, 1985), pp. 71-78.

[17] For Gautier, see note 12 in Chapter I; for Joseph, Joseph Iscanus, *Werke und Briefe*, herausgegeben von Karl Langosch (Leiden und Köln, E. J. Brill, 1970).

thirteenth century, the meter of the *Libro*, the plain fact that its implied audience is Latinless and unlearned, our poem has a personality and a look that is very un-ancient and un-Latin. How could it be otherwise? One might be tempted to attribute its obvious likenesses to certain things in ancient poetry simply to chance: we might indeed be dealing with totally different kinds of discourse. But if the Lucanesque features we have been speaking of are also present in classicizing and archaizing texts of a sort known to our poet, and if, furthermore, his culture is identical to that of their authors, then we can safely incorporate him into the same tradition.

7) OTHER SOURCES?

We conclude here our review of the ancient poetry which directly or indirectly might have had some influence on the structure and fabric of the *Alexandre*. There remains only one important question to ask, whether or not we have left anything out. Is there indeed some text or group of them which might also form part of the background of our poem, one more source, or several, which could partly explain the very special profile of the *Libro*? The possibilities we will consider fall under two headings. The first of these is historiography itself. As I have observed many times, ancient historical texts tend to be full of oratorical devices, and in fact often shape their narratives in ways rather akin to those of the *Libro*. Professor Michael does include Quintus Curtius in the list of sources for the *Alexandre*, though in one case at least the information from this historian may have cone from a gloss on Gautier's poem.[18] In any event, Curtius is the principal source for the *Alexandreis*: indeed, certain stretches of the Latin poem are little more than paraphrases of the older work. On this basis there is no doubt that many of the formal characteristics of Curtius' text survive in the *Libro*, since it in turn follows Gautier. And beyond this it is hardly a secret that ancient historiography generally was read and studied in

---

[18] Michael, Ian, *The Treatment of Classical Material in the 'Libro de Alexandre'*, (Manchester, Manchester University Press, 1970), pp. 289-290. Colker in his edition of the *Alexandreis* transcribes three glosses on his text, two of which have material pertinent to stanza 1970 of the *Libro*; both are glosses to *Alexandreis* IX 4, the Geneva set on p. 338, the Vienna on p. 468. The source for both is obviously Quintus Curtius VIII vi-viii.

the Middle Ages. Sallust is very well known, and so also is Justin's epitome of the histories of Pompeius Trogus.[19] Josephus' *Antiquities* is actually one of the sources of the *Libro*. Why could the *Alexandre*-poet not have absorbed narrative technique from texts like these? One could argue that in medieval times the line between prose and poetry was blurry, and perhaps more pertinently, that some of the *Libro*'s sources are actually prose history – eminently the *Historia* and Josephus' *Antiquities*. In one sense there is no need whatever to exclude historical works from our list of ancient models. The influences on the *Libro* we are speaking of are in any case diffuse, and there is no reason to believe that our poet forgot what Justin may have taught him about storytelling, simply because his Alexander history happened to be in verse. But immediately and in an obvious sense, it is poetry that holds center stage. The mixed media character, the *olla podrida* of description, dialogue, commentary, explanation, summary alongside good evidential narrative, the variety which marks the layout of the *Libro,* is primarily an inheritance from poets, not prose-writers. One could say minimally that among the school-authors there indeed were poets who displayed this mixed style; this chapter to date has been about nothing else. Vastly more significant is the fact that the Lucanesque *Alexandreis* of Gautier de Châtillon is the most extensive source in our poem. As I observed above, much of the variety of exposition in the *Libro* is taken over wholesale from the Latin poem, and when the younger author performs in the mixed style on his own, it is often done to bring a plainer source up to the level of his Gautier passages. The latter sets the standard. The eminent case of this transformation is his set of translations or paraphrases of a historical work (historical for the poet, if not for us), the *Historia de preliis*. We will recall that the *Alexandre*-poet takes great liberties with the relatively unadorned text of the *Historia,* giving it a life and variety which the original does not possess. We could put the question of poetic influence differently. In matters of form and style he generally respects his Latin poetic sources, but treats all the others, historical ones included, with great independence. There are, of course, two extensive Latin poems which are the basis for long stretches of the

---

[19] Manitius, Max, *Handschriften antiker Autoren in mittelalterlichen Biliotekskatalogen* (Leipzig, Otto Harrassowitz, 1935), pp. 76-78 for Justin, and pp. 42-47 for Sallust.

*Alexandre,* the *Ilias latina* and the *Alexandreis.* The *Libro*'s renditions of these texts are at times very free, but its formal and stylistic approach is more or less the same as that of the source. This is especially striking in the *Ilias,* with its lengthy pieces of rapid narrative; the vernacular poem follows suit. But this cautious respect vanishes when the poet is dealing with a prose source. As we have seen more than once, the *Historia de preliis* is for him little more than an excuse to display all his devices and colors: the plain exposition of the source gives way to drama and variety in the final text. One might conclude from this odd set of circumstances that it is narrative poetry and not prose history that is critical here; the norms of composition for the *Libro de Alexandre* are set by poetry.

But what of other influences on our great text? Could there be poets other than Ovid and Lucan who had a hand in giving the work its special profile? This is the second possibility we must entertain. At this point we can hardly afford to be dogmatic. Influences are slippery items, or, to abandon the metaphor, leakage is always possible. Out of hand there are two factors we must take into account. The first is that the twelfth and early thirteenth century canon of *auctores* is small: the list of possible models is not endless. The second follows from the first: other examples of ancient Latin narrative verse which we might be tempted to take into account were almost certainly not accessible to the *Alexandre*-poet. It is most unlikely that any grammarian or poet of the early thirteenth century ever read Valerius Flaccus. The same might be said of Silius Italicus, although one critic, Christensen, claims to find echoes of him in the *Alexandreis.*[20] The *Punica* is, however, interesting for us on other grounds. By the criteria we have laid down Silius is by far the most Lucanesque of the Latin poets after Lucan. It is striking that the very qualities which seem most distinctive in the *Pharsalia* should reappear in a poem whose subject is not mythological, but plainly historical. That these same qualities should also appear in the *Alexandreis,* in Petrarch's *Africa,* in the *Araucana,* in Drayton's *Barons' Wars,* all historical poems, is surely significant. It seems possible that even in antiquity some must have thought that Lucan had invented a new subgenre of epic, unique in its subject-matter and in

---

[20] Manitius (*op. cit.*), p. 125, has only six entries for Valerius Flaccus, and only seven for Silius Italicus. This contrasts with the pages of entries he has for a Lucan or a Juvenal.

his treatment of it. What is generally judged to be Petronius' displeasure with the *Pharsalia* might confirm this view.[21]

That leaves us with Statius,[22] and in a somewhat different category, Claudian. The latter is capitally important for us because he is acknowledged by no one less than Gautier as a model for his own large poem. There is, therefore, no question that Claudian forms part of the background of the *Alexandre*, based in large part on the older Alexander-poem, as we know. I must, however, postpone my discussion of Claudian; when the time comes to speak in detail about the *Alexandreis,* we will deal with him as best we can. For its part, Statius' *Thebaid,* one of the most studied and honored literary texts in history, and a respected *auctor* over many centuries, is surely a work this present essay must take into account. Its formal profile is distinctive. I believe that a study of its influence on medieval and Renaissance poetry, even within the limits of formal and rhetorical analysis, would yield far-reaching results. This is, of course, my conviction with respect to the *Pharsalia*, as I have made clear. An account of the echoes of both in narrative poetry from the twelfth century on would, I am convinced, oblige us to rewrite many pages of literary history. But in the case of Statius the current of influence flows around the *Libro de Alexandre*, not through it. It is of course impossible to describe the style of the *Thebaid* in a few lines. It shares with the *Pharsalia* many qualities, some of which we

---

[21] Petronius, *Satyricon*, ch. 118. The *Pharsalia*, not actually named, is plainly the butt of the criticisms here. One complaint is that Lucan's poem does not make the gods principal actors. Ugo Piacentini, in his study cited, makes their absence from the poem one of his major themes. Reduced to its simplest terms, his argument is this: the wealth of explanation in the *Pharsalia*, the allusion to human motives and to natural causes, is actually meant to replace the intervention of the gods. The latter have been abandoned for philosophical reasons and as a response to the mood of the times, and the gap left by this suppression is filled by this copious reference to worldly causes. Piacentini does take full note of the kinship between the poem and historical texts and, incidentally, develops another theme, Lucan's possible assimilation of his work to didactic poetry, in the style of Manilius. I am not a classicist, but feel impelled to make the following comments. The affinity between the *Pharsalia* and the historiography of his own time and earlier is impressive. Now, the discourse of the historian is already in place, and Lucan, author of a semi-historical poem, does not have to invent this kind of text. On this basis it seems to me that to attribute the Lucanian revolution to extra-literary and extra-rhetorical causes, as Piacentini does, is risky and unnecessary.

[22] Statius, with an English translation by J. H. Mozley, in two volumes (Cambridge, MA, Harvard University Press, and London, William Heinemann, Ltd. 1928). The first four books of the *Thebaid* are in volume I, the rest in volume II.

have already mentioned. Both texts are full of narrator's commentary of all kinds: the great number of apostrophes in either work is actually topical. Both poets show their flair for *sententia* and epigram. Both favor long static descriptive passages full of brilliant *evidentia* which is not progressive or narrative, and both allow themselves lengthy digressions. Both have long stretches of direct discourse. But the narrative proper in the *Pharsalia* and the *Thebaid* go separate ways. Lucan, like Ovid, along with orators and historians, saves his narrative *evidentia*, as I call it, for special occasions: his great scenes are of course remarkable, but they are not omnipresent. But by contrast, almost all the passages of progressive narrative in Statius are evidential. They are so with a vengeance. Some are dazzling: the lines on the treacherous assault on Tydeus and his single-handed victory over his assailants would do credit to Hollywood. The richness of detail is generally remarkable. Narrative in the *Thebaid* is slow. It takes a long time for things to happen. It is not only the long speeches, the digressions, the impassioned apostrophes that impede the flow; at times the storytelling itself unfolds at a very slow pace. The very narrative invention stretches things out. The poet cannot dispatch Capaneus in the final battle with Thebes without convening a council of gods. This is typical: great events in the poem are prepared twenty times over. For a fact, it is not the flow of the poem that is primarily interesting: it is the realization, moment by moment, line by line, scene by scene. Under this aspect the work is simply admirable.

I believe that a study of learned poetry since antiquity would bring to light many texts – isolated passages and indeed whole works – which echoed the style and manner of the *Thebaid*. But alas, as far as I can discover, few of its single qualities and even less of its mix of them show much likeness to those of the *Libro de Alexandre*. If one is to explore the grammarian's world of the early thirteenth century in search of the background of our poem, the *Thebaid* is indeed a logical place to look. The *auctoristae* of the day of course knew the work, and more than one poet imitated it. But the survey of this bit of ground yields little of interest to the student of the *Alexandre*: the explorer returns with little to show. What might be, or perhaps should be, isn't.

I conclude here my discussion of the ancient models, more or less possible, of the *Libro de Alexandre*. But I add as a sort of appendix a few lines on three poems more, all of them certainly in the twelfth-century canon, and which in fairness must also be considered as possible objects of imitation by our vernacular text. We must include them here, because they are narrative, and because they are written in hexameters: if the *Alexandre*-poet knew any of them, as he may have, there is no reason in principle why they may not have had an influence on his narrative style. They are: the *Libri evangelorum IIII* of Juvencus, the *De actibus apostolorum* of Arator, and Sedulus' *Paschali carmen*.[23] One medieval text actually speaks of Sedulus' poem as a *carmen heroicum*, a good twelfth-century equivalent of "epic,"[24] hence a special urgency in this case. The three are Christian poems, as their titles indicate, and this, to my mind, separates them by a wide gap from the other texts we have been considering: the problems they pose as possible models are necessarily quite different from the ones set by Lucan or Statius. The description in the medieval text I have mentioned notwithstanding, we may immediately discount Sedulus' long poem from our argument. Twelfth-century grammarians may have thought it heroic, but for our purposes it disqualifies itself as an example for the *Alexandre*-poet, because it does not contain sustained narratives of any length; it is a series of miracle-stories, taken from both Testaments, each in turn, all culminating in the Resurrection. Other difficulties aside, the *Carmen* simply does not give us long enough stretches of narrative to let us make comparison of any sort with the *Libro*. Juvencus' work, for its part, is a paraphrase in verse of the Gospel-story, and is based largely on Matthew. It sticks fairly close to its text. Its vocabulary and diction are classical, but its narrative manner is mainly that of its source, and we must observe that its very special rhythm and pace have little to do with anything in the composition or layout of the *Alexandre*. I would note particularly that with a few exceptions Juvencus does not expand on his Biblical material. It has been observed that he does offer some lively nature-descriptions, but these aside, there are few instances in which he

---

[23] *C. Vetti Aquilini Iuvenci Libri evangelorum IIII*, recognovit Carolus Marold (Leipzig, Teubner, 1886); the *Paschale carmen* is in *Sedulii opera omnia*, ed. J. Huemer, *Corpus scriptorum ecclesiastorum latinorum*, vol. X (Vindobonae, apud C. Geroldi filium bibliopolae academiae, 1885); *Aratoris subdiaconi De actibus Apostolorum*, ed. Arthur Patch McKinley, *C.S.E.L* (see above), vol. LXXII (Vindobonae, Hoelder-Pichler-Tempsky, 1951).

[24] Huygens, *op. cit.*, p. 29; this is in a passage in the text Huygens calls *Accessus ad auctores*.

turns the plain text of the Gospel into something else, into fully realized scenes; Juvencus simply does not attempt to dramatize his story. We recall that the *Alexandre*-poet at times turns the unadorned information of the *Historia de preliis* into lively and varied narrative sequences. The impulse to do the same with the Gospel-text is wholly alien to our early Christian poet; Juvencus is not the Caravaggio of poetry. Generally speaking, it is hard to imagine that he or his poem had anything to contribute to the formal side of the *Libro de Alexandre*.

That leaves Arator's elegant paraphrase of the Book of Acts. One would have to say that from our point of view the *De actibus* was uninteresting. On one hand, it is indeed very Pharsalian. Its manner of exposition is essentially Lucan's: the narrator's comments are extensive, static set-pieces interrupt the flow of the story, and the dramatic scenes, the ones marked by *evidentia,* are held in reserve for special effect. But that is just the difficulty: since Arator's narrative style is derivative, it is impossible to trace anything in the *Alexandre* to this source in particular. Could our latter-day poet have learned the art of narrative from Arator? It is strictly speaking possible, if inverisimilar: nothing in my argument asserts that the Lucan manner came to the *Libro* directly, though in some sense it may have. But even if the *De actibus* weighed heavily on the art of the *Alexandre*-poet, we are still speaking of a Lucanian influence, not an Aratorian. And if, on the other hand, we are speaking of mediated influence on the *Libro,* the most interesting medium, and the most pertinent, would be the Lucanesque poetry of its own time: this was the point I wished to make moments ago. It makes little sense to appeal to a text from late antiquity on a subject remote from that of our principal text to explain the presence there of certain formal patterns, least of all when these same formulae stare us in the face in the poetry of the twelfth century. Finally, with respect to all three of these Latin Christian poems we can make the following observation. Sacred History is a unique subject-matter. Even the medieval commentator who calls Sedulus' work heroic is arguing by analogy: if epic celebrates the *res gestae* of great men, how much more is the *Paschali carmen* epic, which speaks of the *res gestae* of God Himself. The fact is that Salvation History implies a special sort of sublime, and demands a very particular kind of eloquence, one which has nothing at all to do with that which must surround an Aeneas or an Alexander. The theme of Sedulus' poem, or of Juvencus' is totally unlike that of the *Alexandre*, and therefore, these Christian texts are not likely to have been the critical influence on it, the less so when strictly human heroic poems were everywhere available as models.

## CHAPTER III

## JOSEPH OF EXETER AND GAUTIER OF CHÂTILLON

1) THE CONTEMPORARY WITNESS

In our last chapter we surveyed some of the ancient narrative poems that could have had a part in the shaping of the *Libro de Alexandre*; our attention was focused especially on those elements of the old texts which might have influenced the *Libro* in its rhetorical design or its narrative structure. In an obvious sense, the point in this exercise was to explore the literary background of the medieval poem. But more broadly, our goal was twofold, first, to call up the *Libro* as a witness to a certain tradition, and second, to make it clear that when poets of the twelfth and early thirteenth centuries took ancient texts as models, they were very selective about what they imitated, texts and parts and aspects of them. These two goals are related. As I hoped to show, when these men of letters chose one element of style and rejected another, they were in effect consecrating a very special kind of literary taste, one which was, as we saw, rather more baroque than classical. I would stress that, in using the *Libro de Alexandre* in this general argument about traditions, we are taking only one step along a lengthy journey. The Spanish Alexander-poem is only one witness to the tradition I speak of, only one piece of evidence that the literary bias I alluded to was a reality. But large or small, that testimony is eloquent. The language of the work, a vernacular, is in a sense far removed from the Latinity of any age. Its syntax, as we would expect, is a great deal less adventuresome than that of its principal Latin source, and it is written in a verse-form that has nothing whatever to do with ancient Roman poetry. If the rhetorical patterns the *Libro* inherits from the old poets survive in such a hostile medium, the presence of these turns tells us that in the poet's day the tradition we have spoken of is very much alive.

My argument to date in this study has been simple. Certain post-Virgilian poets belong to the canon of *auctores* studied very generally in the twelfth and early thirteenth centuries; the *Alexandre*-poet, certainly instructed in Latin, must have known these authors. If, then, he lays out his narrative in a way which recalls theirs, the parallelism is most probably not an accident. But for this argument to hold, certain other factors have to be considered. What, generally speaking, were other poets and humanists of his day and shortly before up to? What was their literary bias? What in particular did they see in their *auctores*? More narrowly, what practices did they admire in their models, and which if any did they despise? Unless we can show that the rhetorical patterns which seem to characterize the *Alexandre* were also taken seriously by such contemporaries, the parallelisms we may perceive between our poem and the *Pharsalia* or the *Metamorphoses* may be a fluke: our eminent poet may simply have reinvented the wheel. But as we will see, the case for a mixed media Ovidian-Lucanesque narrative mode in the years around 1200 is very strong.

We will begin by rejecting one option which on the face of it might seem promising. For the moment, at any rate, we will not be examining commentaries, glosses and other secondary material which accompanied the texts of ancient authors as read in the Middle Ages. In the short run this decision might seem positively suicidal, closing off one excellent way of judging how a reader of the twelfth century might have approached a poem from the first. In the case that this secondary matter was actually medieval, we would also be cutting off access to texts which told us what the men of those years actually thought about their *auctores*. We must be very clear about the kind of text these were. One should explain, for example, that many of the commentaries that were in fact studied in the Middle Ages were modest in scope, sober and explanatory, well within the range of ancient "grammar." Thus, one must not labor under the impression that *auctoristae* were single-minded in allegorizing, or in finding in their texts a meaning other than the obvious. As we know, this mode was hardly unfashionable, witness texts like Bernardus Silvestris' on the *Aeneid*. But the less ambitious kind of commentary, if we can call it that, in the style of Donatus' on Terence, or Servius' on Virgil, held its own. Texts of this order were studied in those years, and others like them were produced, which explicated points of lexicon, grammar (in our sense) and syntax, which pointed out rhetorical procedures used by the poet, which clarified obscurities the student might find, and which supplied information about history, mythology or natural philosophy as such might be pertinent. The latter-day examples of such works are many, Arnulf of Orléans' on the *Pharsalia*, and Geoffrey of Vitry's on Claudian's *De raptu Proserpinae*, and others.

The relatively narrow scope of much commentary and literary study in the Middle Ages is often forgotten. There are, as I believe, two reasons for this. In the first place, much emphasis in recent years has been placed on the sort of approach to ancient poetry which I have alluded to, which broadly could be called allegorical. Bernardus reads the first six books of the *Aeneid* as the story of the moral growth and development of an individual over time, and Arnulf of Orléans (the same Arnulf who glosses Lucan) demythologizes the whole of the *Metamorphoses*, reducing each of its stories of gods and demigods to perfectly historical accounts of the doings of ordinary mortals. Essays of this kind, whether Platonic or euhemeristic, seem to have held center stage for modern students, and up to a point, this attention has been fruitful. The second reason why the more sober style of commentary has been overlooked has to do with the appearance within the decade of two very provocative books on medieval literature, A. J. Minnis' *The Medieval Idea of Authorship*, and Judson Allen's *The Ethical Poetic of the Later Middle Ages*.[1] Under pressure, as it seems, of the contemporary interest in literary theory, the two authors, each in his own way, have exploited commentaries, glosses and other secondary matter to try to articulate or reconstuct a general theory of the medieval text. The recognition given these two works is certainly deserved: the enterprise is of course a serious one. But theory is not what ancient and medieval commentaries are about. It is important that we appreciate the purely practical scope of some of these texts: as I have

---

[1] Minnis, A. J., *Mediaeval Theory of Authorship: Scholastic literary attitudes in the later Middle Ages* (London, Scolar Press, 1984) and Allen, Judson, *The Ethical Poetic of the Later Middle Ages* (Toronto, Buffalo, University of Toronto Press, 1982).

insisted, such works aim simply at being useful guides to the student or other reader with a Virgil or Lucan in his hand. A great part of the grammarian's activity lay within the comparatively humble limits I have outlined.

Now, given the practical and local range of all this material, one might guess that it could be a treasure-house of information and comment about the issues that interest us: as we might think, the glosses that touched on rhetorical subjects should prove especially pertinent. But taken as a whole, this large literature disappoints us. It may in great part be the narrowness of our own project that causes the difficulty. The test that I have used to show the presence of certain strains in narrative poetry slips through the cracks of most commentaries. The sort of gloss that concentrates on the figures of rhetoric does not frequently speak of the sort of pattern we have considered as we examined Lucan, Cicero and the *Libro de Alexandre*. This is all a question of fact. In the two indices to Servius that I have in my library I cannot find a single entry for the word *evidentia* or for any of its equivalents, though other rhetorical terms appear there in profusion.[2] Medieval texts of the order of Arnulf's glosses on Lucan are not much more forthcoming. Among the ancients Macrobius is a sort of exception. The *Saturnalia*, not a formal commentary by any means, is in great part a discussion of the *Aeneid* from various points of view; this lengthy work was known and much copied in the Middle Ages. Here indeed we can find some eloquent pages about the poet's expository technique.[3] Occasionally also, certain of the *accessus*, so called, to the poets give in brief a kind of list or repertory of the most prominent rhetorical features of their respective texts. But over all, the landscape is

---

[2] Mountford, J. P. and Schultz, J. T., *Index rerum et nominum in scholiis Servii et Aeli Donati tractatorum* (Ithaca, Cornell University Press, 1930), and Moore, John Leverett, *Servius on the Tropes and Figures of Virgil* (Baltimore, Press of Isaac Friedenwald Co., 1891), pp. 65-66, which contains the index.

[3] In Book IV Macrobius discusses some verses of the *Aeneid* in ways which reveal interests close to ours in this study [*Opera*, ed. J. Willis (Leipzig, Teubner, 1963)]. I would mention also the material discussed in Berthe Marti's article, "Literary Criticism in the Mediaeval Commentaries on Lucan," *Transactions of the American Philological Association* 72 (1941), pp. 245-254. She speaks in particular about the commentary on the *Pharsalia* by Anselm of Laon, which, exceptionally among the works she studies, puts stress on the verisimilitude of certain passages in Lucan's poem. The long section near the beginning on the causes of the Civil War is a special case in point: the background here supplied makes the episodes narrated later all the more believable (p. 252).

bleak. In my reading, at least, Macrobius and certain other scraps are exceptional; there are not many other texts to which we can turn to answer the questions that interest us.

But where one door closes, another opens. There is one area, one body of texts in which twelfth-century perspectives on ancient poetry can be discovered in abundance. I mean the classicizing verse in Latin produced in the years shortly before the composition of the *Alexandre*. In principle one would expect an artful poet in this mode to put on display much of his knowledge of ancient letters and of his perceptions of what these old texts were like. Style, as one would suppose, would be a paramount concern for them: a full range of formal and rhetorical devices reminiscent of one or another *auctor* would be before us constantly as we read these texts. If we were examining narrative poetry, we could surely tell in a moment what sorts of narrative layout in the old poets interested their authors and which not. In a word, if we are interested to know how grammarians and poets shortly before 1200 read and received Ovid and Lucan, or more generally, which poetic *auctores* loomed largest for them, we might expect to find our answers in just this body of medieval verse. And indeed, these texts do not disappoint us. They are very nearly the perfect witness to the tradition, the literary sensibility or broad common style I have been speaking of. We shall be studying two extraordinary poems of the late twelfth century, the *Trojan War* of Joseph of Exeter, and the *Alexandreis* of Gautier of Châtillon; the latter is, of course, the principal Latin source of the *Libro de Alexandre*. The Lucanesque character of this pair of works is actually topical, repeated in modern commentaries and histories of literature,[4] and in this sense our labor is half done: this is precisely the strain we are looking for. In any case, we have here our main argument in little. These two poems, one of which had a direct influence on our *Libro*, are in many ways more like their ancient model than is the *Alexandre*; this is as one would expect. Therefore, if we can find distinctively Lucanesque traits in the vernacular poem, this cannot be an accident: we would certainly be acquainted with the soil from which it sprang, and would thus have a fair idea of how these characteristics came to it.

---

[4] Raby, F. J., *Secular Latin Poetry* (Oxford, Clarendon, 1934, 2 vols.), vol. 2, pp. 134, 137, on Joseph, and Walter of Châtillon, *The Alexandreis*, translated with introduction and notes by R. Telfryn Pritchard (Toronto, Pontifical Institute of Mediaeval Studies, 1986), p. 15, in Pritchard's introduction.

In examining our two Latin epics and in trying to associate each with its ancient models, we will be bringing into play the same tests, the same set of criteria, we have applied to the *Alexandre* itself and to Lucan, Ovid and others. We will consider their use or non-use of *evidentia* in narrative, the various non-progressive elements which the poet may introduce, descriptions, apostrophes, commentaries, or indeed, long digressions. More generally, we will take very seriously the degree to which the narrator's voice is or is not heard in the text, how much he explains and recounts, and how much he simply displays. This test, or agenda, may itself pose a certain difficulty. One might object that the grid we are holding up to these medieval texts is more modern than ancient, that showing and telling, commentary, summary and the rest are categories that smack more of Genette or Wayne Booth than of Quintilian. I would answer in the first place that this set of terms might keep the peace with both, that it might be possible to serve at once God and Mammon. In the second place, I would argue that the characteristics which to my mind set apart Ovid and Lucan and make their influence traceable are few in number. In other words, the grid that we are holding up to all the texts we are studying is a very coarse one. The very simplicity of the project keeps what it has of modernity from being a threat. I might almost want to claim that our analysis throughout these pages might have been intelligible to grammarians of other days; I believe that the texts I have cited of Macrobius and of certain *accessus* are on my side in this matter. Finally, and most important, I would argue that in a study on imitation, which this obviously is, one must be clear about what exactly is being imitated. My set of criteria is nothing other than a list of just such critical traits.

2) Joseph of Exeter

We will begin by examining Joseph of Exeter's great opus. The *Frigii Daretis Yliados* is an ambitious Latin epic poem in six books; it is perhaps the best realized medieval Troy narrative before Boccaccio. The work is, among other things, a very successful classical mock-up; humanists in the sixteenth century took it to be ancient.[5]

---

[5] Joseph of Exeter, *The Iliad of Dares Phrygius*, translated with an introduction and notes by Gildas Roberts (Capetown, A. A. Balkema, 1970), p. xii: here in his in-

As I have suggested, its Lucanesque character is topical, mentioned in the critical literature, and as we shall see, the traits that in my view are distinctive to the *Pharsalia* are everywhere visible in Joseph's poem. But the *Yliados* is a curious production, a mixed performance. From a modern perspective it is not on an historical subject; this sets it apart from Lucan's poem, from Silius Italicus' *Punica*, and indeed, from Gautier's *Alexandreis*. To the objection that to Joseph and his audience the events of the Trojan War recounted in Dares and Dictys were entirely real, one could answer globally that the English poet's plot has much more in common with that of the *Aeneid* or the *Thebaid* than it does with that of Sallust's *Jugurthine War*, and that we could presume that twelfth-century humanists could tell the difference. But beyond this, the *Yliados* falls easily within a pattern grammarians and *auctoristae* of the day speak of often. In the first place, these scholars tended generally to associate poetry with fiction, and in the special case of a poetic work that dealt with historical matters, they had no difficulty in conceiving of a text which was partly fictional and partly truthful. Medieval commentators on ancient epic poems make exactly this judgment about their texts. An *accessus* on Lucan defines epic (*metrum heroicum*) as follows: "Metrum istud [the *Pharsalia*] est heroycum, quia constat ex humanis divinisque personis continens vera cum fictis" (Huygens, p. 44). Judson Allen mentions several medieval *Thebaid* commentaries which have the same definition (pp. 76 and 77, for example). The point is, of course, the fact that the gods play an important role in the action of Statius' work; this sector of the text must surely be read as fiction. Joseph does indeed grant an important part to the pagan gods in his poem, and in this sense and in many others, the theme of the *Yliados* is quite unlike that of the *Pharsalia*.

"Poetic" is a word with many meanings. If we take the word in the twelfth century sense of "fictional," the *Yliados* is certainly poetic, at least in the parts that deal with the gods. But if we wished to use the word in a diffuse modern way, Joseph's poem might also be called poetic on other grounds. The diction is remarkable. Even when the cluster of themes of the moment is prosaic and without

---

troduction Roberts points out that the early printings of the work attributed it to Cornelius Nepos, and that the first to restore it to Joseph was the edition of Samuel Dresemius in Frankfurt, in 1620.

color, the choice of words, the artful hyperbaton, the learned periphrasis, the striving for epigram and brevity generally all give Joseph's verse a tautness and elegance which are in every way notable. His diction has, indeed, an ancient look, and the combination of qualities I have spoken of is one of the elements that marks the poem as an imitation of Lucan. Also Lucanesque and "poetic" – or more simply, designed to arouse affect – are the numerous apostrophes that decorate his text. And once again, there are moments in the narrative when the information conveyed is without distinction, but where the text is loaded with figures, also designed generally to produce affect. The following exmple is typical. In Book IV the Greeks are approaching Troy (in the second of their two assaults on the city):

> Tenedos, in particular, felt the overwhelming anger of the soldiery. It lamented not the torches alone, or the plundering of precious metal, but sighed that it had been annihilated, had been utterly consumed by the frenzy of Greek weapons. The boys had given their beardless throats to the sword, the old men their throats a-tremble, and the young men throats flowing with hair.
> Prima tulit Tenedos graviores militis iras,
> Non solas dequesta faces non rapta metalli
> Pondera, sed prorsus gladii consumpta furore
> Exspirasse gemit. Iugulum puer ensibus affert
> Inberbem tremulumque senex et tiro comantem.
> (IV 343-347, Roberts translation, p. 47; see note 5)

Tenedos is in the first place personified, and a moment later, the slaughter of the males is reduced to particulars, that of the young, mature and aged, each characterized physically; the sword is synecdochic. A few lines earlier we have another personification: "As the Greeks travelled on through the midst of the sea, *and* the drowsy heavings of the waves did not begrudge them the peace and security in which to converse" (IV 324-325; Roberts, p. 47. I have added the *and* to bring the English syntax closer to the Latin, which runs, "Dum mediis spaciantur aquis securaque fandi / Ocia sopitus pelagi non invidet estus".

Various features of Joseph's great work are plainly of non-Lucanian origin. We have already mentioned the large part in the action played by the gods. They and their kin were exiled from the *Pharsalia*, as we know, but they are everywhere visible in the *Yliados*.

Joseph's Allecto, who appears at the beginning of Book II, recalls Virgil's in the *Aeneid*, but also has a strong likeness to the latter poet's Juno, venting her strong feelings that events on earth are an injury to her dignity and standing. Virgilian also is Joseph's personified Rumor, *Fama*, who makes several important appearances in the course of the medieval poem. The Euryalus and Nisus of the ninth book of the *Aeneid* have their avatars in the English *Yliados*: the last moments of Castor and Pollux are very like those of the Virgilian pair. Finally, the battle-scenes are mainly of the Homeric type, series of hand-to-hand combats: the final battle before Troy in Joseph's account is a long and impressive case in point. They have little in common with some of Lucan's, played as growing out of the strategy of the opposing generals.

Joseph's *Yliados* assuredly looks to more than one model: it is in no sense a pastiche of a single poem, or even of the work generally of a single poet. There is, as far as I can judge, little partisanship in the humanism of the twelfth century: to be on the side of Lucan, so to speak, does not set one against Virgil or Statius. Joseph surely does not take sides. The mixed character of the *Yliados* has a great deal to do, as I believe, with the strange profile of the twelfth century canon of authors, with its odd tilt in favor of post-Virgilian Latin. The cut was already made in Joseph's day, and he therefore had little need to express preferences for one *auctor* over another, or for one style over another. The Lucan-factor, if we may call it that, is critical, as we will see presently, but it is one among many. Locating its field is easy: there is indeed a range, an area, an aspect of our poem which is characteristically Lucanian, and we do not have to trace down echoes and reminiscences of the *Pharsalia* one at a time. This area is its patterns of discourse: virtually all the procedures, the species of presentation, of exposition used by Joseph in the *Trojan War* have what we might call a Lucanian lineage. Some are distinctively Lucanesque, while others are shared by other post-Virgilian poets. We are back on our old territory once again: in our medieval Troy-poem we have generous comments on the action, moral and explanatory: some are buried in clauses and phrases which generally advance the narrative, while others stand alone. Many of the latter are in the form of universal propositions, about fortune, about the follies of men, or on other subjects; not a few of these general judgments are in the form of exclamations. The flow of the story is interrupted by long, non-progressive descriptions.

The fine piece on Hesione's wedding feast in Book II fills up dozens of verses. The sixth book begins with a vivid and evidential account of the Trojan army demoralized after the death of Hector:

> The Trojans, in ragged formation, moved their sorrowing standards more sluggishly across the field. Their shields ran with tears, the plumes of their helmets were weighed down with grief, the slender gold of their armour was shattered by repeated sobs, their weapons were a burden to them, and there was no joy, no gladness in the entire army.
> 
> > Segnior explicitis merentia signa catervis
> > Troia movet. Rorant clipei, cristeque gravantur
> > Luctibus, angustum crebris singultibus aurum
> > Rumpitur, arma nocent. Toto nil agmine letum,
> > Dulce nichil. (VI 1-5; Roberts, p. 65)

The text continues with drooping banners, dispirited war-horses, and the trumpets playing mournful music. Armies seen in long shots are often presented in this fashion: details are accumulated, separate actions are mentioned, but the story as a whole does not advance. This formula is of course applied to other subjects as well. The sacrifices offered to the gods by the Trojans at the beginning of Book III are fashioned by Joseph into a splendid scene of just this sort. Many other examples could be cited.

The narrator in Joseph's poem, like the one in the *Pharsalia*, often makes us party to the inner thoughts and feelings of his characters. Sometimes these accounts are routine, even trivial, telling us of the intentions of one or another actor on the scene, or of the general mood of an individual or a group. Occasionally we have quite a bit more. Priam, confronted with the abduction of his sister Hesione, undertakes an inner *deliberatio*:

> Priam's mind, goaded by the hellish frenzies of grief and wakeful sorrow, pulled him now this way, now that. At one moment he was for demanding the return of Hesione under threat of arms, at another he dreaded the thought of war. At length he decided to place his hopes on entreaty, to try the Greeks with flattery.
> 
> > Ecce profundis
> > Curarum Furiis vigilique impulsa dolore
> > Mens Priamum in diversa trahit, nunc Marte reposcit
> > Hesionen, nunc bella timet. Sentencia tandem

> Certior inniti precibus, temptare Pelasgos
> Blandiciis. (II 31-35; Roberts, p.15)

Markedly Lucanesque also, a virtual trademark of the author of the *Pharsalia*, is his fondness for paradox, used to highlight or dramatize a character or an action. Joseph follows the example. Achilles has taken on the whole force of Teuthras single-handed, and we hear immediately of the great cost to his collective enemy: "It was utterly amazing: an army was fleeing, a lone man was putting it to flight" ("Res plena stupore / Turba fugit solusque fugat." IV 381-382; Roberts, p. 48). Nearly as strong is the presentation of Paris about to embark on his mission to take Helen: "The shepherd, Paris, was chosen as the leader of the expedition – once a stranger to the realm, now he was the king's heir" (Dux cepti legitur pastor Paris, advena quondam / Regni, nunc regis heres," III 155-156; Roberts, p. 32). The poet generally invites us to despise Paris, and we are here made to see the anomaly of his position, Paris as shepherd, Paris as former outcast, the king's heir and the leader nevertheless. More striking still is the line on Penthesilea, fighting heroically among the Trojans: "bellatrixque viris dat femina vires." The line comes off poorly in English: "This warrior-girl gave manliness to the men" (VI 568; Roberts, p. 77). This particular paradox has a savor of *comparatio*: men by agreement are stronger and more aggressive than women, yet this woman gives example and encouragement to men, and so must be courageous and strong indeed. One wholly undisguised *comparatio* occurs in the sixth book: "[Hecuba] gazed in wonder at the fires [of Troy], which the flames of Phaethon were unable to equal, and which Rome refused to Nero"; "ignes – / Quos Phetontee nequeant equare faville, Quosque neget tibi Roma, Nero – miratur" (VI 837-839; Roberts, p. 83).

We recall that one of Lucan's procedures most at odds with conventional notions about epic poetry is his allusion in the *Pharsalia* to details of military strategy or of the practical side of warfare. Joseph here follows him part way. Unlike the older poet, he does not give us long sequences in which the execution of battle plans is laid out for us in full detail. But he does not entirely forget the less glamorous aspects of warfare, and in a handful of cases it does seem possible that he is taking Lucan as his model. The sober account of Hercules' tactic in the first war before Troy has a Lucanesque ring:

> Hercules now proceeded with his strategy and divided his fighting-force into three well-balanced units. One group, under Peleus and Telamon, was to attack the actual city of Troy. Another group, under Nestor, was to guard the ships. The third group was to follow Hercules himself. (His watch he shared with his two comrades, one on either side of him.)
>> Dividit ergo acies equi libraminis instar
>> Alcides: pars in Frigios armata penates
>> Iam dictos sortita duces, pars cura relicte
>> Classis disponit cum Nestore parsque secuta
>> Amphitrioniaden sociis partitur utrisque
>> Excubias hinc inde suas. (I 349-354; Roberts, p. 10)

Lest it be thought that this example is trivial, or that a passage telling how a general disposes his lieutenants and their troops is a commonplace, I observe that not one such sequence appears in the whole of the *Aeneid*. Still more prosaic than this one is the detail in Book VI:

> Meanwhile Demophoon, Acamas, and Hippolytus hastened off to fetch the Mysian harvests. A lack of martial corn and audacious wine had blunted the rage of the Greeks, and hunger had fed on their strength.
>> Interea Mesas properat laturus aristas
>> Demophoon Zagamasque, et te, Thesida, volentem
>> Tercia cura vocat. Danaas hebetaverat iras
>> Belligere messis vinique audacis egestas
>> Et vires depasta fames. (VI 65-69; Roberts, p. 66)

The string of personification in the second sentence does lend savor to a basically colorless piece of information. A livelier detail, but equally practical, is Telamon's mining of the walls of Troy:

> Telamon crept stealthily up, hidden and protected by the tortoise formation. He undermined the stability of the wall with his picks, and then when it was tottering forward about to crash headlong, he withdrew. When the dust had settled he was the first to take possession of the city he had smashed open.
>> At testudineo Thelamon defensus amictu
>> Occultum furatur iter silicumque tenorem
>> Ere domat iamque in preceps pendente ruina
>> Cedit et effracta tandem prior urbe potitur.
>>
>>            (I 415-418; Roberts, p. 12)

A description of the walls of Troy rebuilt after the first Greek war is in its first part remarkably unevocative. We are told of the sound construction of the walls, of the larger area they enclosed compared to their predecessors, the number of the gates and their design, and so on (I 483-492; Roberts, p. 13).

In our list of echoes of Lucan in Joseph's *Yliados* we must include one very particular reminiscence, one motif in the later poem plainly copied from the earlier. During the second Trojan war (the Homeric one: the *Dares*, followed by Joseph, tells of an earlier one), the Greeks are threatened by a crisis of leadership. At a decisive moment Palamedes presents himself as Agamemnon's rival as the commander of the Greek forces. Joseph tells us the cause of this serious division: "Envy and greed were the cause – envy which is always brooding over the rights of others, greed which cannot bear the thought of something excellent in the hands of a friend."; "Altera semper / Iura premens Livor et nil insigne Cupido / In socios cessisse ferens coguntque premuntque / Naupliadam" (V 282-285; Roberts, p. 58). One cannot help remembering the beginning of the *Pharsalia* when we read this pair of lines, the long passage on the causes of the Civil War. Chief among them, as we recall, was the mutual envy of Pompey and Caesar: one could not tolerate a superior, nor the other an equal. It is hard to imagine that Joseph did not have these verses in mind in framing the piece about Palamedes' challenge. What is pertinent here is that Joseph is proposing a global moral cause, a general human disposition which in a particular instance produces a practical result. We recall the large role which causes play generally in the argument of the *Pharsalia*, and in particular the space Lucan devotes to detailing human defects to explain the great events of the poem: the long passage in Book I on the causes of the war is the eminent case in point. Particularly notable is Joseph's appeal to greed and envy to explain a relatively minor crisis, much smaller in scope than the one Lucan is dealing with (the Civil War). This confirms our impression that the English poet is consciously imitating Lucan. Joseph is in effect using an elephant gun to shoot a rabbit. This overkill is best explained, as I believe, if we judge that he was willfully trying to give his poem an antique flavor: the simple logic of the narrative does not fully justify the arrangement of the text at this point.

The main focus of this essay is the study of the uses of a practice I have called evidential narrative, the kind that is rich in detail, in which the wealth of minor incidents does not interrupt the flow of the story, or lie outside it, but actually belongs to it. It has been my contention that this mode of storytelling was the normal one in the strictly narrative sections of the earlier epic poems up to and including the *Aeneid*, and that one of the ways that Lucan broke with the model was to make narrative *evidentia* alternate with other sorts of narrative as well as with other forms of discourse. The downgrading of the livelier kind of narrative exposition in favor of the plainer kinds is one of the elements that turn the *Pharsalia* into a distinctive case. The curious fact of history is that the Lucanian pattern survived, and enjoyed much better fortunes than the Virgilian. Where does Joseph's *Yliados* fit into this picture? The examples we have already considered may give us a hint as to what the answer is going to be: Joseph's general conformity to Lucan suggests that the *Yliados* follows the *Pharsalia* in this regard as in others. And this is indeed the case: there are many pieces of plain narrative in Joseph's poem. It also has some fine evidential sequences, and as in Lucan's work, they contrast with the other sort. I have made the point with respect to the *Pharsalia*, and to other works, that the livelier scenes in these poems are sometimes held in reserve to dramatize the more significant moments in the plot. This pattern does not seem to hold in the *Yliados*. There are, as I think, two reasons for this. In the first place, it is my impression that Joseph is not greatly interested in evidential narrative. The impulse of the expert storyteller to brighten and dramatize his tale by suddenly descending to particulars and letting an audience witness a scene on their own seems to be alien to him. In the second place, neither the *Yliados* as a whole nor many sections of it have very much thematic focus. Alexander takes a bad chill while swimming: we see in this event the cruel play of fortune and circumstance. So think many of his chroniclers, Quintus Curtius, Gautier, and the author of the *Alexandre*, and all three give us a fully realized scene to drive home the point. There are not many analogous moments in Joseph's poem. On the whole, then, narrative in the *Yliados* is slow, abstract, and mediated; *evidentia*, what there is of it, occurs in static descriptive passages, as we have seen, and as a matter of routine, in the battle-scenes, which are of the Homeric type, or of the sort that appear in the *chansons de geste*, with hand-to-hand combats, blood flowing on the ground, riderless horses, and shouts and wails. Beyond this, stretches of extended evidential narrative are rare, and are applied with no special skill. One must add, however, that occasional enlivening touches do appear in otherwise plain passages: Joseph is especially artful in his management of these.

In Joseph the business end of narrative, the actual moving of the story from one moment to the next, the *Yliados*, in a word, without the speeches, the apostrophes, the descriptions, and such like, is made up in great part of rapid exposition, poor in detail, of the sort that I have pointed out in Ovid and Lucan. Our Troy-poem is one more eminent case of narrative *evidentia* evaded. Here are some instances of relatively unadorned story-exposition in the *Yliados*. Laomedon prepares for the first Greek onslaught:

> The Trojan king ordered the defense of his native land, and all the barbarians rushed to arms. Confident that he would burn their ships and scatter the Greeks into the sea, the king ordered his army to march to the shore. He was obeyed, and quickly all leapt into the waves. The Nereids, not accustomed to such frightful events, gaped in horror at the sight of arms and were terrified by the uproar.
>
> Patriumque armaverat orbem
> Principis edictum Frigii, ruit omnis in arma
> Barbaries; flammisque rates consumere fisus
> Et Danaos sparsurus aquis ad litora Martem
> Dux migrare iubet, paretur et ocius omnes
> Fluctibus insiliunt. Solite nil tale timere
> Nereides visa arma stupent horrentque tumultum.
>
> (I 355-361; Roberts, p. 10)

The rush to arms, vivid up to a point, is nevertheless a global event, made up of many particulars. "The king ordered" occurs twice in English, but the Latin has different expressions; both utterances are speech acts, given in indirect discourse. We recall that reported speech is relatively uncommon in Virgil, but is everywhere in Lucan. We are given the motive for the king's second order: the Trojans are to march to the shore in order to destroy the enemy fleet. The Nereids at the end are a fine touch, particularizing and gratuitous; details like this occur usually in isolation. A few lines later on we have the aftermath of Laomedon's death:

> When their king was slaughtered, the Trojans ran. The enemy plundered the wealth of the city. Some thirsted to appease their

anger with countless slaughter. At length a kingly voice rebuked
the plundering mobs of raging Greeks.

> Fit fuga Dardanidum mactato principe. At hostis
> Civiles predatur opes, pars cedibus iras
> Innumeris explere sitit. Vox regia tandem
> Castigat rapidos Danao grassante tumultus:
> (I 440-443; Roberts, p. 12)

The "kingly voice" turns out to be that of Hercules; a short speech by him follows. That unidentified voice is itself an elegant evidential detail, and like the one in our preceding quotation, it stands pretty much alone. The flight of the Trojans could easily be the subject of a great scene, with clouds of dust and taunts from the enemy, but as in the case of the rush to arms at Laomedon's order, Joseph recounts the event globally, without details. The poet gives us one inner disposition, a collective one, the bloodthirst of the Greeks.

Our next quotation is out of series; it is a non-progressive summing up, functioning also as a transition. We are told at the end of Book I that Priam was absent during the first attack on Troy, but that he returns to bring great prosperity to his realm. Book II begins as follows:

> Now Priam prospered, fortunate in the many children of his loins, fortunate in his marriage, fortunate in the lands of his inheritance – if only the Gods, if only the Fates had allowed it, if only it had been permitted to the lucky to continue in their good fortune.
> 
> > Iam floret Priamus populoso pignore felix,
> > Felix coniugio, felix natalibus arvis,
> > Si superi, si fata sinant, si stare beatis
> > Permissum. (II 1-4; Roberts, p. 15)

The proposition in the main clause (the Latin syntax is close to the English) once again is a summing up of many particulars. The if-clause (Latin "si") makes us party to the narrator's knowledge of the end of the story, and works also as a moralizing reflection on fortune and mutability. At the beginning of Book III Priam and the Trojans have come to agree that Paris should indeed go to bring back Helen. There are dissenting voices, however. Helenus delivers a long prophecy, which is unheeded, but Panthus' prophecy, much briefer, does have its effect. His words are, "Pergamum will fall to the Greeks, if Helen enters the city of the Trojans." Then comes the following:

> The captains were convinced, and the plebs changed their cry. Oh, how more readily do men listen to old things than to new! They all agreed that there was more of Apollo in the prophecy Panthus quoted from the past than in the one Helenus was himself now delivering. Nevertheless the thought of Hesione still tormented the confused mind of Priam; he thrust from him the advice of the Gods: he heard the truth and yet dared to be deceived. He helped the Fates when he rejected what they had to say.
>> Hiis iam facta fides ducibis vulgique tumultus
>> Flectitur. O quanto priscis nova mollius urgent!
>> Plus superi constant Pantho memorante futura
>> Quam dicente Heleno. Priami tamen egra lacessit
>> Consilia Hesione; superos premit, audit et audet
>> Dux falli fatisque favet, cum fata recuset,
>> (III 104-109; Roberts, p. 31)

The Trojans' reaction to Panthus' words is told briefly. Once again, we could imagine an elaborately realized scene at this point. A *sententia* follows, the line about the caution of humans. The invasion of *sententiae* into other sorts of discourse is topically one of the traits of Silver Latin. "All agreed" is indirect discourse. Priam's inner thoughts come next: these deliberations have a great bearing on the plot, since they are what effectively send Paris off on his ill-fated mission. The section concludes with a comment by the narrator, in the form of a Lucanian paradox, "superos premit, audit et audet / Dux falli fatisque favet, cum fata recuset" (III 108-109). One could remark here that the wordplay, "audit et audet" is not un-Lucanian.

Consider the following:

> When the presence of Helen was made known to Paris he deserted the fleet. Confident of his beauty and fully aware of the handsomeness of his face, he followed Helen here and there, wherever she went, tirelessly dogging her steps.
>> Postquam Helenes Paridi patuit presentia, classem
>> Deserit ac forme fidens et conscius oris
>> Huc illuc gressum librans, qua Tindaris ibat,
>> (III 223-225; Roberts, p. 34)

Nothing could be plainer than "deserted the fleet." Paris' self-confidence is of course an inner disposition. The "here and there," "huc illuc," and what follows is the mildest sort of *evidentia*. A few lines earlier we have: "And so the report hurtled headlong through all the cities of Cythera that Paris the son of Priam had come: from all sides the plebs flocked to the harbour to meet him" (III 218-220; Roberts, p. 34). "Hurtled headlong" and "flocked" exaggerates the effect of the Latin, which runs, "Ergo Citheriacas preceps it fama per urbes / Priamiden venisse Parim, plebs undique portus / Occursu complet." Nothing in Nature exists in a pure state, but this comes as close to being a simple report as we can imagine.

The following turn of plot may seem un-Homeric to some. This is the medieval, post-*Dares* version of the encounter with Dolon:

> Ulysses and Diomedes showed him [Dolon] the olive branch. They said they were envoys and begged to be admitted to Priam. They were taken to the king, they said what they had to say, they returned – all this in short order. The war was suspended for three years, and on this they shook hands. But warlike Hector railed against the treaty and the delay imposed by the truce. He guessed that the broken Greeks would of necessity regain their strength over so long a period.
>
>> Illi Palladia legatos arbore pandunt
>> Exorantque aditus. Iam regis copia, iam res
>> Edita, iam redeunt. Tres suspenduntur in annos
>> Dextris bella datis. At federa Martius Hector
>> Incusat pacisque moras, fractisque novandas
>> Inachidis tanto coniectat tempore vires.
>
>> (V 394-400; Roberts, p. 60)

With the exception of the olive branch and the handshake all this is indirect discourse. Our next quotation could serve as a counter-example:

> A truce and their pledged word put arms to sleep for a year. Both camps lay open to either army: the defenders were allowed to see the Greek tents and the enemy could gaze at the homes of the Trojans.
>
>> Pax arma soporat
>> Inque annum iurata fides. Utrique cohorti
>> Utraque castra patent; fas civi Graia videre
>> Carbasa, fas hosti Frigios lustrare penates.
>
>> (VI 69-72; Roberts, p. 66)

This is fine and elliptical. We are not told directly of the content of the treaty, but discover it from its practical effects. The one touch that separates this passage from pure reporting is the personification of the arms, asleep for a year. Our last quotation in this series takes us to the ceremonies on the anniversary of Hector's death. Achilles is present, and it is here that he first sees Polyxena and falls in love with her. The effect was devastating:

> He forgot the practice of arms and lost interest in battle. Already he was willing to return, to lead back his national contingent, to throw the whole army into confusion, if the royal maiden would be given to him as a companion for his bed, as a reward for his withdrawal. He sent word of this to Priam by way of the Phrygian, Sergestus, who had his closest confidence in every secret dealing. There would be peace, Achilles declared, and the entire war would have to be concluded with a treaty, if the Myrmidons followed his orders and returned.
>
> Ergo nec armorum meminit nec prelia curat
> Iamque redire velit patriosque reducere cetus
> Et totam turbare aciem, si regia detur
> Virgo sibi consorsque tori preciumque recessus.
> Instruit hiis Friga Sergestum, cui proxima in omne
> Archanum regale fides, pacemque futuram
> Asserit et totum cogendum in federa Martem,
> Si reduces sua Mirmidones precepta sequantur.
> (VI 90-97; Roberts, p. 66-67)

Obviously, the *style indirect libre* in the last sentence of the English is not in the Latin, which has simply a pair of infinitive phrases: "he declared *that* there would be peace, *that* the whole war" &c. would be a fairer rendering. The entire section is essential to the plot: Achilles' move does indeed persuade his men to go home with him (although moments later they change their minds). His inner disposition explains the decision he is about to make. His intention to withdraw and his message to Priam are, of course, in indirect discourse.

What this series of quotations represents is in effect the bricks and mortar of Joseph's narrative, the ordinary normal way the plot is made to unfold. Obviously, these selections are not all alike: summary, generalization, indirect discourse, the reporting of motives, thoughts and feelings are distributed differently in each selection.

The gratuitous detail that lets the audience visualize an event distinguishes some of them, but what is notable about our texts generally is that this mode is not prevalent in them: these touches are isolated. Our selections are typical. The bulk of the storytelling in the *Yliados* is, like that of our quotations, abstract, mediated – recounted, not shown, heard clearly in the voice of the narrator – and poor in particularizing detail. As I have pointed out, this is not the whole story. There are pieces of narrative in Joseph that are fully evidential, the battle scenes, for example, and as we would expect, the speeches themselves move events along. But it is the plainer mode that is most in evidence, even if it is not universal. And indeed, it is the very mixture of styles that is characteristic: that mosaic, un-Virgilian as it is, is the mark of narrative in other sorts of texts, in histories, in judicial speeches, as well as in poetry.

We will conclude our examination of Joseph of Exeter by considering the role played in his poem by direct discourse. Ancient epic poetry of all periods features speeches of various lengths and of different degrees of significance, put into the mouths of its characters, and the *Yliados* can hardly afford to do otherwise. But curiously, the importance of this sector of the poem is rather less than it has in its models. It is not as large, for one thing: a smaller proportion of the text is made up of direct speech. A count of verses in the *Aeneid* and the *Thebaid* tells us that more than a third of each is made up of direct speech, and in the case of the *Pharsalia* the fraction is slightly less than a third.[6] I have not made my own sounding, but a rapid reading makes it obvious that the proportion in the *Yliados* is quite a bit smaller. With one exception Joseph's speeches run from moderate length to brief. The long one is actually a piece of narrative, much like Aeneas' long recital which makes up Books II and III of the *Aeneid*: in Joseph, Paris' long utterance in Book II also gives us some of the prehistory of the poem's action, in this case of his judgment of the three goddesses. Otherwise, as I say, the speeches in the *Yliados* are not remarkable for their length. In one sense their relative shortness breaks the bond between this poem and Silver epic, an affinity otherwise strong. Story, as I would insist, is the great casualty in Roman narrative poetry after Ovid: the interest passes to other features of the text. Thus, Lucan gives us a sort of anthology, or vaudeville, a collection of set pieces, digressions

---

[6] Marti, op. cit., p. 80.

and scenes, strung together by a slim thread of story and a strong thematic focus. Statius simply slows things down, as well as presenting his own large repertory of digressions and other non-progressive matter. It is not an exaggeration to say that to a great extent both poems use narrative as an excuse to present other sorts of material. One feature of both the *Pharsalia* and the *Thebaid* is the long speech which brings the action to a dead stop: the grass grows, as it were, between events at either end. Lucan, for example, gives us the old man's account of the Marius-Sulla moment-in-history, and the priest's discourse on the sources of the Nile. In both cases the content itself of the speech is not in any way designed to advance the plot, though it may add a great deal otherwise to the context or to the poem as a whole. This typically Lucanian procedure is entirely absent from Joseph's poem. The point or meaning of the small role of direct discourse in the *Yliados* is hard to specify: it is certainly distinctive. One might reflect, however, that the direct style is mimesis par excellence: as long as it prevails, nothing is being reported, but instead, the audience is hearing the very words of Cato or Caesar. Indeed, some ancient writers on rhetoric describe certain forms of direct speech in a way which makes plain its affinity to *evidentia* (for example, Quintilian IX ii 32-3). It seems to me possible that Joseph's preference for modes of presentation that are abstract, or mediated, in which the narrator's voice carries the burden of the argument, may well explain why other voices are relatively so faint in his poem.

3)  GAUTIER DE CHÂTILLON

The other great humanistic epic poem of the late twelfth century, one of the best known and most studied texts of later years, is, of course the *Alexandreis* of Gautier of Châtillon. It will be my intention in the pages which follow to show that the system of exposition in this work is nearly the same as the one we have discovered in Joseph's *Yliados*. My larger point is that the poetics, if we can call it that, which the two poems share is one that is very widely known and used, effective in the *Libro de Alexandre*, for example, and in many poetic texts written since. The similarity of the narrative style of the *Alexandreis* and the *Yliados* is a telling one, because in other respects the two works are so very unlike. I return to an old theme, the contrast between poetry and history. I made the point pages back that the *Yliados* was not on an historical subject as was the *Pharsalia*. The possible truth of this proposition seemed to evaporate, when we reflected that Joseph and his audience almost certainly thought that the Trojan War as recounted by Dares actually happened. We might add that as a practical matter in Joseph's time poetry and history were in many ways more closely allied than one might think. But as I insisted, there is still a great difference between the *Yliados* and an historical text, and a great likeness with respect to subject and plot to ancient epic, Lucan excepted. We may replay this opposition with respect to Joseph's poem and the *Alexandreis*. In the first place, the theme of the *Yliados* is one actually treated elsewhere in poetry, and for its part, the matter of Gautier's work is in fact dealt with elsewhere in historical texts. The differences go further. Joseph's Troy-poem has to do with the perennial themes of epic, individuals and families, heroes and gods, and their interaction, especially in warfare. The *Alexandreis*, on the other hand, is about affairs of state, the acts of an exemplary ruler and world conqueror, all a proper and typical subject for a history. We must further note that Gautier's poem is a biography; no surviving ancient epic poem ever told the complete life's story of its principal character. In a word, style does not seem to follow function: the whole narrative mode shared by Gautier's poem and Joseph's is not common to them simply because they tell exactly the same kind of story. If, as I suggested, this pattern of exposition, adapted to epic by Lucan, was applied by Silius Italicus in the *Punica* because it too was an historical epic, that whole motive was dead by the late twelfth century when Gautier and Joseph composed their poems. The style had gone into orbit, wholly free of its origins.

4) CHRIA

The common mode I speak of will of course be the theme of this section of our study, but for the moment let us postpone airing it directly, and instead start to look without prejudice at the *Alexandreis* by itself. It is of course impossible to characterize Gautier's long poem in a few pages. Perhaps the safest way to begin is to plunge into particulars. There is an important rhetorical pattern which occurs in it several times in which it inherits not from Lucan or any of the ancient poets, but from its principal source, the *Historia Alexandri regis* of Quintus Curtius (ed. E. Hedicke, Leipzig, Teubner, 1908); the figure is the *chria*. The term *chria*, as we know, covers a wide area: the rules allow for quite a bit of variety. Broadly, *chria* is an edifying anecdote, usually about a famous person. It frequently ends in a witty or memorable saying. The utterance preceded by an account of when, where and how it was produced could itself stand as a sort of *chria*, but this is only one possibility among several. One might remark without humor that the story of George Washington and the cherry tree, with its I-cannot-tell-a-lie dénoument, is a perfect and exemplary *chria*. The genre has many uses. It may stand alone. The *Facta et dicta memorabilia* of Valerius Maximus, a book of enormous prestige in the Middle Ages and after, is a large collection of free-standing *chriae*. The figure may decorate other kinds of discourse: moral philosophers delight in it, and as the text of Quintus Curtius makes clear, historians do not despise it. The various offshoots of the history of Julius Valerius, whose echoes in the *Libro de Alexandre* are so numerous, are in large part a succession of *chriae*. We may note incidentally that many of these survive in the Romance text; the famous episode of the exchange of gifts and letters between Darius and Alexander is a series of three such anecdotes, all meant to illustrate the greater cleverness and wisdom of Alexander (stanzas 780-819, after *Historia de preliis*, as in A. Hilka, *Der altfranzösische Prosa-Alexanderroman* I, 29-30, 34-35). One of the triplet, Darius first letter and the Greek's response, actually appears in Gautier's poem, having found its way there from Julius Valerius' history.[7] Here are some futher *chriae* from the harvest of Gautier of Châtillon. Alexander, having conquered the city of the Uxii, is resolved to destroy all the inhabitants, including its ruler Medates. But Sisigambis, the mother of Darius, now a prisoner of the Macedonian, intercedes for all, and the then temperate and virtuous young king accedes, treating his former enemies with generosity. His change of heart is testimony to his moral excellence: "If fickle Fortune had put this city in the hands of a victorious Darius, his own mother would not have gained more from him than this enemy gave his conquered foes"; "Si uaga uictori Dario Fortuna dedisset / Vrbem pre manibus, non impetrasset ab illo / Plura

---

[7] *Julii Valerii Epitome*, ed. Julius Zacher (Halle, Verlag der Buchhandlung des Waisenhauses,1867), I:36, 38.

parens quam que uictis dedit hostibus hostis" (VI 142-144, Pritchard translation; see note 4). The parallel passage in Curtius, scarcely different, is in Book V (iii 12-15). Alexander, in pursuit of the Persian king, hears that he is in chains, prisoner of the treacherous Bessus and Narbazanes. The Greek is outraged. The chase must go on, he says, but our goal now is to save his life, if possible: "It is just as important to spare this now broken man, when he has begun to be wretched, as to be able to crush a rebel"; "Non minus est, postquam cepit miserabilis esse, / Parcere confracto quam frangere posse rebellem" (VII 115-116). Exceptionally, this utterance has no analogue in Curtius. Darius' wife, also a prisoner of Alexander, dies, a victim of stress, caused by her unhappy situation, compounded by the difficulties of constant travel. The Persian, informed of her passing, assumes that she died refusing Alexander's advances, but once assured of the young king's chaste behavior towards her, the bereaved husband is deeply moved. In a prayer to Jove he pleads:

> "first, I beseech you, grant stability to my kingdom both for myself and my people. But if you have already determined that it should be taken away from me, and if fate's imperious will bids that the kingdom of Asia be transferred from me to another, let this man, who is so respectful an enemy and so merciful a conqueror, have my kingdom after me."
> "Primum, queso, michi regnum stabilite meisque.
> Quod michi si tolli iam prefinistis et a me
> Transferri fati iubet imperiosa uoluntas,
> Regnum Asiae me post hic tam pius hostis habeto
> Tam clemens uictor." (IV 62-66)

Once again, these words are very nearly the same as those of Curtius in the analogous passage (IV x 34). As a result of Alexander's courtesy and consideration, Darius offers him a large part of his domain as well as the hand of his daughter. The Macedonian summons his council to discuss the offer; all are silent except Parmenion, who recommends acceptance. Alexander rejects his counsel:

> "I too, if I were Parmenion, should prefer the offer of money to glory, and should prefer to be without distinction than to gain glory and honour without riches. But, as it is, Alexander reigns free from care beneath poverty's mantle. I boast that I am a king,

not a merchant. Away with the seller of fortune! I have nothing for sale. If it is agreed that they should be returned [the other royal prisoners], I am of the opinion that it would be more agreeable for these to be returned gratis and sent back as a gift rather than at a price. For, if a price attends gifts, gratitude does not follow, nor do commercial transactions command thanks."

>                          'a me,
> Si essem Parmenius, oblata pecunia palmae
> Preferretur' ait 'mallemque inglorius esse
> Quam sine diuiciis palmam cum laude mereri.
> At nunc securus sub paupertatis amictu
> Regnat Alexander. regem me glorior esse
> Non mercatorem. fortunae uenditor absit.
> Nil uenale michi est. si reddendos fore constat,
> Gratius hos gratis reddi donoque remitti
> Censeo quam censu. precium si dona sequantur,
> Gratia non sequitur, nec habent commercia grates.'
>                                         (IV 131-141)

This too is taken almost verbatim from Curtius (IV xi 14-16). Parmenion always seems to be cast as the mean-spirited foil to Alexander. On the eve of the battle of Gaugamela-Arbela, the great lieutenant recommends a night-attack on the Persians, and all of his fellow-officers concur. Alexander rejects his advice, as he had before. He answers in a style not unlike that of his first response to Parmenion. He calls the night-attack the way of the robber, and some lines later says:

> "I prefer a king to grieve for his ill fortune and unfair lot than to be ashamed of a victory won by night. Victory is not worth so much, that posterity should read that I conquered by guile, and that cunning should lessen the glory."
> 'Malo peniteat fortunae et sortis iniquae
> Regem quam pudeat parti de nocte tryumphi.
> Vincere non tanti est ut me uicisse dolose
> Posteritas legat et minuat uersutia palmam.' (IV 363-366)

This too runs close to Curtius (IV xiii 8-9).

How did the *chria* find its way into the *Alexandreis*? The question is on the face of it ridiculous. Every example I have cited but one comes to the Latin poem by express mail from Curtius. The two texts include the same *chriae* at analogous moments in the plot:

Gautier does no more than follow his predecessor in this matter. But in another sense the whole question is not at all trivial. The *Alexandreis* is of course much shorter than the *Historia Alexandri regis*, and on this basis alone, Gautier had to perform major surgery to get Curtius' text down to the right size. By necessity and by choice, the poet treats all of his sources with great freedom, with respect to both matter and form as well as to extent. There is absolutely no reason why the author of the *Alexandreis* could not have eliminated systematically every single *chria* he found in the *Historia*. He of course did nothing of the sort. One must emphasize that, however passively he may have been following Curtius at any particular moment, the appearance of the figure in his text would surely have to be part of his design. He knew perfectly well what a *chria* was. He could hardly have been ignorant of the rules governing *chriae*; they appear in Priscian's Latin paraphrase of Hermogenes' *Progymnasmata*, which was frequently appended to the Latin grammar of the former as a final section.[8] The grammar itself is, of course, one of the most widely studied books on record. Beyond this, Gautier's reading might well have included Valerius Maximus' work, a well-known collection of *chriae*, as we have seen, and he must have encountered many more examples in his other reading, aside from the *Historia*. The figure belongs by full right to the design of the *Alexandreis*. Its presence there is one of its distinctive marks: it is a significant element of its form.

A discussion of *chria* at this point in the study may seem to be out of series. Our focus to date has been on poetry, on how a group of writers in verse over the years kept certain practices alive against expectations. But no one has ever suggested that *chriae* were prominent or characteristic of ancient Roman poetry of any period. And on the other hand, discussions of rhetorical devices that belong almost exclusively to prose and very infrequently to poetry have not figured large in this essay. But in a sense, Gautier, the incorporator of *chriae* into his text, is the latest in a long line of our star performers from antiquity; Ovid and Lucan, the two poets we have examined in greatest detail, are remarkable precisely because they incorporate into their style devices more characteristic of prose than of poetry. The point is an obvious one in the case of Lucan, but it holds quite as much and in the same way for Ovid, whom we might

---

[8] Manitius, op. cit., has twelve pages of entries for Priscian, 305-317.

consider, in a conventional sense, at least, more poetic. The narrative summary, the stretches of indirect discourse, and all the other ostensibly prosaic patterns are as much his as Lucan's. Thus, the total hospitality which Gautier offers all the devices of prose generally, including *chria*, is in no way unique. What should be stressed above all is that the flagrant affair the poet carries on with the *Historia Alexandri regis* does not engender a monster. The *Alexandreis* is a text within a tradition, not its first representative, and certainly not its last.

## 5) The Art of Gautier

*Chria* is not the most interesting feature of our great Alexander-text. The poet's competence in general may be. His work is, among other things, a poem of fine effects. It is not simple indulgence which leads us to make this point. In a way, it has been unfortunate that so much of this investigation has been focused on prosaic things, or to put it irreverently and indeed inaccurately, about how poets manage to be and remain dull. In the face of this imbalance, it seems to me pertinent to try to display Gautier at his best and most fully grounded in his art. And as we shall see, this attempt is in no way going to distract us from our main goals. In Book VIII, Alexander, about to cross the river Tanais, is met by a delegation of Scythians, who try to dissuade him. Their spokesman represents his people as unwarlike, living a simple life close to Nature, loving justice and respecting each other as equals, and intractable to domination of any sort. He rebukes Alexander for his ambition and his misguided aspirations, but offers him friendship and an alliance on equal terms. He warns Alexander that if he refuses the offer, they will take up arms, and that his victory, if he achieves it, will be costly (VIII 371-476). This speech is nearly identical to the one in Quintus Curtius (VII viii 12-30). But the lines in Gautier immediately following are entirely his own:

> So he spoke, but, nevertherless, Alexander drew up his men in formation and prepared to attack the Scythians. Having crossed the river with great effort, he dislodged the enemy in a confrontation of strength, and at length, but not without losing a number of his men, compelled Scythia to submit to Macedonian rule.

> Sic ait, at Macedo nichilominus agmine facto
> Arma Scitis inferre parat, multoque labore
> Flumine transmisso, collatis uiribus, hostem
> Deicit et tandem, sed non sine cede suorum,
> Imperio Macedum Scitiam seruire coegit, (VIII 477-481)

One should note that this is the perfect example of the rapid narrative poor in particularizing details, the minimal exposition I have referred to so frequently. It is a summary in the literal sense: it replaces a long passage in Curtius which gives a full and rich account of the whole action. The very brevity of the account in the *Alexandreis* makes it dramatic. It is successful in a totally different way from its analogue in the *Historia*. Its very bareness connotes Alexander's brutality, and the comments, "with great effort," and "not without losing a number of his men," offered without any corroborative detail, convey by their very bluntness the valor of the enemy and his own overconfidence. And above all, the contrast between the brevity of the account and the relative luxury of the preceding speech, more than 100 verses long, as well as the fact that, against appearances, the pair function as members equal in weight, the Scythian's offer, Alexander's response, give the five short verses a force and a power that is wholly remarkable. We must remember that the sense of the Scythian's speech is also the sense of the poem as a whole. The audience is indeed expected to see in the barbarians a dignity and virtue lacking in Alexander, and the envoy's reproaches to him for his ambition and for the vanity of his goals parallel sentiments set down elsewhere in Gautier's text. The short account is thus the other member of the balance, the assurance to the audience that the sometime nobility of character of the king of Macedon has been corrupted. The poet's hand here is sure: the means he uses are not extraodinary, but his application of them is deft and artful.

The scene in Gautier of the discovery of the dying Darius is another fine moment in the poem:

> The stench of slaughter and death's anger was not abated until Alexander curbed the frenzy of his sword, and those bloodthirsty young warriors held back from shedding blood. Then, indeed, the surviving body of men were driven along like cattle, but without suffering injury. However, there was no one in the

whole column who could reveal to the Greeks any trace of Darius. Each Persian waggon was searched, but nowhere did they come across the king's corpse and fate's dishonour. For the king's yoked team had abandoned the beaten track and, with their chests pierced with javelins, had come to a halt in a remote valley, bewailing their own and Darius' death.

Not far from there a murmuring stream glided by with its petulant babble, it alone holding sway over the spring herbage. For its parent this stream had a crystal clear spring which poured out of a rock. After squeezing its drops through the rock's inner crevices, it flowed along and watered the dry clods with its nectar. To this stream a panting Macedonian, Polystratus, was led to revive his parched lips with water, for he was tired after battle and lashed by the storm of thirst. He beheld the small chariot covered with abandoned skins and also the wounded animals which belonged to Darius who was even now breathing out his life. Seeing this, he approached nearer and came upon Darius, pierced through with many wounds. He had a wild look in his eye and lay on the borders between death and the very end of life. When he was asked in the Persian language who he was, as far as one could judge from his voice, he rejoiced and said &c.

   Nec cedis rancor nec funeris ira quieuit
Donec Alexandro gladii reuocante furorem
Cedibus abstinuit cedi deuota iuuentus.
Tunc uero intactum pecudum de more superstes
Agmen agebatur, nec erat uestigia toto
Agmine qui Darii Grais ostendere posset.
   Singula scrutantur Persarum plaustra nec usquam
Dedecus inueniunt fati regale cadauer.
Regis enim trito deserto calle iugales,
Pectora confossi iaculis, in ualle remota
Constiterant, mortem Dariique suamque gementes.
Haut procul hinc querulus lasciuo murmure riuus
Labitur et uernis solus dominatur in herbis.
Patrem riuus habet fontem qui rupe profusus
Purus et expressis per saxea uiscera guttis
Liquitur et siccas humectat nectare glebas.
Ad quem uir Macedo post Martem fessus anhelo
Ore Polistratus sitis incumbente procella
Ductus, ut arentes refoueret flumine fauces,
Curriculum Darii uitam exhalantis opertum
Pellibus abiectis iumentaque saucia uidit.
   Vidit et accedens confossum uulnere multo
Inuenit Darium turbatum lumina, mortis

> Inter et extremae positum confinia uitae,
> Cumque rogaretur Indo sermone quis esset,
> Gauisus, quantum perpendi ex uoce dabatur,
> 
> (VII 229-254)

Darius' words to Polystratus follow. The source of this passage is not in this case the *Historia Alexandri regis* but Justin's epitome of the histories of Pompeius Trogus. Here is his version:

> Alexander travelling rapidly arrived the next day. He found out there that Darius was being carried at night in a closed wagon. Having ordered his army to follow, he pursued the fugitive king with 6000 horse: on his way he fought many dangerous battles. He advanced many miles, and since he had not come on any trace of Darius, he allowed the horses to recover their breath. As one of the soldiers hastened to a nearby spring, he came upon Darius, afflicted by many wounds, but still breathing. When he [the soldier] spoke to the captive, he [Darius] recognized him as a countryman.
> 
> Alexander quoque citato cursu postera die supervenit; ibi cognovit Dareum clauso vehiculo per noctem exportatum. Iusso igitur exercitu subsequi cum sex milibus equitum fugientem insequitur, in itinere multa et periculosa proelia facit. Emensus deinde plura milia passuum cum nullum Darei indicium repperisset, respirandi equis data potestate unus ex militibus, dum ad fontem proximum pergit, in vehiculo Dareum multis quidem vulneribus confossum, sed spirantem adhuc invenit.[9]

We notice immediately that the best feature of the passage in Gautier, the mild reversal, is already in Justin: Alexander, in pursuit of the Persian, can find no trace of him, but one of his men comes upon him by chance. I observe in parentheses that Justin, plain-spoken, never much admired for his prose, is nevertheless particularly apt at narrating just such sudden changes of fortune: his account, for example, of the great Macedonian's death takes the reader totally by surprise. To Justin's simple recital Gautier adds several elements. Least interesting of all, perhaps, is the explanation of why Alexander did not succeed in finding Darius: his captors had left

---

[9] Iustinus, *Trogi Pompei historiarum philippicarum epitoma*, recensuit Iustus Ieep (Leipzig, Teubner, 1876), XI xv:3-5, p. 77; the translation is mine.

the beaten path. I need not remind the reader of the importance rhetoricians assign to explanation in narrative, and the essential role they give it in establishing verisimilitude. Gautier moralizes the episode. The Persian troops are driven on "like cattle," and Darius' abused body is equated with "fate's dishonour." The incorporation of moral comment in the very body of the narrative is characteristic of Gautier, and as we have seen, is in no way peculiar to him: it is far from uncommon in the other texts we have studied. The scene in the *Alexandreis* in which Polystratus actually finds Darius has some new evidential touches. To Justin's account of the king dying "afflicted by many wounds" the poet adds the wounded animals and the wild look in Darius' eye. But most successful of all is the description of the fountain where the soldier goes to quench his thirst. The lines are not especially distinguished in themselves, but in context, delaying as they do the reader's discovery of Darius' tragic end, they are very effective. They are the more so because they describe something pleasant, leaving the reader ill-prepared for the sad matter which follows it: the final scene is by contrast the more pathetic.

In common with Joseph of Exeter and unlike Lucan, Gautier realizes his battle-scenes largely as successions of hand-to-hand combats. For the most part they are entirely new, replacing very different ones in Quintus Curtius. Let us look at part of one splendid example of the species, the beginning of the Arbela-Gaugamela sequence at the beginning of Book V of the *Alexandreis*. After a learned periphrasis in which the narrator gives us the date of the encounter, we have the following:

> When he saw Alexander in the distance, blazing forth with his fiery helmet, the Indian Aristomenes, lavishly goading his elephant with ten blows of the lash, buried his sword with its poisoned tip in Alexander's shield. But, though the shield itself was dented, the suit of armour protected his body. Thereupon, Alexander turned against the elephant with his spear and, where the trunk joined its side, with his sword he laid open its viscera. With a dreadful crash, the monstrous beast collapsed. After the elephant's headlong fall, the merciless, avenging sword then cut off Aristomenes' head. "Ours is the victory, yes, ours it is" repeated the Greeks. The Persians massed together, and a thick rainstorm of missiles flew round the king. But neither javelins nor the axe more savage than the sword, could move the man

whom, under Fortune's guidance, undaunted virtue was protecting.

> Quem procul ut uidit galea flammante choruscum
> Indus Aristomenes, denis elephanta flagellis
> Prodigus excutiens medicata cuspide ferrum
> Inmergit clipeo, sed eo lorica retuso
> Tutatur corpus. at Magnus harundine monstro
> Obuiat, et qua se lateri promuscida iungit,
> Vitales aperit ferro mediante latebras.
> Fit fragor ingentem monstro faciente ruinam.
> Sed cum precipiti cecidisset belua lapsu,
> Vltor Aristomenen et parcere nescius ensis
> Acephalum reddit. 'nostra est uictoria, nostra est!'
> Ingeminant Graii. Persae glomerantur in unum,
> Missiliumque frequens regem circumuolat imber.
> Sed nec gesa mouent nec seuior ense bipennis
> Quem duce Fortuna uirtus infracta tuetur. (V 11-25)

This fine scene goes on in this style for pages. I do not need to point out to my reader all the details that make this passage a first-rate example of narrative *evidentia*. All the stops are out: we know exactly where Alexander's spear struck the elephant and how he escaped the threat of Aristomenes' poisoned sword. And so it is in the rest of the sequence. Homer could do no better. I would call attention especially to the speed with which things get under way. I repeat that this is literally the first piece of the action: we are thrown into the middle of things in a few short verses. But matters do not end here. As in other passages in the *Alexandreis*, it is not only the internal make-up of the passage that makes it effective. It is also impressive in context: it forms a sharp contrast with the verses at the end of Book IV which lead up to it: the pages on the preparations for the battle move very slowly, just as slowly as the lines on the beginning of the battle move fast The whole passage is very close to the analoguous one in Curtius (IV xii-xiii), but the poet adds details of his own. Here is Gautier's long list. Alexander chooses the site of the coming battle; both armies raise terrifying shouts. But events are cut short because of the failing light. Apollo retires, says the poet; the periphrasis for the sunset occupies seven verses. Alexander stands on a hill and surveys the Persian army: he is compared to Tiphys, piloting the Argo over stormy seas. Alexander confers with his generals. Parmenion recommends a night-attack, and his fellow officers concur, but Alexander rejects the plan as ignoble: Gautier gives us his speech in direct discourse. Darius in fact anticipates an attack under cover of darkness, and his forces can be seen on the ready, lighted up by countless fires. Alexander contemplates the scene, and cannot decide what measures he will take: restless and uneasy, he shuffles over various plans in his mind. The goddess Victoria intervenes. She abandons the temple on the Tiber and journeys at length to call upon Sleep, and implores him to visit Alexander: this is an elaborate sequence, populated by many personification deities, Justice, Clemency, Peace and so on. Uncharacteristically, Alexander actually oversleeps: his lieutenants have to awaken him. But he comes to himself serene and confident: we are given a short speech of his, expressing this optimistic mood. He is armed and Bucephalus is summoned. He settles on the battle-formation of the day, and explains to his troops how they may best deal with the Persians' scythed chariots. A deserter warns Alexander that Darius' men have planted the ground with pointed spikes. The Macedonian harangues his troops. It is only at this point in the text that Gautier finally throws us into the action. He tells us simply, "the armies clashed together"; the bluntness of the account and its suddenness is itself a fine touch.

This whole sequence, covering the events of a few hours, takes up more than 300 verses, more than half of Book IV. It is very nearly as long as the parallel text in Quintus Curtius; its size is thus disproportionate in the *Alexandreis*, as a whole much shorter than the *Historia*. The change of pace at the opening of the new book is effective: after pages of very slow narrative, we are thrust, suddenly and dramatically, into one of the liveliest and busiest sequences of the whole work. The poet knows the ropes. More than once, I have spoken of the artful narrator who saves his purple patches for the critical moments in the text. Gautier is such an artist. I should stress that the *Alexandreis* as a whole is notable precisely for its evasion of *evidentia*. What the Arbela passage and others like it clearly show is that the plainer stuff in the poem is not always inert matter: there are moments when its role is clearly to make the brilliant sequences, the most visual ones, all the brighter by contrast.

## 6) The Plain Style

The aim over all of this examination of the *Alexandreis* is to show that its method of presentation, its discursive mode, is of a certain type, heavily mediated, full of commentary and static description, explanatory, verisimilar rather than evidential, in which story is advanced in great part by summary, in which brilliant scenes and livelier narrative are held in reserve as special effects. Obviously, this whole pattern of style is not simply a model, a Weberian ideal type. Broad reading makes it clear that it is effective in a great many texts, of different periods, in prose and verse alike. It should be obvious that at this point much of our work in tying the *Alexandreis* into this system has already been done. In our direct examination of the *Libro de Alexandre,* for example, we occasionally looked across at features and details of its main Latin source in a way that made this connection clear. And more particularly, in my discussion, just concluded, of the felicities in Gautier's text, a number of themes surfaced which are pertinent to this project: rapid narrative, moral comment, etiology, *evidentia* as an occasional resource, all stared us in the face, telling us where the *Alexandreis* stood. Our list of differential traits is not going to be endless, to be sure, but certain features of its narrative style do require a still closer look.

There is summary itself, rapid narration that informs more than it evokes. As is the case in the *Yliados*, a great deal of the storytelling in the *Alexandreis* is of this kind. The sort of exposition in force at the beginning of the Arbela-sequence, in which many successive stages in a longer happening are detailed, is undoubtedly important within the poem, but it actually does less of the narrative work, so to speak, than does the plainer kind. I need not remind my reader one more time that the evasion of narrative *evidentia* is one of the main themes of this study, and I would insist that the preference of Gautier and others for the plain style is one of the ways in which their narrative practice parts company with the narrative practice of ancient epic up to the time of Virgil. Summary is thus nothing less than an index to the sort of unclassical taste I have so often considered in the course of this investigation. Now, what is especially interesting about the bits of rapid narration in Gautier is what we could call their pedigree: the history of each obliges us to focus on the genuinely prosaic and informative character of the genre. Thus, many of them are of one of two types. Some are little more than close paraphrases of equally rapid pieces in the *Historia Alexandri regis*, whereas others are genuine summaries, passages that give us the substance of much longer stretches in Curtius. The paraphrases, virtual metrical versions of the *Historia*, obviously cannot help having the character and profile of prose: if they seem to have less in them of Virgil than of an historical text, it is because that is what they are. One should observe in general that plain narrative is acceptable in history as it ordinarily is not in certain kinds of poetry. As for the genuine summaries, they are global and impoverishing by their very nature, by definition. Here is a selection of examples of both kinds. The condensations already in Curtius will be treated first. The historian, after telling us of the defeat of Porus, gives us a very brief account of Alexander's plans and hopes for a drive futher east at the very beginning of Book IX. This matter passes into the *Alexandreis* expanded but still very short, and with an element of genuine narrative:

> At a gallop, he hurriedly hastened to turn the fighting against the farthest nations, and to add the peoples of the Ocean to his camp. And so, subjecting to himself the Indians and the farthest climes of the world quicker than the South Winds, he roamed about from one people and king to another.
>    laxis propere festinat habenis
> Orbis in extremas conuertere prelia gentes
> Oceanique suis populos adiungere castris.
> Ocior ergo Nothis Indos extremaque mundi
> Clymata subiciens, populos regesque pererrat,
>
>                                  (IX 331-335)

The story marches in seven-league boots. One should emphasize that these lines, condensed as they are, are not meant to convey peripheral matter, or to sum up hastily what is going to be told in greater detail further along. Global and abstract, they nevertheless are designed to convey the main story; they contain information that cannot be found elsewhere in the poem. Gautier, after the description of Darius' wife's tomb, sends Alexander off on his march to meet the Persian force:

> Alexander, having completed the traditional funeral rites at the tomb and offering sacrifices to the dead, gave swift orders for the striking of camp, and at a rapid pace advanced furiously against the foe. He also bade Menidas, content with a few choice soldiers, to explore the plains, where the Persians and their king were hiding. Mazaeus, catching sight of this man in the distance, hastily gathered his detachments together and returned to his camp. But Darius, in his eagerness to fight a decisive battle on the open plains, reformed his lines for battle and, as he wandered among his troops, he armed their hearts with his warnings, in addition to protecting them before battle with arms.
>
> Magnus ut exequiis tumulo de more peractis
> Inferias soluit, festinus castra moueri
> Imperat et rapido cursu bachatur in hostem,
> Et Menidan raro contentum milite campos
> Explorare iubet ubi rex Persaeque laterent.
> Quo procul inspecto Mazeus prepete cursu
> Contraxit turmas et sese in castra recepit.
> At Darius, patulis auidus decernere campis,
> Instaurat bellis acies, cuneosque pererrans
> Pectora tam monitis honerat quam prestruit armis.
>
> (IV 275-284)

Alexander's order is a speech-act, reported in indirect discourse. So also is Darius' warning. His eagerness and Menidas' contentment are subjective dispositions. The sole particularizing touch is Mazaeus' look from afar. The version in Curtius (IV xii 1-5) has barely a few details more. The episode I have already alluded to of the Persian deserter who, on the eve of Arbela, informs Alexander that his enemy has planted the battle ground with spikes is also told plainly:

> While he warned and fortified his men, and strengthened their hearts with words, a Persian deserter, escaping from the Persians, crossed over to the king, and told him that Darius with hidden cunning had planted iron implements in the ground – caltrops by name. Although Darius could not overcome his enemy by force, he hoped nevertheless to trap them by tenacious hooks, and swallow up the Greeks in a hidden calamity. Once he had received this news, lest the Persian was lying and seeking to trap his men with his words, the king ordered him to be placed under guard. Nevertheless, he himself had that spot marked and

shown to his men, where the Babylonian king, relying on the cunning of a Ulysses, had planted hooks in the ground. So that lofty valour might not be rebuffed and fall victim to guile, Alexander ordered the spot suspected of treachery to be shown to all, and when shown to be guarded against.

>  Dumque monet munitque suos, dum pectora dictis
> Roborat, elapsus a Medis transfuga Medus
> Transmeat ad regem, Darium qui ferrea terrae
> Instrumenta refert astu mandasse latenti,
> Muricibus nomen quibus, et si uiribus hostem
> Vincere non possit, retinere tenacibus uncis
> Sperat et occulta Graios sorbere ruina.
>   Quo semel accepto, Medus ne ficta loquatur,
> Ne capiat sermone suos, rex imperat illum
> Seruari, tamen ipse locum fecitque notari
> Monstarique suis ubi rex Babilonius arte
> Fretus Vlixea terrae mandauerat uncos.
> Neue repulsa dolis, succumberet ardua uirtus,
> Omnibus ostendi iubet ostensumque caueri
> Suspectum de fraude locum. (IV 532-546)

The passage has a few moralizing expressions, the "hidden cunning" and the "cunning of a Ulysses"; it specifies motives three times, Darius' for planting the hooks, Alexander's, for taking the Persian prisoner, and his again, for showing his men the critical spot. Otherwise, the narration is straight and simple. Finally, as we have noted, the hasty account of the taking of Susa in Gautier is like its analogue in Curtius, but the latter, unlike the poem, does not make a sharp contrast between this action and the taking of the city of the Uxii: the short account and the long are side by side in the *Alexandreis*, but separated by other matter in the *Historia Alexandri regis*. The version in the poem could not be more simple: "all most willingly accepted Susa when that city was handed over by its citizens, and when the soldiers had been cheered by its many treasures, tempestuous Alexander turned his army against the stronghold of the Uxii."; "omnes / Accepere animis, Susam tradentibus urbem / Ciuibus et multis hilarato milite gazis, / Agmen ad Vxias conuertit turbidus arces" (VI 63-66). In the Latin, as we can see, the line and a half about Susa is actually an absolute construction.

These passages are entirely typical. There are many more bits of rapid narrative in Curtius which get transplanted into the *Alexandreis*; none are formally very different from the ones we have cited.

In some ways, the bits of rapid narration in Gautier that summarize longer passages in Curtius are rather more interesting than those that follow him closely. The *Alexandreis* is of course a much shorter text than the *Historia Alexandri regis*, and its author must at times treat his sources very freely. In the Latin poem some episodes in Curtius are dropped completely. Others are radically altered. Most characteristically in these Gautier conveys only the barest essence of the parallel passage in his source. Now, the less space a narrative unit occupies in the text, the less weight will it carry with its audience, or so some would believe: nothing underlines the importance of a subject-matter more than the plenty of words that is devoted to it, and nothing diminishes that significance to the reader more than dismissing it quickly. And yet, things do not always work out that way in Gautier. We could, for example, cite his account of Alexander's attack on the Scythians: its very brevity was what seemed to make it eloquent. Here are some more summaries in the *Alexandre* in which something comparable takes place. The first I will leave in context: our whole selection is part plain and part ornamented. Here is the plain part. The battle of Issus has just been fought. The Greek soldiers take spoils, sometimes with scant courtesy. But then we have:

> But with their majesty unimpaired and, likewise, their modesty, Darius' whole household, his mother and royal wife, his sister and his son, were carried to the Greek camp in chariots of gold – such was Alexander's clemency.
> Maiestate tamen salua saluoque pudore
> Tota domus Darii, genitrix et regia coniunx
> Et soror et natus, tanta est clementia regis,
> Curribus auratis in Dorica castra uehuntur. (III 234-237)

This plain account of Gautier is preceded by a sequence of very different character:

> They [Alexander's men] proceeded next against the unwarlike throng of women. After they had torn their necklaces from their marble necks, rings were wrenched off, and the ear lost its earring. The soldiers proceeded to embrace married women, and virginity suffered violence. Intercourse took place in the open, and bloody hands handled private parts. Some contracted the stigma of unhallowed intercourse; but others grieved and came

for pardon. For the fact that force had been brought to bear mitigated the fault of the sufferer, and compulsion lessened blame.
>    Itur in inbelles agmen muliebre cateruas.
>    Quarum ubi marmoreo rapuere monilia collo,
>    Extorti torques, et inaures perdidit auris.
>    Itur in amplexus nuptarum, uirginitasque
>    Vim patitur. coit in patulo tractatque pudenda
>    Sanguinolenta manus. coitus pars altera labem
>    Contrahit incestus, uerum pars altera luget
>    Et uenit ad ueniam, pacientis namque reatum
>    Vis illata leuat, minuitque coactio culpam. (III 225-233)

Gautier's simple and informative account of the capture of Darius' family and its treatment by Alexander is preceded by a horror-show, full of unpleasant details. The contrast is effective: the passage on the captives holds its own precisely becuase of the accompanying Hollywood production. Now this whole passage, both parts of it, replaces a long sequence in Curtius in which the evidential style of the rape-scene is sustained throughout to the end: we are given every stage in the capture of the royal party, and of their treatment by Alexander. Why should it be otherwise? The material treated is important, bearing on the nobility and virtue of Alexander: they deserve no less than a fully realized scene. But as we have seen, the shorter version in the Latin poem is effective in its own way: in context, its brevity works in its favor. The conclusion we need to draw from this instance and others like it in the *Alexandreis* is that here as elsewhere in the poem rapid narrative is perfectly capable of conveying weighty and significant material, and that the same work that can be done in a long version can also be done in a short. One need not think of the simple and informative style as second best, a draft-horse assigned to only routine cargoes: our poet in fact entrusts to it some of the most critical and important material in the work.

I add in parentheses that Gautier suppresses an elegant *chria* from the passage in Curtius. Alexander is short, and Sisigambis mistakes the taller Hephaestion for his lord. She apologizes for the error, but Alexander graciously says of his officer and friend, "This man is Alexander too."

I offer one more passage in Gautier which summarizes a longer one in Curtius. We pick up the story immediately after the campaign against the Uxii:

> Without delay, having divided his forces with Parmenion, he ordered him to track down Darius with caution, and told him to go by the road through the plains. He himself, however, retained the chosen cavalrymen and made for the high ridges whose backs turn and run without interruption into Persia.
>
> > Nec mora, diuisis cum Parmenione cateruis,
> > Imperat ut Darium caute uestiget, eumque
> > Campestri iubet ire uia, tamen ipse retentis
> > Delectis equitum iuga tendit in ardua, quorum
> > Perpetuum excurrit uergens in Persida dorsum.
> >
> > (VI 145-149)

This is reasonably close to what might be called minimal narrative. It does include one bit of indirect discourse, Alexander's order, and one metaphor to relieve the bareness, the mountain ranges as backs of horses which "run" into Persia ("excurrit"). As I have suggested, a great deal of the story in Gautier's poem is conveyed in passages no less austere than this. Our episode goes on. The function of the verses I have quoted is to get us into the next big campaign, the advance into Persia. But the importance of this latter action is expressed not by an amassing of lively detail, or even by the length of the passage, but by a commonplace, an appeal to Fortune: "On no other occasion did Alexander endure more serious dangers, or learn through experience that Fortune remains always fickle, inconsistent and never eternal for anyone."; "Non alias Macedo, grauiora pericula passus, / Experto didicit semper uariamque sibique / Dissimilem et nulli fortunam stare perhennem" (VI 150-152). The actual march is told with the most modest *evidentia*: we are given "the mere by-way" he had to follow, and the "circuitous routes," and we are told that the enemy attacked him from above. But then, the dénouement takes us back to the global and abstract terms of the opening: "Finally, at the heavy cost of his men's blood and after many trials, he crushed the enemy standards in a confrontation of rival strength, and the arms of the conquered lay under those of the conquerors"; "multaque suorum / Sanguinis impensa post tot discrimina tandem / Hostica confregit collato robore signa, / Victaque sederunt uictricibus arma sub armis" (VI 157-160). The interest of this passage is very nearly the same as that of the one of the captivity of the royal family. Our lines in Book VI recount in brief the events Curtius presents in a long and fully developed episode (V iii16-23). To give us a moral equivalent, Gautier gives us a small group of mild attention-getters framed by two bits of lean and abstract narrative. I would add that the rapidity of the last eight verses is made effective as it comes to rest in a handsome *epiphonema*, "Victaque sederunt uictricibus arma sub armis" (160).

7) THE PROSE OF WARFARE

Lucan, as I am convinced, was for many generations the one great exemplary narrative poet, one with few rivals among the *auctores*. Most of the traits I have been pointing out in later poetry are the very ones which generally set his work apart from that of his predececessors, and at the very least, make it unusual in ancient narrative poetry. As we recall, one of these anti-poetic qualities is verisimilitude, the accumulation of materials in narrative which make it not lifelike, but plausible, or in other terms, fully intelligible. I remind my readers parenthetically of my old theme. Verisimilitude may be thought of as one of the ways of evading *evidentia*: the event that is explained does not have to be evoked. Now, one whole subclass of verisimilar motifs in Lucan is the one that has to do with the practical aspects of warfare, broadly, with strategy. We of course heard a faint echo of this Lucanian strain in Joseph of Exeter's poem. The reverberations are quite a bit louder in Gautier, and this is the next feature of the *Alexandreis* that I wish to consider. I would begin by observing that Gautier loves verisimilitude generally, and that this bias has much the same significance in his production that it has in Lucan's: our medieval poet explains more than he displays. The point should be fairly obvious. We have caught him in the act, so to speak: many of our references and quotations have made it clear that bits of explanation, the specification of the motives of the characters, the allusion to the circumstances which make an action or a turn of events understandable are all planted widely throughout Gautier's text. His comments on strategy and the bricks and mortar of military action are especially prominent. There are very particular reasons for this. Gautier's Alexander-poem, through Quintus Curtius, is an heir to the historical tradition of Alexander-narratives, as opposed to the legendary. There are elements of both in his text, but the historical prevails by a large factor. Alexander was, of course, a man at arms, and logically enough, a great many of the old texts devote long pages to the detail of the military actions in which he played a leading part, the disposition of troops, their movements in battle, the natural advantages of one battleground over another, problems of supply, and the rest; space is given eminently to the foresight of the generals, especially Alexander's, which takes all of these elements into account, as he and they pursue victory. Curtius, for all of his fine phrases and moralizing, preserves a great deal of this material. His accounts of Issus, Gaugamela and the rest are exemplary historical expositions, paying full attention to the way the Macedonian prevails, following the action of the battle step by step. He also tells us in detail about the king's activities between battles which bear on his success in them and on his military advantage generally. Gautier, as we know, replaces some of this material with his own, but other pieces of it he leaves virtually unaltered. Here, with a minimum of comment, are a few of these passages. We recall that on the very morning of the battle of Gaugamela-Arbela Alexander warns his troops of the Persias' scythed chariots, and tells them to confront these strange weapons in open formation, showering their drivers with javelins (IV 527-531). This corresponds to its parallel text in Curtius (IV xiii 33). I add in parentheses that in the *Historia* this detail is but one item in a long list of dispositions made by Alexander before the battle. In a way that should be familiar to us Gautier sums up all this matter in the global statement that Alexander makes all the arrangements for the coming battle. Two verses is all that is allotted to this proposition: "Alexander, therefore, divided his army into its proper sections, and arranged his line of battle in proper order."; "Ipse suis igitur distinguens partibus agmen / Disponensque aciem quo debuit ordine," (IV 526-527; this is obviously not a complete sentence in Latin). Gautier does somewhat better in his line on the disposition of troops for the battle of Issus: the phalanx forms the front line, facing the body of the enemy; Nicanor commands the right wing, surrounded by a body of lieutenants, Parmenion holds the left, with his own generals in turn, and Alexander himself commands the horse, on the right with Nicanor (II 422-429). Earlier in the same book, Alexander's generals are in doubt as to what piece of terrain would favor them most in the coming battle. At that moment, the Greeks are encamped in a mountainous area, and under Parmenion's urging, the leaders decide to wait there for the enemy force: in his view, the narrow valleys would put the larger Persian army at a disadvantage (II 262-268). This scene parallels one in

Curtius (III vii 8-10). Still earlier in the book, Alexander's long view is emphasized: in Gautier's account, after taking Cappadocia, the king rushes to the plains to spare himself an encounter with Darius in the mountain passes – tactical considerations are plainly different here from the ones faced by Parmenion! (II 96-98). Exceptionally, this detail is not from Curtius, but from Justin (XI viii 1-3). In the decisive battle against Porus, the Macedonian wins by a ruse. The Indians are in firm possession of one of the banks of the river Hydaspes: a Greek crossing is virtually impossible. Alexander, however, has a double, whom he has dressed to look like him, and who takes over the king's role completely there on the river bank. The real king, meanwhile, takes a force along the river for some distance and makes a safe crossing out of sight of the Indians, who, taken up completely by the movements of the false king, are in time surprised by Alexander and defeated. The episode is in both Gautier and Curtius (G., IX 148-195; C., VIII xiii 17-27; xiv 1-2). As we recall, both the *Alexandreis* and the *Historia* tell of the secret access to the city of the Uxii: Alexander approaching this difficult quarry is informed by the natives that a hidden road "would bring the Greeks to the city without the knowledge of its citizens" (G.'s version, VI 63-76; Curtius' account is at V iii 7-8). The prosy particulars of the first assault itself are given in the poem in the lines immediately following:

> Timber suitable for making hurdles and mantelets was cut, and erected in the narrow passage in a curved tortoise, so that, protected by means of such a defence through the enthusiastic efforts of the carpenters, the armed young warriors could undermine the walls completely. But the approach was difficult, since the earth had never been cut and threatened trouble with its sharp crags and rocks. Alexander was not only fighting a dour enemy, but had also to struggle with the place and the living rock protected by its natural position. Nevertheless, the lightly armed companies, preceded by their leader, began to climb up the narrow, precipitous terrain.
>> Cesaque materies faciendis cratibus apta
>> Et pluteis curua testudine surgit in arcem,
>> Artificum ut studiis tali munimine tuta
>> Funditus erueret muros armata iuuentus.
>> Sed grauis accessus cum dura minetur acutis
>> Cotibus et saxis succidi nescia tellus.

> Nec solum Macedo cum duro dimicat hoste,
> Sed locus est cum quo pugnandum uiuaque cautes
> Natiuo munita situ; tamen arta subibant
> Et prerupta leues duce precedente cohortes. (VI 77-86)

The analogous passage in Curtius is in his Book V iii 7-8.

It cannot be emphasized too strongly that the rehearsal in narrative poetry of prosaic military matters, tactics, materiel, and so on, is entirely distinctive: it is a strong indication of the influence of Lucan, direct or indirect. One could note, incidentally, that later poems of unquestionably Lucanesque character, frank imitations of the *Pharsalia*, preserve just this feature. A striking instance is Michael Drayton's *Barons' Wars*:[10] many verses of this fine poem are given over to the practical problems of both sides in the struggle between Edward and his vassals. The poet tells us at length, for example, how the king, much weaker than his barons, tries to weaken them by organizing a march through the middle of England and splitting their forces in two. Drayton's diction at this point, as we should note, is remarkably plain; there is no need to quote the passage.

## 8) The Failure of Narrative

In an earlier chapter I spoke of what could be called the failure of narrative, the fact that in Lucan, and even in Statius, story seemed to be assigned a relatively minor role in the make-up of the text, yielding place to exclamations, digressions, speeches, descriptions, commentary and other non-narrative forms and material. I even suggested that in the *Pharsalia* and the *Thebaid*, the plot came close to being an excuse, a framework on which to hang other sorts of matter. Since both Lucan and Statius cast long shadows over

---

[10] Drayton, Michael, *The Barons' Wars, Nymphidia, and Other Poems*, with an introduction by Henry Morley (London, George Routledge and Sons, 1887), p. 26. On the Lucanesque character of *The Barons' Wars* I would cite La Branche, Anthony, "Drayton's *The Barons Warres* and the Rhetoric of Historical Poetry," *Journal of English and Germanic Philology* 62 (1963), pp. 82-95. Germaine Greer's brief study, *Shakespeare* (Oxford and New York, Oxford University Press, 1986), p. 78, speaks in passing about Elizabethan historical poetry, and mentions in particular Samuel Daniel's *The Civil Wars*, a work written a few years before Drayton's poem, and Drayton's immediate model.

poetry of later ages, one might guess that in the learned Latin poetry of the twelfth century story might also be a semi-exile. We may indeed say that neither in the case of Joseph's poem nor in that of Gautier's is elegant narrative flow the great merit of the work. We must qualify this: both poems, especially the *Alexandreis*, have sections in which the story is told very effectively, but taken as a whole, neither work has a large narrative structure that is particularly adroit or otherwise admirable: the merits of each, such as they are, lie elsewhere. Why is this? In the case of Gautier's poem there are answers of two kinds. The first has to do with its dependence on the *Historia* of Quintus Curtius. Gautier, as we know, preserves a great deal of the material, and indeed, many of the very words of Curtius' text: there are whole long sequences that are virtually identical in the poem and the history. Some of these passages are the ones in which the plot is made to advance, but in others it moves forward little or not at all. The critical matter here is the fact that the *Alexandreis* as a whole is much shorter than the *Historia*. This means that each section which is common to both occupies relatively more space in the poem than in the history. Therefore, if the portion in question is a speech or a description, or a section in which the story unfolds slowly, that means that a smaller fraction of the poem as a whole will have narrative movement: things stand still or creep along for relatively longer stretches of time. Examples are legion. We have already seen several. The Scythian ambassador's speech to Alexander brings things to a stop in poem and history alike, but the king's practical response is much briefer in the poem. An even more notorious example is the one in Book VIII of the poem, in which Philotas, accused of plotting to kill Alexander, delivers an endless harangue in his own defense: it is taken almost literally from Curtius. But the narrative arrest that it represents is much more considerable in the *Alexandreis* than in the *Historia*. We recall also that the long narrative on the preparations for the battle of Arbela, the story of the events of the night before and of the morning of the encounter, pays out very slowly in both texts, and therefore relatively much more slowly in the poetic one. Gautier is no fool, and does not make decisions lightly; so, in any case should we imagine him. The whole architecture of the *Alexandreis* is simply designed to cheat narrative. Quintus Curtius' *Historia* is a brilliant work, but like good history, it is rambling and discursive, at the service of many goals and ends: whatever its merits, it does not read like a detective story. But the découpage Gautier subjects it to weakens the narrative flow even more.

Even in isolation, Gautier's poem reveals him as at bottom feeling little responsibility towards narrative. As we have repeated so often, the action of the *Alexandreis* is explained, interpreted, is the occasion of comments about life and the world, is, in a word, presented in such a way that its significance will be beyond doubt. But outside of certain episodes, the simple flow of events is not what is interesting, and nothing in the narrative presentation itself is designed especially to make it so. Then, there is also the issue raised by the figure *evidentia* and its evasion. The story does not, so to speak, tell itself: we do not witness the events narrated, but have to be told about them. In the language of modern poetics, we would characterize Gautier's text as heavily mediated. The narrator's voice is heard loudly, as it judges, analyzes, exclaims, and above all, calls attention to itself. The narrator is the middle-man, as it were, putting his own trade-mark on the actions he recounts. I remark also that the *Alexandreis* summarizes a great deal, a fact that may seem to vitiate my point: summaries recount plain facts without interventions from the narrator, so it seems. But not so. As I have insisted in my remarks on the *Pro Milone*, summary is itself heavily mediated discourse. A summary tells us what we could not possibly know from first-hand experience: events have to be sifted out and evaluated before anyone can summarize. Modern theoretical texts are sometimes misleading on just this point. Summary along with other factors makes the layer of mediation in Gautier's poem very thick, quite as thick, for example, as the corresponding sector of the *Pharsalia*. One reason for this dimension in our text is obvious: the work depends heavily on an historical composition in prose, Curtius' on Alexander: mediation is, after all, hardly a scandal in an historical text. But lumping together the element of mediation in the *Alexandreis* with its halting narrative, we may wish to ask whether the special profile and structure of our Latin poem might not have part of its origin somewhere else still. An answer to this question lies, as I think, in the presence in our Alexander-epic of the poet Claudian. Let us begin by noting that this extraordinary man of letters leaves his footprint in the *Alexandreis* twice. It has been pointed out that in Book X Nature's journey to the Underworld to procure the death of Alexander is traceable partly to a remark in the *Pharsalia* that at the height of his power death came to

Alexander, and that only Nature had the power to end his career (X 41-42), and partly to a passage in Claudian's *In Rufinum*, in which Allecto goes down to Hell to try to disrupt the peace of Theodosius' reign.[11] There is no need to go into details, but indeed, the parallels between Claudian's passage and Gautier's are everywhere visible, and the dependence of the later text on the earlier is virtually certain. Gautier, like many cultivated medievals, knew Claudian very well. But there is more. In another passage in the *Alexandreis* Claudian is actually named. Alexander has entered Babylon, and is received with a splendor and ceremony the poet calls unique in history, greater than that accorded Julius Caesar after Pharsalus, or Octavian (here called Augustus) after Actium. The applause and celebration were deserved, says the poet, because

> in comparison with this prince, the whole series of other leaders will be mere commoners, be they those made notable by the Spaniard's poem, composed in lofty style, or by Claudius [sic] in his noble lines. Lucan would then be sorry to have sung such a splendid poem about Caesar and the downfall of Rome and, likewise, great Honorius would give way before the arms of the Macedonians.
> Tota ducum series, uel quos Hyspana poesis
> Grandiloquo modulata stilo uel Claudius altis
> Versibus insignit, respectu principis huius
> Plebs erit ut pigeat tanto splendore Lucanum
> Cesareum cecinisse melos Romaeque ruinam
> Et Macedum claris succumbat Honorius armis.
> (V 504-509)

What is significant here is, of course, the pairing of Claudian and Lucan. It is striking, in the first place, that Gautier speaks of the *Pharsalia* as being primarily about Caesar (virtually celebrating him) and the fall of Rome. We recall that the Marqués de Santillana refers to the *Pharsalia* as the "gesta Magnea,"[12] that is, also as a celebration of one man, in this case not Caesar, but Pompey (called "Magnus" in the poem). Claudian, for his part, is the author of a set

---

[11] In Pritchard's note on this passage in his translation, p. 232.
[12] *Defunssión de don Enrique de Villena*, in Marqués de Santillana, *Poesías completas*, ed. Manuel Durán, 2 vols. (Madrid, Castalia, 1975 and 1980), vol. 1, pp. 228-236, line 8, p. 228.

of panegyrics on Honorius. Gautier's meaning here is entirely clear: he is associating his own work with that of these two poets who, to his mind, are up to the same business as he, that of celebrating the great. Matters do not end here. Gautier tells us elsewhere that epic poetry, his and others', is designed primarily to exalt the memory of its heroes. As we recall, Alexander on the site of Troy is made to declare Achilles fortunate, he who had Homer to perpetuate his memory. The point is that Gautier in latter days has been the poet to play the same role with respect to Alexander as did Homer with Achilles. What Gautier is conveying in these two passages is his conviction that the genre or mode of the text he is composing is epideictic, simply, the speech of praise or blame, and in this sense, the appearance of the name of Claudian, author of panegyrics, is the perfect index.

The untutored modern reader perhaps makes little sense of these views, least of all with reference to the *Pharsalia*. Can we nowadays receive Lucan's poem as a "gesta Magnea" or indeed, "Cesárea"? The work may strike some as in its way Zolaesque, a narrative without a hero. There is in it, surely, a strong feeling of the transpersonal, the social and collective, in the references to Rome in serious crisis, and the cosmic, the working out of a large, unfriendly fate. We are brought up short thinking about the poem as simply panegyric. And on the other hand, the comparison with Claudian seems odd. His works on historical-contemporary subjects are for us very unlike epic as we think of it, and in any case, wholly dissimilar in their large conception to the *Pharsalia*. Some of them are not primarily narrative works at all. The panegyrics, properly speaking, follow the agenda laid down for the description of the person in many handbooks of ancient rhetoric (see, for example, Cicero *De inventione* I:34-38). Claudian is a supreme poet, his own man and not a slave to rules, but the formal pattern is nevertheless visible in these poems. In the panegyrics he tells us of the hero's forbears, the place of his birth, the circumstances surrounding this event, especially the prodigious ones, those attending his youth which promised greatness, his education, his virtues, qualities of mind, those of his body and physical bearing, his great deeds, and so on. Narrative is not wholly alien to this form: some of the stops on this line must obviously be in chronological order, birth before education, for instance, or lineage before birth. But the description of Honorius' qualities, important elements in the series, are not at all the subject of narrative properly speaking: they are states, not events. The Honorius pieces and the others cast in the same mold are sometimes made up of long speeches, often on themes not closely bound to their occasion: they may touch, for example, on philosophical subjects, on the nature of virtue, or of wisdom. What bits of genuine narrative that do appear in these works are brief, barely enough to get us from one set-piece to the next, and are schematic, global, lacking in detail. The genre itself makes small demands on narrative, and Claudian does not often give us more than the statute requires. His less formal pieces on contemporary themes are themselves not remarkable for their narrative flow. It has been observed that they are not wholly unlike their panegyrical fellows. Cameron in his classic study of the poet remarks that "all Claudian's major poems, epics no less than panegyrics and invectives, consist of little but a succession of speeches and descriptions." [13] This is true not only of the occasional-contemporary poems: "*Rapt.* [*De raptu Proserpinae*] too is constructed on the same pattern of speeches and descriptions, linked by passages of seldom more than a dozen or so lines of narrative" (p. 264).

It is striking, incidentally, that Cameron speaks of "epics," referring to occasional poems so poor in narrative. Here is the agenda of the *Gothic War*.[14] We begin with a series of *comparationes*. Tiphys, the pilot of the Argo, artful to the point of prodigy as he eluded disaster between the clashing cliffs, was the savior of the ship and its crew. But, says the poet, greater yet was Stilicho, who saved Rome from destruction. Another mythical term of comparison is offered, only to be surpassed by the heroism and capacity of Stilicho. The general is praised directly in an apostrophe, and in another Rome is assured of her safety thanks to him. After all, the threat to Heaven itself at the hands of the giants in time came to naught. The Goths' spectacular rise and subsequent fall comes next, followed by the observation that the Romans' clemency towards them effectively spares the city a final attack. Then Stilicho is described, and is compared to other great and famous men at arms. All of these matters have taken up 165 verses of the 647 that make up the poem. And it is only at this point that we are given anything like a chronological

---

[13] Cameron, A., *Claudian: Poetry and Propaganda at the Court of Honorius* (Oxford, Clarendon, 1970), pp. 262-263.

[14] Claudian, ed. and translated by M. Platnauer (Cambridge, MA, Harvard University Press, and London, William Heinemann Ltd., 1922).

sequence of events. A long verse paragraph has an account of the ravages of the Goths throughout Europe: the lands they have overrun are listed in turn. An *exclamatio* gives us the peril that threatened Italy itself. But hope came in the person of Stilicho. We return to Rome's desperate situation, the apparent invincibility of the enemy, the omens which many considered unfavorable. Stilicho is of course the man of the hour: Claudian gives us a long speech of his, words that restore courage and hope in Roman hearts. Global and figurative language follows: "The dark shadow fled and Italy dared raise her head once more"; "ausaque tum primum tenebris emergere pulsis / Hesperia" (verses 316-317). At long last, we are given a genuine bit of story, albeit rapid and summary:

> Where Larius clothes his banks with shady olive-trees and with his fresh water imitates the sea's salt waves, Stilicho crossed the lake with all speed in a small boat. Next he ascended those mountains, inaccessible in winter, with no thought for the season or the weather.
>
> protinus, umbrosa vestit qua litus oliva
> Larius et dulci mentitur Nerea fluctu,
> parva puppe lacum praetervolat; ocius inde
> scandit inaccessos brumali sidere montes
> nil hiemis caelive memor. (319-323)

But immediately well-enough gets disturbed: an extensive lion-simile follows. The passage through Raetia comes next, but the episode is told in the form of an extensive rhetorical figure, Nature at her most threatening, all ice and snow: "Such was the country over which Stilicho passed in mid winter"; "Per talia tendit / frigoribus mediis Stilicho loca" (348-349). A form of *ratiocinatio*, a figure of amplification in which we are told of the forces, natural or human, that the hero manages to overcome; the audience is left to judge on its own his power and capacity (Quintilian VIII iv 20). At this point we have reached verse 403. There is little point in going on. Another "epic," the *War against Gildo*, 526 verses long, settles down to plain story-telling in the narrator's voice only a few verses from the end. Cameron tells us plainly that Claudian is not good at narrative. This is unfair. There are a number of fine scenes. The bloody and gruesome end of Rufinus, told in the invective against him, is a splendid dramatic sequence, well-paced, beautifully realized generally. But the long occasional poems, panegyric and other, are simply not narrative in any fundamental way. They allude to genuine events, and sometimes arrange things in chronological order, but in the sense that story is fundamental to Homer, Virgil, and even Lucan, in the poems of Claudian it is not.

How, then, is it that Gautier can link Claudian with Lucan, and associate his own work with that of both? Obviously, what is at issue here is the kind of reading Gautier makes of the ancients. It is very unlike ours. The gap for us between the *Pharsalia* and Claudian's *In Rufinum* is enormous: we would surely put them into different genres. But for Gautier the two belong together, and the link between them is in no way problematic. The common theme is, of course, praise and blame. Let us for the moment set aside the difficulties we may have in reducing the *Pharsalia* to epideictic. The fact is that the association of texts we call epic with the element of praise and blame is no special whim of Gautier. We have already seen a glimmer of the idea in Santillana's reference to the *Pharsalia* as "gesta Magnea." The notion is exceedingly widespread. Here is a hasty proof. Judson Allen's study, *The Ethical Poetic of the Later Middle Ages*, is a scrutiny of hundreds of *accessus*, glosses and commentaries produced over several centuries, and many of his texts refer, explicitly and otherwise, to the equivalence of heroic poetry and praise of an individual. Separately, an *accessus* to Sedulius' *Paschale carmen* speaks of *carmen heroicum*, that is, an epic poem, as about the great deeds of kings and nobles – "heroico enim carmine gesta regum et ducum scribebantur antiquitus" (Huygens, p. 29). In Conrad of Hirsau's comment on the *Thebaid*, we are told that Statius presented Adrastus as a model king so that he could serve as an example to Vespasian. Professor Craig Kallendorf, in a fundamental study of Petrarch, has pointed out that the Italian poet and humanist regarded epideictic as of the essence of ancient epic generally and as the mainspring of his own heroic poem, *Africa*.[15] This case is instructive, as we must note. The *Africa* itself,[16] in spite of its large debt to Virgil, indeed, in spite of the fact that it is supposed to be an imitation of the *Aeneid*, is really a rogue epic, poor

---

[15] Kallendorf, Craig, "Petrarchan Poetics and the Literature of Praise and Blame," paper read at the Sixth International Congress of the International Society for the History of Rhetoric, July 15-20, 1987.

[16] Petrarca, Francesco, *L'Africa*, edizione critica per cura di Nicola Festa (Firenze, G. C. Sansoni, 1926).

in narrative, with perhaps more affinities to its author's own *Trionfi* than to any ancient narrative poem.

But even disregarding the motive of praise and blame, we must confess that the statute underlying all these elements, the reading of old poems, the composition of new, is very broad. Defining this statute is not altogether easy. If within the secondary material from Gautier's own time we look particularly at *accessus*, we find that the classification of literary texts follows two lines. The commentator may assign the work under study to a particular literary genre, or he may include it under one of the large divisions of knowledge. The first road is from our point of view very perilous. One must explain that the grammarian's prologue to an *auctor*, called *accessus*, followed a fairly rigid agenda: in the "type C prologue," in the terms of R. W. Hunt),[17] the commonest sort, the explicator had to tell first something of the life of the author, then, his matter, his intention, the utility of the text, and the section of philosophy to which it belonged. Obviously, it is the last item on this list that concerns us: the possible divisions of knowledge/philosophy are, hastily, the seven liberal arts, plus ethics. As I have said, there is a second system of classification of texts: one may inquire about the *qualitas* of a poem, a term not inaccurately translated "genre." Often *qualitas* is effectively discussed without the word actually being used. Epic does not fare particularly well within this system. In the first place, more often than not, our prologues do not speak of *qualitas* at all: in the little collection of *accessus* published by Huygens only four out of twenty-nine of the texts speak of *qualitas*, and in Conrad of Hirsau's *Dialogus super auctores,* a very similar text, the count is four out of twenty-one. Among the poets appearing in the above set whose *qualitas* is not mentioned are Homer (mainly the *Ilias latina*), Statius, and the Virgil of the *Aeneid*. Not a promising outlook, exactly. Occasionally, as we have seen, one does find the *qualitas* of a text we call epic characterized as *metrum heroicum*, or *carmen heroicum*, a fair enough equivalent. But even this fact is less assuring than it seems. There are several extant *accessus* and similar writings in which we are given a detailed and rich morphology of *qualitates*, but in which the epic genre, *metrum heroicum*, does not appear at all: pastoral, lyric, satire, comedy and tragedy and others may be de-

---

[17] Hunt, R. W., "A Fragment of a Manuscript from the Abbey of St. Victor in Paris," *Bodleian Library Record* 4 (1952), pp.124-126.

scribed, but epic goes begging. In one very interesting such case, the prologue to the glosses of Arnulf of Orléans on the *Pharsalia* – an epic text to say the least –, the term *carmen heroicum* or its equivalents do not appear at all. We are indeed taken on a tour of *qualitates*, we hear about lyric, comedy and the rest, but we are told that Lucan's poem is a special case, a mixture of history and poetry, kind unspecified. Here is Arnulf's text (in my translation):

> Just as Juvenal is a pure satirist, and Terence a pure comic poet, and Horace in his odes, a pure lyric poet, this poet [Lucan] is not pure, but is both poet and historian. For he follows history ["historiam suam prosequitur"] and makes up nothing, and on this basis he is called not a poet simply, but a poet and an historian.
>
> Sicut Iuuenalis purus est satiricus, Terencius purus comedus, Horacius in odis purus liricus, non est iste poeta purus, sed poeta et historiographus. Nam historiam suam prosequitur et nichil fingit, unde poeta non simpliciter dicitur, sed poeta et historiographus.[18]

Epic is the outsider, once again. By contrast to Arnulf's text, the prologue to William of Conches' glosses on the satires of Juvenal[19] gives us a complete discussion of the genre satire. The case is not unique. Indeed, most *accessus* which raise the issue of *qualitas* give a fair account of the genre of the work being treated.

One would conclude that for the grammarians of the twelfth century the question of the genre of the *Aeneid*, the *Pharsalia*, or the *Thebaid* was not a very important one. But more broadly, the very notion of genre, the notorious *qualitas* of all these commentaries and *accessus*, does not seem to loom very large for them. The practical sense of this is clear. If one were a reader or student alive and well in 1180 with a copy of any of these poems in hand, one might find that the prose warm-up, the student's introduction, would say not a word about the work's *qualitas*. One might learn a great deal else about Virgil's poem, or Statius', but would most probably set aside one's reading without being reminded once that there was such a thing as an epic genre, or that the work in hand might be-

---

[18] *Arnulfi Aurelianensis glossvle super Lucanum*, ed. Berthe Marti (Rome, American Academy in Rome, 1958), p. 4.

[19] Guillaume de Conches, *Glosae in Iuvenalem*, ed. with introduction and notes by Bradford Wilson (Paris, Vrin, 1960), p. 45.

long to it. What sort of classificatory scheme would a typical *accessus* offer such a reader instead? As I suggested, it would tell him which part of philosophy the work belonged to. Philosophy, as we must note, consists of three parts, logic, physics, and ethics. Logic in turn is broken down into grammar, rhetoric and dialectic, and physics, into arithmetic, geometry, music and astronomy/astrology: in other words, logic equals the trivium, and physics, the quadrivium, the whole adding up to seven liberal arts, plus ethics.[20] The *Aeneid*, or the *Pharsalia* has to fit into one of these slots. Which one? The vote is unanimous: both belong to ethics. But here is our next large difficulty. Very nearly all the poetry in the twelfth-century canon of *auctores* also belongs to ethics, the satires of Juvenal, Persius, and Horace, the *Bucolics* of Virgil, all of Ovid, except, possibly, the *Fasti*, the comedies of Terence, the *Disticha Catonis*, and so on. Not only that, the list includes works in prose, Boethius' *De consolatione*, and Cicero's *De amicitia*. One might rightly conclude that the generic identity of the *Aeneid* was left shivering and comfortless, out in the cold. More generally, one would judge that the grammarians were serving very thin broth as far as the discussion of literary kinds is concerned. And yet, the classification is not at all frivolous. Most of the poets on the twelfth-century list belong to ethics because they depict human behavior, hardly a trivial reason. We are of course speaking now of poetry at large, certainly not merely epic. But whatever the merits of the scheme, we can hardly say that the plain differences between Lucan's poem and some of Claudian's, or between many other such contrasting pairs, are very well provided for within it.

We started this discussion with a serious anomaly, the sense expressed by Gautier that Lucan's poem and those of Claudian belong in the same heap, even though to us they seem very unlike. The anomaly is compounded by the fact that Gautier means to throw his own work, much more like Lucan's than like Claudian's, into the same heap. But the anomaly evaporates, as it were, twice first, if we reflect that Gautier most probably thought that his two ancient models, as well as his own poem, were in the business of praise and blame, and second, if we observe that the inclusion of much poetry and some prose under the heading "ethics" makes the boundaries between what are for us different genres very blurry,

---

[20] Conrad of Hirsau's account is typical: see Huygens, p. 83.

and in any case unimportant. The point of all this discussion is that Gautier's composition of an epic poem in which narrative globally is not a very interesting factor may have to do with the very ill-defined status of the work in the poet's own mind. His model undoubtedly is Lucan, who himself pares down the importance of story. But beyond that, if Gautier also associated his work more broadly with texts that were not meant to be narrative at all, he would have had even less reason to dramatize or highlight story in his work. And so, the halting story-line in the *Alexandreis* is not such a strange matter after all: it could well be a part of the poet's conception, something entirely intentional.

## 9) NARRATIVE IN THE *LIBRO DE ALEXANDRE*

As we approach the end of this study, we cannot fail to return, even if briefly, to our main subject, the *Libro de Alexandre*. My purpose in examining the poems of Joseph and Gautier was to add something to our understanding of the Spanish poem's immediate background. Obviously, and for what it is worth, I have in some measure done this. This essay has shown that the distinctive features of certain blocks of ancient Latin poetry which seem to reappear in the *Libro* are also present in some of the narrative verse of its own time or immediately before. Early in this chapter I spoke of overkill, as though our scrutiny of the two medieval Latin texts gave us much more of Lucan than we needed to understand the *Alexandre*. In some instances such overshooting may have taken place, but in one which I wish to consider I believe we have a parallel, a close match, perhaps against appearances. The issue is the slowness or the awkwardness of the narrative. Here, surely is a case in which a characteristic of, let us say, the *Alexandreis* disappears completely from the *Libro de Alexandre*. One is tempted to generalize: the story lumbers in the Latin poem, but it is lively and varied in its vernacular analogue. Gautier's poem is abstract and full of talk: its narrative stumbles both because of the extraneous matter that keeps interrupting it, and because of the poor concept the text expresses of narrative itself. But in the *Libro de Alexandre*, on the other hand, narrative never sags: it is lively and varied, and the layout of its story is always satisfying. One does, of course, have to hedge things here: on a small scale, in particular episodes, narrative in Gautier looks after itself very well, and if we admire the flow of the narrative in the *Libro*, we may sometimes attribute this style and economy to the poem's main Latin source. But if on a larger scale the Latin poem lags, the Romance one runs with grace and style, if not great speed: so one is inclined to think. And yet, every single element that appears to bog down narrative in the *Alexandreis* is also present in the *Libro*. It too moralizes, has long descriptions, explanations and digressions; it also has its share of purely informative story-telling. One could even point out that the *Libro* compounds the difficulty on its own. Its variety of sources, the unlikeness of their styles, the unlikeness of the treatment they receive in the definitive text, all would seem to stand in the way of a smooth narrative development: we recall, for example, the special character of the *Ilias latina* and of its adaptation in our text, and how different the narrative presentation in the Trojan War episode is from that of the other sections. Where, then, does the truth lie? Is our impression that the *Alexandre*-poet is a better story-teller than Gautier a fair one?

We may begin by reflecting that the difference between the two texts may in fact have little to do with the elegance or non-elegance of the narrative of each. Whatever the nature of its story-line, the *Alexandreis* is not a failure: one indeed might want to call it a very beautiful poem. It must in any event be read on its own terms, as a classicizing, archaistic poem, aimed at an audience that is small and select, which could savor its look backward. With respect to the *Libro de Alexandre* also, we must look to the total performance: it is for its part a vernacular text, with few responsibilities to its literary past, aimed at an audience which, large or small, is certainly not select. It is in the ordinary sense an entertaining poem: its aim is to please just this body of listeners. Without putting a fine point on the question, one could describe the *Libro* as a script for a gifted public entertainer, a *juglar* who stood before an audience which would have only the vaguest notion of who Venus was, and would derive no pleasure from an allusion to the story of Euryalus and Nisus. The transformation the Latin text undergoes in the *Alexandre*, and the wealth of rhetorical devices the poet employed to bring all its material to life for his unlettered hearers would be the subject of another study. But in principle, there is absolutely no need to believe that all these profound changes have to do simply with enlivening story, or with the pruning down of the non-narrative part.

The *Libro* is in no way whatever like the streamlined versions of the *Guzmán de Alfarache* that leave out all the philosophical and theological material. A simple and obvious term of comparison may serve to clear the air. The *Libro de buen amor* is a supremely entertaining poem, but the proportion of its text that belongs to the principal narrative is relatively small. Even this story-development in itself is informal and little organized. What is more, some of the book's funniest passages are actually digressions of some sort, and many of these are not narrative in any sense at all. But what else can we say? The Archpriest's wonderful book flies. In its own way so does the *Alexandre*. In a word, the color and variety of this great poem are the qualities of its discourse in general, and it is a great mistake to attribute them to its narrative exclusively.

10) A WORD IN CONCLUSION

The original proposition of this study was that the narrative style of the *Libro de Alexandre* was unlike that of Virgil. I conclude by reminding the reader that this same style, that of the *Libro* and in general terms of the *Alexandreis* and the *Yliados* as well, is far from universal in the period of any of these texts. Indeed, one could argue that some forms of medieval Romance poetry represented the opposite pole in this matter. Gautier's poem, as we know, shares with the *chanson de geste* just one structural element, one set-piece, the battle-scene made up exclusively of hand-to-hand combats. Regardless of the other sources one might propose for this pattern, one thing is certain: in formal terms the *Alexandreis* resembles a vernacular Romance epic song of its time in virtually no other way. Ignorance is not at issue: Gautier knew the vernacular epic. Geon, the Persian warrior at the battle of Arbela, is a medieval wild man, ugly, dark-skinned, unnaturally large, the wielder of a club. This typical figure belongs by proper title to the *chanson de geste*: we need only remember Raincourt in the *Song of William* and similar characters in other songs. But with Geon and the standard battle-narrative the similarity between the *Alexandreis* and the contemporary epic comes to an end.

Let us explore some very well-known territory. Here are some familiar verses:

> Ya quiebran los albores     e vinié la mañana,
> ixié el sol,     ¡Dios, qué fermoso apuntava!
> En Casteión     todos se levantavan,
> abren las puertas,     de fuera salto davan
> por ver sus lavores     e todas sus heredades;
> todos son exidos,     las puertas abiertas an dexadas
> con pocas de gentes     que en Casteión fincaron;
> las yentes de fuera     todas son derramadas.
> El Campeador     salió de la çelada,
> corre a Casteión     sin falla.
> Moros e moras     aviénlos de ganançia
> e essos gañados     quantos en derredor andan.
> Mio Çid don Rodrigo     a la puerta adeliñava,
> los que la tienen,     quando vieron la rrebata,
> ovieron miedo     e fue dese[m]parada.
> Mio Çid Ruy Díaz     por las puertas entrava,
> en mano trae     desnuda el espada,
> quinze moros matava     de los que alcançava.
> Gañó a Casteión     e el oro e la plata,
> sos cavalleros     llegan con la gananançia,
> déxanla a Mio Çid,     todo esto non preçia[n] nada.[21]

It is a mistake to overgeneralize, but it is surely safe to say that beautiful passages like this one, with its very selective and artful marshalling of particularizing detail, make up one of the strains that compels us to listen to the *Poema de mio Cid*. In the Roncesvalles sequence of the *Song of Roland* we are told that "Roland is proof and Oliver is wise." The verse is impressive in its context – most verses of the poem are –, but in logical terms it is entirely redundant: the text up to that point has been telling us nothing else. Telling is not the right word. The *Chanson* has been displaying with great vigor the polarity between its two heroes: the proposition is not there, but the prowess and wisdom have been before our eyes from the beginning of the poem. In the first sequence at the court of Charlemagne the text does not tell us that the rash and impulsive Roland is the only person present who talks sense. It does not tell us that Charles himself, hieratic, larger than life, 200 years old, is a flawed king, whose judgment fails him in critical matters. It does not tell us that his wisest nobles are totally agreed on a plan which in time will bring destruction to his finest knights and to a large

---

[21] *Poema de mio Cid,* ed. Ian Michael (Madrid, Castalia, 1976), verses 456-475.

part of his force. The *Roland* is memorable for its presentation of all these states of affairs, but it does not tell us of a single one.

It is way beyond the scope and intention of this study to try to explain the abyss that separates the *Poema de mio Cid* and the *Chanson de Roland* from the *Libro de Alexandre* and texts like it. If one had to say in a line what kept these narrative modes apart, one could put it simply that the practice of the *juglar* and that of the grammarian belong to two very different institutions, and that it was unimaginable that the pair could have influenced each other any way but superficially. But my real point in commenting on the *Cid* and the *Roland* is that the narrative technique of both, along with that of the *chanson de geste* in general, is close to that of Virgil. This is not a question of style in any conventional sense. The "style of Virgil," the distinctive sensibility, the moods the poetry evokes, the rise and fall of the hexameters obviously has nothing whatever to do with the *Roland*. But as I have insisted so many times in this study, the *Aeneid*, like the *Roland*, *shows* much more than it *tells*. To get a sense of this we need only look at any ancient commentary: in Servius, for example, gloss after gloss is given over to making explicit the motives and causes Virgil keeps to himself, explanations in plain Latin that tell us what the poet does not say at all. What is genuinely remarkable is that the *Alexandre*, and, along with it, twelfth-century Latinity were so little inclined to follow Virgil, even when poetic narrative organized essentially like his was at hand and very well-known to all. From our own vantage point it seems incredible that at the time no one made the connection. Simple explanations for this anomaly are hardly possible. To be sure, any institution runs in large part on inertia, and grammar and the study of the *auctores* up to the thirteenth century cannot have been an exception. Whether one looks at manuals of instruction, *poetriae*, or at long sophisticated poems like those of Gautier and Joseph, one concludes that in their day poetic narrative had to be heavily mediated: one might say that that was the law. Behind this routine, this inertia, there undoubtedly lay the fact that the canon of authors in those days was tilted steeply in favor of Silver Latin; I have done my best to convince my readers of that. But in the long run, the reason the *Alexandre* is put together the way it is, and the reason the large body of doctrine and example that lay behind it has the profile it does, the factors, in a word, that underlie the matter of this book, must remain a mystery.

# BIBLIOGRAPHY

*Ad Herennium*, edited and translated by Harry Caplan (Cambridge, MA, Harvard University Press, and London, Wm. Heinemann Ltd., 1954).
Allen, Judson, *The Ethical Poetic of the Later Middle Ages* (Toronto, Buffalo, University of Toronto Press, 1982).
Anderson, Theodore M., *Early Epic Scenery* (Ithaca, Cornell University Press, 1971).
*Apollonii Rhodii Argonautica*, ed. Hermann Fränkel (Oxford, Clarendon, 1961).
*Aratoris subdiaconi De actibus Apostolorum*, ed. Arthur Patch McKinley, *Corpus scriptorum ecclesiastorum latinorum*, vol. LXXII (Vindobonae, Hoelder-Pichler-Tempsky, 1951).
*Arnulfi Aurelianensis glossvle super Lucanum*, ed. Berthe Marti (Rome, American Academy in Rome, 1958).
Artiles, Joaquín, *Los recursos literarios de Berceo* (Madrid, Gredos, 1968).
Barthes, Roland, "Introduction à l'analyse structurale des récits," *Communications* 8 (1966), pp. 1-27.
———, "L'effet du réel," *Communications 11* (1968), pp. 84-89.
Bly, P. A., and Deyermond, A. D., "The Use of *Figura* in the *Libro de Alexandre*," *The Journal of Medieval and Renaissance Studies* 2 (1972), pp. 151-181.
Boethius, *De topicis differentiis*, in Migne, J. P., *Patrologia latina*, vol. 64, (Paris, published by the editor and his successors, 1891).
Bonner, Stanley F., *Roman Declamation* (Liverpool, University of Liverpool Press, 1949).
Cameron, Alan, *Claudian: Poetry and Propaganda at the Court of Honorius* (Oxford, Clarendon, 1970).
Cascales, Francisco, *Tablas Poéticas*, edición y notas de Benito Brancaforte (Madrid, Espasa Calpe, 1975).
Christensen, Heinrich, *Das Alexanderlied Walters von Châtillon* (Halle, Verlag der Buchhandlung des Waisenhauses, 1905).
Cicero, *De Inventione, De optimo genere oratoris, Topica*, edited and translated by H. A. Hubbell (Cambridge, MA, Harvard University Press, and London, Wm. Heinemann Ltd., 1949).
———, *De oratore*, in two volumes, Books I and II, with an English translation by E. W. Sutton, completed with an introduction by H. Rackham, Book III, with an English translation by H. Rackham (Cambridge, MA, Harvard University Press, and London, William Heinemann, Ltd., 1942).
———, *Select Political Speeches*, translated by Michael Grant (Hammersmith, Penguin, 1969).
Claudian, edited and translated by M. Platnauer (Cambridge, MA, Harvard University Press, and London, William Heinemann Ltd. 1922).
Currie, H. McL., *Silver Latin Epic* (Bristol, Bristol Classical Press, 1985).

Curtius, E. R., *European Literature and the Latin Middle Ages*, trans. Willard R. Trask (New York, Pantheon, 1953).

Díaz y Díaz, M. C., "Tres notas sobre cultura latina medieval en la región palentina", *Actas del I Congreso de Historia de Palencia*, tomo IV, *Edad media latina y humanismo renacentista en Palencia, lengua y literatura, historia de América* (Palencia, Diputación Provincial de Palencia, 1985), pp. 9-28.

Drayton, Michael, *The Barons' Wars, Nymphidia, and Other Poems*, with an introduction by Henry Morley (London, George Routledge and Sons, 1887).

Dutton, Brian, "French Influences in the Spanish *Mester de Clerecía*," *Medieval Studies in Honor of Robert White Linker* (Valencia, Castalia, c. 1973), pp. 73-93.

Erasmus, Desiderius, *De duplici copia verborum ac rerum commentaria duo*, in *Desiderii Erasmi Rotterdami opera omnia*, ed. J. Leclerc, (Leiden 1702-1706), 10 vols, vol 1.

Faulhaber, Charles, "Latin Poems from Palencia," *Romance Philology* 43 (1989), pp. 59-69.

Fraker, Charles F., "Aetiologia in the *Libro de Alexandre*," *Hispanic Review* 55 (1987), pp. 277-299.

———, "Repetition, Old and New: the *Libro de Alexandre*," in *Studies in Honor of Sumner M. Greenfield*, edited by Harold L. Boudreau and Luis González del Valle (Lincoln, Nebraska, Society of Spanish and Spanish-American Studies, 1985), pp. 95-106.

Gariano, Carmelo, *Análisis estilístico de 'Los milagros de nuestra Señora'* (Madrid, Gredos, 1965).

(Gautier de Châtillon) *Galterii de Castelione Alexandreis*, edidit Marvin L. Colker (Patavii in aedibus Antenoreis, 1978).

———, Walter of Châtillon, *The Alexandreis*, translated with introduction and notes by R. Telfryn Pritchard (Toronto, The Pontifical Institute of Mediaeval Studies, 1986).

Genette, Gérard, *Figures* III (Paris, Seuil, 1972).

———, *Narrative Discourse Revisited*, translated by Janet E. Lewin (Ithaca, Cornell University Press, 1988).

Goldberg, Harriet, "The Voice of the Author in the Works of Gonzalo de Berceo and in the *Libro de Alexandre* and the *Poema de Fernán González*," *La Corónica* 8 (1980), pp. 100-112.

Gonzalo de Berceo, *Poema de santa Oria*, edición, introducción y notas de Isabel Uría Maqua (Madrid, Castalia, 1981).

Greenia, George, *The 'Alexandreis' and the 'Libro de Alexandre': Latin versus Vernacular Direct Discourse*, PhD dissertation in Romance Languages and Literatures, University of Michigan, 1984.

Greer, Germaine, *Shakespeare* (Oxford and New York, Oxford University Press, 1986).

Guillaume de Conches, *Glosae in Iuvenalem*, ed. with an introduction and notes by Bradford Wilson (Paris, Vrin, 1960).

Heinze, Richard, *Virgils epische Technik* (Leipzig and Berlin, Teubner, 1908).

Hilka, A, *Der altfranzösische Prosa-Alexanderroman* (Geneva, Slatkine Reprints, 1974 reproducing the Halle edition of 1920).

*Homerus latinus, id est, Baebii Italici Ilias latina*, *Poetae latini minores*, post Aemilivm Baehrens iterum recensvit Fridericvs Vollmer, Vol II, fasc. III (Leipzig, Teubner, 1913).

Hunt, R. W., "A Fragment of the Manuscript from the Abbey of St. Victor in Paris," *Bodleian Library Record* 4 (1952), pp. 124-126.

Huygens, R. B. C., *Accessus ad auctores, Bernard d'Utrecht, Conrad d'Hirsau, Dialogus super auctores* (Leiden, E. J. Brill, 1970).

Iustinus, *Trogi Pompei historiarum philippicarum epitoma*, recensuit Iustus Ieep (Leipzig, Teubner, 1876).
Iuvencus, C. *Vetti Aquilini Iuvenci Libri evangelorum IIII*, recognovit Carolus Marold (Leipzig, Teubner, 1886).
Joseph Iscanus, *Werke und Briefe*, herausgegeben von Karl Langosch (Leiden und Köln, E. J. Brill, 1970).
———, (Joseph of Exeter), *The Iliad of Dares Phrygius*, translated with an introduction and notes by Gildas Roberts (Capetown, A. A. Balkema, 1970).
*Julii Valerii Epitome*, ed. Julius Zacher (Halle, Verlag der Buchhandlung des Waisenhauses, 1867).
Kallendorf, Craig, "Petrarchan Poetics and the Literature of Praise and Blame," paper read at the Sixth International Congress of the International Society for the History of Rhetoric, July 15-20, 1987.
Kelly, Douglas, "The Scope of the Treatment of Composition in the Twelfth- and Thirteenth-Century Arts of Poetry", *Speculum* 41 (1966), pp. 261-278.
LaBranche, Anthony, "Drayton's *The Barons Warres* and the Rhetoric of Historical Poetry," *Journal of English and Germanic Philology* 62 (1963).
Lausberg, H., *Manual de retórica literaria*, trans. José Pérez Riesco (Madrid, Gredos, 1975), 3 vols.
*Libro de Alexandre: Texts of the Paris and Madrid Manuscripts*, edited by Raymond Willis (Princeton and Paris, Princeton University Press, Elliott Monographs 32, 1934).
Lucan, *The Civil War*, ed. and translated by J. D. Duff (Cambridge, MA, and London, Harvard University Press, and Wm. Heinemann Ltd., first published 1928).
Macrobius, *Opera*, ed. J. Willis (Leipzig, Teubner, 1963).
Manitius, Max, *Handschriften antiker Autoren in mittelalterlichen Biliotekskatalogen* (Leipzig, Otto Harrassowitz, 1935).
Marcos Marín, Francisco, "La confusión de las lenguas: Comentario filológico desde un fragmento del *Libro de Alexandre*," *El Comentario de textos, 4: La poesía medieval* (Madrid, Castalia, 1983), pp. 148-184.
Marti, Berthe, "Literary Criticism in the Mediaeval Commentaries on Lucan," *Transactions of the American Philological Association* 72 (1941).
———, "Lucan's Narrative Technique," *La parola del passato* 30 (1976), pp. 82-89.
Martindale, Charles, *John Milton and the Transformation of Ancient Epic* (London and Sydney, Croom Helm, 1986).
Mena, Juan de, *La Yliada en romance*, según la impresión de Arnao Guillén de Brocar (Valladolid, 1519), edición, prólogo y glosario por Martín de Riquer (Barcelona, Selecciones Bibliófilas, 1949).
Michael, Ian, *The Treatment of Classical Material in the "Libro de Alexandre,"* (Manchester, University of Manchester Press, 1970).
Minnis, A. J., *The Mediaeval Theory of Authorship: Scholastic Literary Attitudes in the Later Middle Ages* (London, Scolar Press, 1984).
Moore, John Leverett, *Servius on the Tropes and Figures of Virgil* (Baltimore, Press of Isaac Friedenwald, 1891).
Mountford, J. P., and Schultz, J. T., *Index rerum et nominum in scholiis Servii et Aeli Donati tractarum* (Ithaca, Cornell University Press, 1930).
Ovid, *Metamorphoses*, ed. with a translation by Frank Justus Miller (Cambridge, MA, and London, Harvard University Press, and Wm. Heinemann Ltd., originally published in 1916), two volumes.
Pérez Rodríguez, Estrella, "Un tratado de gramática dedicado a Tello Téllez de Meneses," *Actas del I Congreso de Historia de Palencia*, tomo IV, *Edad media latina y humanismo renacentista en Palencia, lengua y literatura, historia de*

*América*, (Palencia, Diputación Provincial de Palencia, 1985), pp. 71-78.
Petrarca, Francesco, *L'Africa*, edizione critica per cura di Nicola Festa (Firenze, G. C. Sansoni, 1926).
Piacentini, Ugo, *Osservazione sulla tecnica epica di Lucano* (Berlin, Akademie-Verlag, 1963).
*Poema de mio Cid*, ed. Ian Michael (Madrid, Castalia, 1976).
Quinn, Kenneth, *Latin Explorations* (London, Routledge and Kegan Paul, 1963).
Quintilian, *The Institutes of Quintilian*, edited and translated by H. E. Butler (Cambridge, MA, Harvard University Press, and London, Wm. Heinemann Ltd., 1920-1922, four volumes).
Raby, F. J., *Secular Latin Poetry* (Oxford, Clarendon, 1934, 2 vols.).
Rico, Francisco, *Alfonso X y la "General estoria," tres lecciones* (Barcelona, Ediciones Ariel, 1972).
———, "La clerecía del mester", *Hispanic Review* 53 (1985), pp. 9-23.
Santillana, Marqués de, *Poesías completas*, ed. Manuel Durán, 2 vols. (Madrid, Castalia, 1975 and 1980).
*Sedulii opera omnia*, ed. J. Huemer, *Corpus scriptorum ecclesiastorum latinorum*, vol.X (Vindobonae, apud C. Geroldi filium bibliopolae academiae, 1885).
The Elder Seneca, *Declamations*, in two volumes, translated by M. Winterbottom (Cambridge, MA, Harvard University Press, and London, William Heinemann, Ltd., 1974).
Statius, in two volumes, translated by J. H. Mozley (Cambridge, MA, Harvard University Press, and London, William Heinemann, Ltd., 1928).
Such, Peter T., *The Origins and Use of the School Rhetoric in the 'Libro de Alexandre'*, PhD dissertation, Cambridge University, 1979.
Thalmann, Betty Cheney, *'El Libro de Alexandre': a Stylistic Approach*, PhD dissertation, Ohio State University, 1966.
Thierry of Chartres, *The Rhetorical Commentaries of Thierry of Chartres*, ed. Karin M. Fredborg (Toronto, Pontifical Institute of Mediaeval Studies, 1988).
Uría Maqua, Isabel, "El Libro de Alexandre y la Universidad de Palencia," *Actas del I Congreso de Historia de Palencia*, tomo IV, *Edad media latina y humanismo renacentista en Palencia, lengua y literatura, historia de América* (Palencia, Diputación Provincial de Palencia, 1985), pp. 431-442.
———, "Sobre la unidad del Mester de Clerecía del siglo XIII. Hacia un replanteamiento de la cuestión," *Actas de las III Jornadas de Estudios Berceanos* (Logroño, Diputación Provincial, 1981), pp. 179-188.
Wilkinson, L. P., *Ovid Surveyed* (Cambridge, Cambridge University Press, 1962).
Willis, Raymond "'Mester de clerecía', a Definition in the *Libro de Alexandre*," *Romance Philology* 10 (1956-1957), pp. 212-224.
Woodman, A. J., *Rhetoric in Classical Historiography* (London and Sydney, Croom Helm, and Portland, Oregon, Areopagitica Press, 1988).
Zanker, Graham, *Realism in Alexandrian Poetry: a Literature and its Audience*, (London, Sydney and Wolfboro, New Hampshire, Croom Helm, 1987).

# NORTH CAROLINA STUDIES IN THE ROMANCE LANGUAGES AND LITERATURES

I.S.B.N. Prefix 0-8078-

## Recent Titles

"LA QUERELLE DE LA ROSE": Letters and Documents, by Joseph L. Baird and John R. Kane. 1978. (No. 199). -9199-1.
TWO AGAINST TIME. A Study of the Very Present Worlds of Paul Claudel and Charles Péguy, by Joy Nachod Humes. 1978. (No. 200). -9200-9.
TECHNIQUES OF IRONY IN ANATOLE FRANCE. Essay on Les Sept Femmes de la Barbe-Bleue, by Diane Wolfe Levy. 1978. (No. 201). -9201-7.
THE PERIPHRASTIC FUTURES FORMED BY THE ROMANCE REFLEXES OF "VADO (AD)" PLUS INFINITIVE, by James Joseph Champion. 1978. (No. 202). -9202-S.
THE EVOLUTION OF THE LATIN /b/-/u/ MERGER: A Quantitative and Comparative Analysis of the B-V Alternation in Latin inscriptions, by Joseph Louis Barbarino. 1978. (No. 203). -9203-3.
METAPHORIC NARRATION: THE STRUCTURE AND FUNCTION OF METAPHORS IN "A LA RECHERCHE DU TEMPS PERDU", by Inge Karalus Crosman. 1978. (No. 204). -9204-1.
LE VAIN SIECLE GUERPIR. A Literary Approach to Sainthood through Old French Hagiography of the Twelfth Century, by Phyllis Johnson and Brigitte Cazelles. 1979. (No. 205). -9205-X.
THE POETRY OF CHANGE: A STUDY OF THE SURREALIST WORKS OF BENJAMIN PÉRET, by Julia Field Costich. 1979. (No. 206). -9206-8.
NARRATIVE PERSPECTIVE IN THE POST-CIVIL WAR NOVELS OF FRANCISCO AYALA "MUERTES DE PERRO" AND "EL FONDO DEL VASO", by Maryellen Bieder. 1979. (No. 207). -9207-6.
RABELAIS: HOMO LOGOS, by Alice Fiola Berry. 1979. (No. 208). -9208-4.
"DUEÑAS" AND DONCELLAS": A STUDY OF THE DOÑA RODRÍGUEZ EPISODE IN "DON QUIJOTE", by Conchita Herdman Marianella. 1979. (No. 209). -9209-2.
PIERRE BOAISTUAU'S "HISTOIRES TRAGIQUES": A STUDY OF NARRATIVE FORM AND TRAGIC VISION, by Richard A. Carr. 1979. (No. 210). -9210-6.
REALITY AND EXPRESSION IN THE POETRY OF CARLOS PELLICER, by George Melnykovich. 1979. (No. 211). -9211-4.
MEDIEVAL MAN, HIS UNDERSTANDING OF HIMSELF, HIS SOCIETY, AND THE WORLD, by Urban T. Holmes, Jr. 1980. (No. 212). -9212-2.
MÉMOIRES SUR LA LIBRAIRIE ET SUR LA LIBERTÉ DE LA PRESSE, introduction and notes by Graham E. Rodmell. 1979. (No. 213). -9213-0.
THE FICTIONS OF THE SELF. THE EARLY WORKS OF MAURICE BARRES, by Gordon Shenton. 1979. (No. 214). -9214-9.
CECCO ANGIOLIERI. A STUDY, by Gifford P. Orwen. 1979. (No. 215). -9215-7.
THE INSTRUCTIONS OF SAINT LOUIS: A CRITICAL TEXT, by David O'Connell. 1979. (No. 216). -9216-5.
ARTFUL ELOQUENCE, JEAN LEMAIRE DE BELGES AND THE RHETORICAL TRADITION, by Michael F. O. Jenkins. 1980. (No. 217). -9217-3.
A CONCORDANCE TO MARIVAUX'S COMEDIES IN PROSE, edited by Donald C. Spinelli. 1979. (No. 218). 4 volumes, -9218-1 (set), -9219-X (v. 1), -9220-3 (v. 2); -9221-1 (v. 3); -9222-X (v. 4).
ABYSMAL GAMES IN THE NOVELS OF SAMUEL BECKETT, by Angela B. Moorjani. 1982. (No. 219). -9223-8.
GERMAIN NOUVEAU DIT HUMILIS: ÉTUDE BIOGRAPHIQUE, par Alexandre L. Amprimoz. 1983. (No. 220). -9224-6.

---

When ordering please cite the ISBN Prefix plus the last four digits for each title.

Send orders to:   University of North Carolina Press
P.O. Box 2288
CB# 6215
Chapel Hill, NC 27515-2288
U.S.A.

# NORTH CAROLINA STUDIES IN THE ROMANCE LANGUAGES AND LITERATURES

*I.S.B.N. Prefix 0-8078-*

## Recent Titles

THE "VIE DE SAINT ALEXIS" IN THE TWELFTH AND THIRTEENTH CENTURIES: AN EDITION AND COMMENTARY, by Alison Goddard Elliot. 1983. (No. 221). *-9225-4.*
THE BROKEN ANGEL: MYTH AND METHOD IN VALÉRY, by Ursula Franklin. 1984. (No. 222). *-9226-2.*
READING VOLTAIRE'S CONTES: A SEMIOTICS OF PHILOSOPHICAL NARRATION, by Carol Sherman. 1985. (No. 223). *-9227-0.*
THE STATUS OF THE READING SUBJECT IN THE "LIBRO DE BUEN AMOR", by Marina Scordilis Brownlee. 1985. (No. 224). *-9228-9.*
MARTORELL'S TIRANT LO BLANCH: A PROGRAM FOR MILITARY AND SOCIAL REFORM IN FIFTEENTH-CENTURY CHRISTENDOM, by Edward T. Aylward. 1985. (No. 225). *-9229- 7.*
NOVEL LIVES: THE FICTIONAL AUTOBIOGRAPHIES OF GUILLERMO CABRERA INFANTE AND MARIO VARGAS LLOSA, by Rosemary Geisdorfer Feal. 1986. (No. 226). *-9230-0.*
SOCIAL REALISM IN THE ARGENTINE NARRATIVE, by David William Foster. 1986. (No. 227). *-9231-9.*
HALF-TOLD TALES: DILEMMAS OF MEANING IN THREE FRENCH NOVELS, by Philip Stewart. 1987. (No. 228). *-9232-7.*
POLITIQUES DE L'ECRITURE BATAILLE/DERRIDA: le sens du sacré dans la pensée française du surréalisme à nos jours, par Jean-Michel Heimonet. 1987. (No. 229). *-9233-5.*
GOD, THE QUEST, THE HERO: THEMATIC STRUCTURES IN BECKETT'S FICTION, by Laura Barge. 1988. (No. 230). *-9235-1.*
THE NAME GAME. WRITING/FADING WRITER IN "DE DONDE SON LOS CANTANTES", by Oscar Montero. 1988. (No. 231). *-9236-X.*
GIL VICENTE AND THE DEVELOPMENT OF THE COMEDIA, by René Pedro Garay. 1988. (No. 232). *-9234-3.*
HACIA UNA POÉTICA DEL RELATO DIDÁCTICO: OCHO ESTUDIOS SOBRE "EL CONDE LUCANOR", por Aníbal A. Biglieri. 1989. (No. 233). *-9237-8.*
A POETICS OF ART CRITICISM: THE CASE OF BAUDELAIRE, by Timothy Raser. 1989. (No. 234). *-9238-6.*
UMA CONCORDÃNCIA DO ROMANCE "GRANDE SERTÃO: VEREDAS" DE JOÃO GUIMARÃES ROSA, by Myriam Ramsey and Paul Dixon. 1989. (No. 235). Microfiche, *-9239-4.*
CYCLOPEAN SONG: MELANCHOLY AND AESTHETICISM IN GÓNGORA S "FÁBULA DE POLIFEMO Y GALATEA", by Kathleen Hunt Dolan. 1990. (No. 236). *-9240-8.*
THE "SYNTHESIS" NOVEL IN LATIN AMERICA. A STUDY ON JOÃO GUIMARÃES ROSA'S "GRANDE SERTÃO: VEREDAS", by Eduardo de Faria Coutinho. 1991. (No. 237). *-9241-6.*
IMPERMANENT STRUCTURES. SEMIOTIC READINGS OF NELSON RODRIGUES' "VESTIDO DE NOIVA", "ÁLBUM DE FAMÍLIA", AND "ANJO NEGRO", by Fred M. Clark. 1991. (No. 238). *-9242-4.*
"EL ÁNGEL DEL HOGAR". GALDÓS AND THE IDEOLOGY OF DOMESTICITY IN SPAIN, by Bridget A. Aldaraca. 1991. (No. 239). *-9243-2.*
IN THE PRESENCE OF MYSTERY: MODERNIST FICTION AND THE OCCULT, by Howard M. Fraser. 1992. (No. 240). *-9244-0.*
JORGE LUIS BORGES AND HIS PREDECESSORS OR NOTES TOWARDS A MATERIALIST HISTORY OF LINGUISTIC IDEALISM, by Malcolm K. Read. 1993. (No. 242). *-9246-7.*
DISCOVERING THE COMIC IN "DON QUIXOTE", by Laura J. Gorfkle. 1993. (No. 243). *-9247-5.*

When ordering please cite the *ISBN Prefix* plus the last four digits for each title.

Send orders to:   University of North Carolina Press
P.O. Box 2288
CB# 6215
Chapel Hill, NC 27515-2288
U.S.A.

The Department of Romance Studies Digital Arts and Collaboration Lab at the University of North Carolina at Chapel Hill is proud to support the digitization of the North Carolina Studies in the Romance Languages and Literatures series.

www.ingramcontent.com/pod-product-compliance
Lightning Source LLC
Chambersburg PA
CBHW030655230426
43665CB00011B/1098